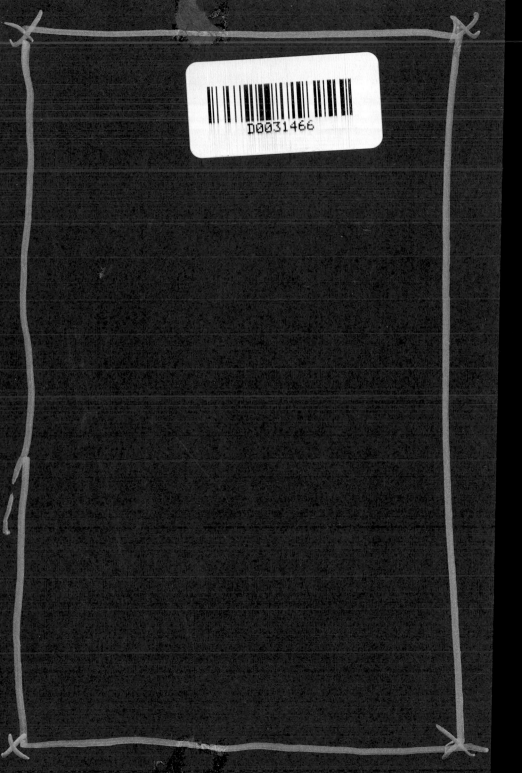

THE STATES AND THE NATION SERIES, of which this volume is a part, is designed to assist the American people in a serious look at the ideals they have espoused and the experiences they have undergone in the history of the nation. The content of every volume represents the scholarship, experience, and opinions of its author. The costs of writing and editing were met mainly by grants from the National Endowment for the Humanities, a federal agency. The project was administered by the American Association for State and Local History, a nonprofit learned society, working with an Editorial Board of distinguished editors, authors, and historians, whose names are listed below.

Nebraska

A Bicentennial History

Dorothy Weyer Creigh

W. W. Norton & Company, Inc.
New York

American Association for State and Local History
Nashville

Published and distributed by
W. W. Norton & Company, Inc.
500 Fifth Avenue
New York, New York 10036

Library of Congress Cataloging in Publication Data

Creigh, Dorothy Weyer.
Nebraska : a Bicentennial history.

(The States and the Nation series)
Bibliography: p.
Includes index.
1. Nebraska—History. I. Series.
F666.C83   978.2   77–5425
ISBN 0–393–05598–1

3 4 5 6 7 8 9 0

To the memory of Weyers, Careys, Creighs
rugged Nebraska homesteaders of yesterday
and to their descendants
Frank and Mabelle Carey Weyer
and especially
Tom
Mary Elizabeth, Tommy
Johnny and Jaimie Creigh

Contents

Illustrations

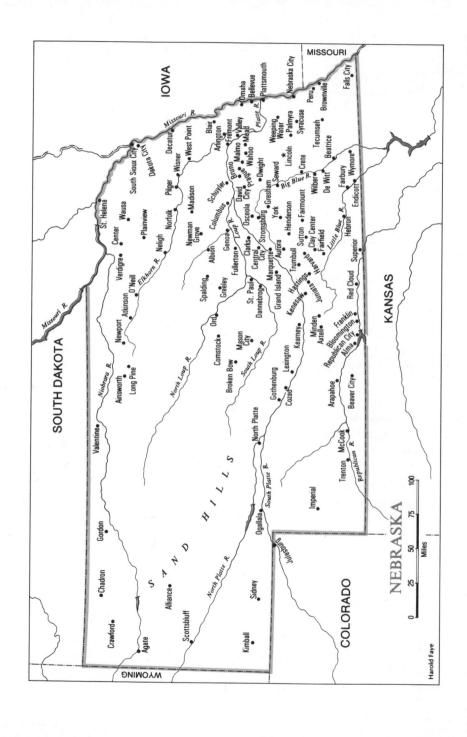

Harold Faye

Invitation to the Reader

IN 1807, former President John Adams argued that a complete history of the American Revolution could not be written until the history of change in each state was known, because the principles of the Revolution were as various as the states that went through it. Two hundred years after the Declaration of Independence, the American nation has spread over a continent and beyond. The states have grown in number from thirteen to fifty. And democratic principles have been interpreted differently in every one of them.

We therefore invite you to consider that the history of your state may have more to do with the bicentennial review of the American Revolution than does the story of Bunker Hill or Valley Forge. The Revolution has continued as Americans extended liberty and democracy over a vast territory. John Adams was right: the states are part of that story, and the story is incomplete without an account of their diversity.

The Declaration of Independence stressed life, liberty, and the pursuit of happiness; accordingly, it shattered the notion of holding new territories in the subordinate status of colonies. The Northwest Ordinance of 1787 set forth a procedure for new states to enter the Union on an equal footing with the old. The Federal Constitution shortly confirmed this novel means of building a nation out of equal states. The step-by-step process through which territories have achieved self-government and national representation is among the most important of the Founding Fathers' legacies.

The method of state-making reconciled the ancient conflict between liberty and empire, resulting in what Thomas Jefferson called an empire for liberty. The system has worked and remains unaltered, despite enormous changes that have taken place in the nation. The country's extent and variety now surpass anything the patriots of '76 could likely have imagined. The United States has changed from an agrarian republic into a highly industrial and urban democracy, from a fledgling nation into a major world power. As Oliver Wendell Holmes remarked in 1920, the creators of the nation could not have seen completely how it and its constitution and its states would develop. Any meaningful review in the bicentennial era must consider what the country has become, as well as what it was.

The new nation of equal states took as its motto *E Pluribus Unum*—"out of many, one." But just as many peoples have become Americans without complete loss of ethnic and cultural identities, so have the states retained differences of character. Some have been superficial, expressed in stereotyped images— big, boastful Texas, "sophisticated" New York, "hillbilly" Arkansas. Other differences have been more real, sometimes instructively, sometimes amusingly; democracy has embraced Huey Long's Louisiana, bilingual New Mexico, unicameral Nebraska, and a Texas that once taxed fortunetellers and spawned politicians called "Woodpecker Republicans" and "Skunk Democrats." Some differences have been profound, as when South Carolina secessionists led other states out of the Union in opposition to abolitionists in Massachusetts and Ohio. The result was a bitter Civil War.

The Revolution's first shots may have sounded in Lexington and Concord; but fights over what democracy should mean and who should have independence have erupted from Pennsylvania's Gettysburg to the "Bleeding Kansas" of John Brown, from the Alamo in Texas to the Indian battles at Montana's Little Bighorn. Utah Mormons have known the strain of isolation; Hawaiians at Pearl Harbor, the terror of attack; Georgians during Sherman's march, the sadness of defeat and devastation. Each state's experience differs instructively; each adds understanding to the whole.

The purpose of this series of books is to make that kind of understanding accessible, in a way that will last in value far beyond the bicentennial fireworks. The series offers a volume on every state, plus the District of Columbia—fifty-one, in all. Each book contains, besides the text, a view of the state through eyes other than the author's—a "photographer's essay," in which a skilled photographer presents his own personal perceptions of the state's contemporary flavor.

We have asked authors not for comprehensive chronicles, nor for research monographs or new data for scholars. Bibliographies and footnotes are minimal. We have asked each author for a summing up—interpretive, sensitive, thoughtful, individual, even personal—of what seems significant about his or her state's history. What distinguishes it? What has mattered about it, to its own people and to the rest of the nation? What has it come to now?

To interpret the states in all their variety, we have sought a variety of backgrounds in authors themselves and have encouraged variety in the approaches they take. They have in common only these things: historical knowledge, writing skill, and strong personal feelings about a particular state. Each has wide latitude for the use of the short space. And if each succeeds, it will be by offering you, in your capacity as a *citizen* of a state *and* of a nation, stimulating insights to test against your own.

James Morton Smith
General Editor

ACKNOWLEDGMENTS

I am indebted to many people for the help they have given while this manuscript was in progress: various staff members of the Nebraska State Historical Society, especially Marvin Kivett, James Potter, Paul Riley, and Donald Snoddy. To Dr. Frederick Luebke of the University of Nebraska, who read the section on the German immigrants and provided much help; Erma Ourecky of Wilber, Dr. Vladimir Kucera of Lincoln, and Miss Helen Kucera of Hastings, who helped with material about the Czechs; Pastor Martin Lingwall of Hastings, who supplied information about the Swedes; Ronald D. Johnson, librarian at Dana College, and Dr. Niels M. Johnson of Blair, who helped with material about the Danes; and many others who provided assistance with the chapter on ethnic groups.

The librarians at Hastings College, especially Marie Russell, and at the Hastings Public Library, for locating dissertations and hard-to-find books; Dr. Vernon Carstensen of the University of Washington, for his overall criticism and help with the manuscript as a whole; Dr. Gene Gressley of the University of Wyoming, for his help with the chapter on the cattlemen; Darrell Bauder, Milton and Marie Klint, and others who supplied information for the chapter on farming; Barry Combs of the Union Pacific historical department; Dr. Richard Bartlett of Florida State University of Tallahassee.

Charles C. Osborne, who read the manuscript in its entirety; Gerald George, The States and the Nation editor; and Jane Whitehead, the copy editor; Joe Golden of the Office of Planning and Programming of the State of Nebraska; and many, many others who supplied specific information or general ideas.

Betty Bixby Ford and Cathy Kohmetscher, who spent tedious hours at the typewriter on the various drafts of this book.

My parents, Dean Frank E. and Mabelle Carey Weyer, who celebrated their sixtieth wedding anniversary while the book was in process, whose recollections of early pioneer days were priceless; my father's contributions went far beyond editorial help, for he read proof, researched data on education, ran errands—a shuttle service to the duplicating machine—and was a constant support.

Most of all, to my husband and children for their endurance and fortitude in living through the domestic chaos that came about while this book was in the making.

Preface

$\mathcal{T}$HROUGH the years, more words have been published about the area that was Nebraska Territory than possibly any other region in the United States.

The books have ranged from sensational potboilers about cowboys and Indians to scholarly volumes of governmental history. The writers have seen the story of Nebraska as the six blind men saw the elephant, each one a different segment. Some have seen only the lurid details of the physical warfare of man against man, others only the significance of Nebraska politically in the story of the development of the United States, still others only the struggles of the sod-house era.

The history of Nebraska is colorful. The geographical area is vast, for the original Nebraska Territory encompassed the central portion of the continental United States, the Great Plains that were completely unlike any other land. The development of the present-day civilization has been rapid, for Nebraska was opened to white settlement less than one hundred twenty-five years ago. As a territory, Nebraska was born in political battle; as a state, she has played a role far more significant nationally than the size of her population would indicate. Her story has been one of constant struggle against nature, between cultures, even at times seemingly for economic survival.

Because a detailed, overall history of the state is impossible to compress within the confines of one small volume, and because others have written well of other facets of Nebraska history, I have concentrated on the story of the people who now comprise the population of the state, telling who they are, where they came from, and how they have adapted the land to their own uses, the interrelationship of man and the land.

The analogy with the elephant is apt. The first white men in any numbers to know Nebraska were the travelers on the Oregon Trail who, for some reason, referred to their adventures as "seeing the elephant." The elephant they saw has grown in size and complexity, its appendages now being its government, its political relationship with the rest of the country, its business and industry and economic growth, its cultural and artistic contributions, its relationships with the native Americans whose culture it destroyed, and its people generally. I like to think that in this book I have touched the backbone of the elephant.

1 August 1976   Dorothy Weyer Creigh

Nebraska

1

The Nebraska Psyche

$\mathcal{T}$O know Nebraska is to know the land and the people and their interdependence, for they are so closely intertwined that each affects the other. Whether they are farmers in the rolling cornlands of the east, ranchers in the semiarid Sandhills of the west, wheat farmers of the broad prairie lands, or townspeople manufacturing farm equipment or selling grain or meat, Nebraskans are dependent upon the soil. The land has made the people what they are—self-reliant, physically vigorous, elemental, and long-lived—and they have learned to adapt the land, to change it and, in increasing ways, to control it. This is the story of Nebraska.

Although Nebraska is prairie country, treeless, grass-covered plains stretched out across the center of the continental United States, her lands range from woodlands in the east, to broad prairies in the central and western parts, rolling Sandhills in the northwest, and even unexpected waterfalls on the Snake and Minnechaduza streams in the northwest.

Only three percent of her land is forested, most of that lying along her eastern reaches, overlooking the Misssouri River, which runs north and south to form the eastern boundary of the state. There the land is undulating, the alluvial lowlands sustaining native stands of oak, walnut, and cottonwood trees, climate and topography not unlike those of Iowa, her neighbor across the river.

Three-fourths of the state lies west of the 98th meridian,

3

stretching out into flat, treeless expanses, mile after mile of fertile loess soil warmed by the brilliant golden sunlight. Much of the land lies on a vast inland sea, created eons ago as glaciers melted. The plains extend westward, the land increasing gradually in elevation from less than a thousand feet above sea level in the southeast to more than five thousand feet in the west.

In the central northwestern regions the Sandhills rise, eighteen thousand square miles of sandy, treeless dunes and lake-studded valleys unlike any other in the world, covered with native grasses and wildflowers which ripple in the breeze. Beyond lie the high plains, and far off in the northwestern corner, the buttes and canyons of the Wildcat Hills and the Pine Ridge with their stands of pine.

Three rivers traverse the state from west to east, the Niobrara in the north, called *L'Eau Qui Court* (Running Water) by early-day French fur trappers; the Republican in the south, named *La Nacion de la Republica* in jest by the Spaniards commemorating a band of Pawnees who refused to move with other tribesmen to another location (the Spaniards likened the situation to that of the colonists in New England, who at that time were fighting to establish the Republic); and, in the middle, the broad, shallow Platte, named by the French, the word meaning flat, and called, not without justification, the "mile-wide, inch-deep river." The sandy-bottom Platte, too shallow to be navigable except by early-day bull-boats—canoes made of buffalo skins—was ridiculed by early travelers. Washington Irving considered it the most magnificent and useless river, and Mark Twain suggested that, laid on end, it would be a respectable river. Other, smaller rivers flow from west to east, but the Platte is the ribbon that ties the varying parts of Nebraska together, her broad valley providing one of the finest natural roadways in the world, the great highway to the west.

The story of Nebraska was unpromising in its beginnings. Early-day travelers considered Nebraska part of the Great American Desert, for that part lying beyond the 98th meridian had no trees and little rainfall; for years it was considered an impenetrable barrier dividing the lands east from the lands west, almost a land of no return. In 1806 Zebulon Pike, the first American explorer through the area, wrote of "barren soil, parched and dryed up for eight months in the year" that would "become in time equally celebrated as the sandy desarts of Africa," [1] and Major Stephen H. Long reported in 1820 that "it is almost wholly unfit for cultivation;" his chronicler, Dr. Edwin James said that it was "an unfit residence for any but a nomad population." [2] From Long's expedition onward, maps recorded the land as the Great American Desert.

Later on, as restless travelers plunged through it, the transcontinental pioneers hurrying to the gold fields of California or the fertile lands of Oregon regarded it a bothersome area to endure before reaching the Promised Land. Only after other, more desirable lands were settled did the frontiersman seek Nebraska for herself. Even as late as autumn 1969, Nebraska was called a nothing-land, for Frederick V. Grunfeld, writing in *Horizon* magazine, described a part of Spain as ". . . a vast parched plain . . . a rather vague region," saying that "no one ever goes there just to see it; La Mancha is the Nebraska of Spain." [3]

From this land, once scorned, have come fruitfulness and plenty. Nebraska contributes to the nation and to the world the bounty of her soil, hundreds of millions of bushels of corn and wheat, and thousands of tons of beef and pork each year. But even more than material goods, she gives a particular spirit of tenacity, determination, and audacity to America, and has fostered men of letters, political authority, and artistic ability.

Perhaps the rigors of living, which Colonel Richard I. Dodge described in a book published in England in 1877, have made Nebraskans what they are; to survive in Nebraska, you must be something special. "All Plains animals have extraordinary vitality," he said, "and nothing but the breaking of the backbone or a shot in the brain will certainly bring one down." [4] Although he was talking about animals, not man, that same indomitable

1. Zebulon M. Pike, *Account of Expeditions to the Sources of the Mississippi, 1805–1807* (Philadelphia, 1810), quoted by James C. Olson, *History of Nebraska* (Lincoln: University of Nebraska Press, 1955, 1966), p. 3.

2. Stephen H. Long, report quoted by Olson, *History of Nebraska*, p. 3.

3. Frederick V. Grunfeld, "La Mancha," *Horizon* 11 (Autumn 1969):42.

4. Richard Irving Dodge, *The Plains of the Great West* (1877; New York: Archer House, 1959), p. 112.

vigor, transposed into emotional, psychological, and physical factors, has produced some remarkable results in Nebraska's people.

Who were these people who transformed the land? For the most part, they were ordinary men who possessed a vision of freedom, independence, the chance to make a living for themselves and for their families through their own labor. From the settled parts of this country and from the crowded areas of northern Europe they came, seeking land and wide-open spaces, hoping that with muscle and determination they could create a new existence. They were not heroes, but because of their imagination, dogged perseverance, and continual optimism, they achieved heroic stature.

The country they found in central and western Nebraska was completely unlike any they had known before; no previous experience could prepare them for the treeless prairie. With few of the natural resources they were accustomed to, they had to "make do," a term that still typifies the ingenuity and resourcefulness that Nebraskans apply to all activities. Almost overnight they evolved a unique way of living, creating a sod-house–windmill–barbed-wire culture. Since there was no wood or stone for building, they made their houses of dirt and grass —and called the sod Nebraska marble; since there was no wood for fuel, they burned dried cow manure and called it Nebraska coal. The sod houses are gone now, but the inventive spirit and the broad sense of humor remain.

Nebraskans today reflect the qualities of their pioneer fathers—the stubbornness that would not let them be defeated, the friendliness and generosity that makes no man a stranger on the prairie, the stoicism of the farmer watching his crop shrivel and die in front of his eyes, the daring of the cattleman betting his all on the turn of the market. The raucous violence of the frontier is not long past nor are the days of bleakness; all the elements of Nebraska's past have combined to create a breed of forceful, energetic, free-ranging souls. Nebraskans possess audacity tempered with caution, honesty and trust, creativity, ambition, and most of all, force, determination, and drive.

But Nebraskans seem not to realize their greatness. They tend to underestimate their accomplishments. Only when outsiders discover and announce their successes will Nebraskans themselves believe them. When national polls proclaimed the Big Red football team of the University of Nebraska Number One, the entire state succumbed to Scarlet Fever; eighty thousand people jammed the highways to pack into the stadium on golden October afternoons, wearing red clothing to show their patriotic fervor, and even engaging a legislative committee in discussion about the distribution of football tickets. Earlier, when Nebraska led the nation in beef production, her license plates proclaimed "Beef State," but when other states made fun of the line, the legislature quietly dropped it.

Unlike Texans, who legendarily believe that everything about their state is bigger than any other state, Nebraskans tend to underrate their own. Although the city folk—one-third of the population of the state live in two cities, Omaha and Lincoln—are less inclined than the country folk to believe small, yet they too are victims of the Nebraska tendency toward deprecation. When the major Omaha newspaper carried a story in 1975 congratulating the community for its artistic efforts, the headline read:

NYC DANCER FINDS OMAHA AS GOOD A PLACE AS ANY.[5]

One of the most endearing qualities of Nebraskans is their lack of braggadocio, of arrogance.

But they have not always been so unassertive. During her boisterous, formative years Nebraska had her share of flamboyant booster types: Buffalo Bill Cody, for instance, whose long curls flowed behind him as he galloped his resplendently saddled bronco, performing all over the world; the silver-tongued Orator of the Platte, William Jennings Bryan, declaiming in mellifluous tones in his recurrent campaigns for the presidency of the United States; the enthusiastic supporters of almost any raw, bleak, prairie village who were confident that their town, their state, their land, was the most promising in the whole wide world; the settlers themselves—all praised the land loudly.

Outsiders knew about the country then. The national press—newspapers, magazines, pulp publications—all peddled colorful accounts of buffalo hunts, the hairbreadth struggles of man against nature; and the stories were read and believed in New

5. *Omaha World-Herald,* out-state edition, July 19, 1975.

England, in Bristol, in Hamburg. Nebraska was often in the
press in the late nineteenth century; the name itself evoked a
mental image of adventure, physical prowess, and victory of
man against the elements.

So convincing were the stories, so alluring the land, that almost over night the population of Nebraska leapt from a few
thousand in 1860 to more than a million in 1890, a figure that
has not doubled yet; villages and farmsteads sprang up on the
prairie; schools, churches, governments, other institutions, leapt
into being. Everything happened at once in an atmosphere of
wonder and anticipation.

But the decades since then have been different. Intermittent
years of defeat, of blown-out fields lost to dust storms, of heat
waves shriveling crops in the row, of grasshoppers, high winds,
blizzards, and bank closings, left Nebraskans stripped of their
ability to crow loudly. They began to realize that no amount of
bragging could bring forth rain or stop the winds, that work
rather than words would create the kind of life they wanted.
They kept their confidence in the land, but added to it back-
breaking labor and imaginative daring, and renewed their faith
in their own ability to control it. Now they are quiet, hesitant to
mention their own accomplishments. Their innovations in land
management and productivity, in political theory, in various
other realms of living go largely unnoticed and unheralded by
the rest of the world. The horn that tooted so noisily a century
ago is now rusty with disuse.

Nebraskans are contradictory. They originally acquired land
at low cost from government homestead programs or bought it
at minimal fees from the railroads, whose hospitality and services they accepted gratefully. But they are nonetheless vocal
against government handouts and are suspicious of Big Business.

They are ultraconservative politically, often re-electing good
ribbon-cutting officials and defeating those who upset the *status
quo,* but for forty years they re-elected George W. Norris, the
Fighting Liberal, to the United States House of Representatives,
later to the Senate. They have had Populist governments, pio-
neered initiative and referendum in the country, adopted the
only unicameral, or single-house legislature in the United

States, and are the only state to obtain all their electricity from government-owned power plants.

They are frugal—"squeezing the buffalo on the nickel until it bellows" is the common phrase—but they spend tremendous amounts to equip their farms, many having half-million-dollar inventories in machinery and stock. Although they may spend fifty thousand dollars for a single piece of equipment—a self-propelled combine, for instance, capable of cutting and reaping grain—they may balk at a dollar for paint on the barn.

They are slow to make changes—unless the changes relate to farming procedures, which mean money in the bank. They utilize techniques developed from research and experimentation of agronomists, geneticists, chemists, and other specialists, add their own expertise, and have increased their land productivity tenfold in a matter of decades.

They are practical, not given to artistic pursuits, yet they have contributed to the world a disproportionate number of painters, writers, composers, musicians, and actors: Willa Cather, Mari Sandoz, Roscoe and Louise Pound, Howard Hanson, Harold Lloyd, Henry Fonda, Robert Taylor, Johnny Carson, Dick Cavett, and many more. Their forty-year-old university-sponsored literary magazine, *Prairie Schooner,* has outlived most others of its kind and continues to attract distinguished manuscripts from all over the world. The University of Nebraska Press ranks among the most respected publishers in the field of American history. Nebraskans say they are indignant about modern art, writing hundreds of letters to the editor to protest abstract sculptures along the Interstate highway—the first such program in the country—but they are proud of their tradition-breaking capitol, completed in 1932 and generally acclaimed as one of the most innovative public buildings in America. Typically, for Nebraska, it was completely paid for as it was built, not one stone being bought on credit. For years Nebraska prided herself as the White Spot of the Nation, having neither bonded indebtedness nor sales nor income taxes; she paid as she went, and she spent frugally.

Nebraskans are imaginative. From the dry flatlands they have created forests and lakes. More than three-fourths of their land was treeless; they evolved Arbor Day, now a national tree-planting holiday, and they have two national forests, the trees man-planted on the wide-open prairies. The earliest nickname for their land was the Tree-Planter State. Their land was plagued periodically by droughts of beyond-Biblical proportions, yet occasionally and sometimes simultaneously parts of it were inundated by floods; the Republican River flood of 1935, in the middle of the dust-bowl years, drowned 104 persons. Nebraska now has one of the largest earthen-construction dams in the world for flood control, and a series of smaller dams, the new lakes providing water for irrigation, power, fishing, and sailing regattas.

Nebraskans are emotional about their land. Since the beginning of settlement, which isn't long as such things go, residents of the land have either been enthusiastic promoters, praising the broad sweep of lush prairie land, the sparkling skies and clear air, and the peace, or they have cursed the fates that consigned them there, damning the winds, the lonesomeness, the extreme temperatures. There seems to be no middle ground; no one who knows Nebraska is neutral about her. It's a land of wide-open spaces and few people; although in land size, Nebraska is larger than all of New England with most of New York thrown in for good measure, it has mighty few people, fewer than twenty per square mile. In the rolling Sandhills grasslands, where there are fifty or seventy miles between settlements—not towns—it's possible to see almost that far across the rippling grama grasses.

From this land, most of it semiarid, with a harsh climate of great temperature extremes, have come rugged, stubborn, independent persons who, for the most part, still live according to the pioneer tenets of hard work, honesty toward their fellowman and trust in him, and faith—in God, mankind, nature, and life in general. They have freedom of spirit, openness, and are generous of themselves.

Part of their tenacity comes from having to face the vagaries of nature, for in this inland area temperatures range from below zero—the lowest recorded was 47 below—to well above 100 degrees. During the drought year of 1934, more than eighteen consecutive days were recorded at more than 100, and in 1899, the officially recorded temperature reached 118 degrees. The brilliant sunshine that bathes the country in golden light can change into a furnace blast. Some of the toughness of Nebraskans comes from having to live with the wind, which can change from a breeze to a raging gale in a matter of moments.

Nebraskans' stubbornness also reflects to some degree their ethnic backgrounds, for although Nebraskans helped create the American melting pot, their European origins are predominantly German, Scandinavian, and northern European. There is little of Latin emotionalism, levity, and bubble in the composite Nebraskan. An old saw, not proved but oft-repeated nonetheless, says that in Nebraska anyone with a Scandinavian name is assured of victory at the polls, unless, of course, as sometimes happens, Swanson and Johnson are running against each other. The original homesteaders, moving westward with the frontier, came from New England, either directly or indirectly by way of Michigan, Pennsylvania, Ohio, or elsewhere; they, too, were earnest, no-nonsense types, coming from economic adversity, intent on establishing permanent homes, and realizing that whatever they accomplished would be the result of their own hard work. They knew that if there was a pot of gold at the end of the rainbow, they'd have to do the spading themselves to get it.

Nebraskans have long been highly literate, bringing literacy with them from New England, which had a well-established public school system, and from Europe, for many of the immigrants from northern Europe were well educated. Those few who could neither read nor write also recognized the worth of literacy and insisted that their children acquire as much academic education as possible: the high school diploma, the college degree, were marks of great distinction. Although there was never any question about establishing a public school system in Nebraska—the Northwest Ordinances of 1785 and 1787, and the Organic Act of the Territory of 1854 prescribed such procedure—territorial Nebraskans organized schools quickly, adding academies, colleges, and other private schools with equal enthusiasm. So engrained is the school philosophy that some Nebraskans are loath to give up any schools, equating quantity with quality and withstanding appeals to consolidate school districts; with 1,241 school districts, some with only one or two pupils, Nebraska has more districts than any other state.

Nebraskans love their wide-open spaces, but they cherish

whatever provides convenience to bridge that space. They were early enthusiasts of automobiles and airplanes; an automobile factory operating in the village of Angus between 1907 and 1909 produced more than four hundred Fuller automobiles, for instance; and in 1926, the largest single shipment of cars ever consigned to a single firm to that date went to Hastings, 126 Chevrolet coaches, landaus, coupes, sedans, touring cars, roadsters, and a few trucks. But when it came to roads, Nebraska frugality won over Nebraska automobile fervor. Until the 1960s, the state lagged behind many others in paving highways and maintaining secondary roads, and even now in the sparsely populated Sandhills where the soil is light, some less-traveled roads are scarcely more than trails.

Nebraskans were early-day airplane buffs, almost every village in the state claiming an airfield by the late 1920s. When Hollywood made a movie, "The Great Waldo Pepper," about begoggled barnstorming pilots, it was appropriate that the mythical locale be Nebraska; that's where they really were! Charles Lindbergh was just one of many young aviators when he learned to fly in Lincoln. Now some businessmen and large numbers of ranchers fly their own planes, almost every ranch of any size has an airstrip, and members of an organization called Flying Farmers pilot their own planes to attend Fly-Ins, as the meetings are called. At a wintertime farm sale on a Sandhills ranch, frozen Ell lake in front of the residential compound was covered with small planes, scores of ranchers having flown in to bid on stock and machinery. The broad flatlands and cloudless skies made Nebraska a natural for wartime airfields during World War II; Army Air Corps installations were located at Harvard, Bruning, Lincoln, Grand Island, Kearney, Ainsworth, Alliance, Fairmont, McCook, Scottsbluff, and Scribner; and the headquarters of the Strategic Air Command are located just outside Omaha. Ironically, the paucity of population means that commercial air schedules are almost nonexistent in the state except for the major cities of Omaha and Lincoln.

Nebraskans were engrossed with radio in its early years; the land lying on the underground water table provided exceptional conductivity for radio waves emanating from towers grounded there. The first commercial relay station in the world for shortwave radio began in mid-Nebraska in 1923, its signal being heard as far away as Africa and Australia; KFKX broadcast special Christmas Day messages to Admiral Richard E. Byrd's staff at Little America in the Antarctic in 1925. The state now is blanketed by a sophisticated public-service television network, a network of nine stations providing educational programs to even the most remote regions.

Nebraskans are long-lived. Early-day promoters praised the climate for its healthfulness, and present-day scientific investigation has proved that Nebraskans do have astonishing longevity. An area west of Lincoln, south of the Platte river—Adams, Butler, Clay, Fillmore, Hamilton, Jefferson, Polk, Saline, Seward, Thayer, and York counties—has been identified as having the lowest death rate in the country for middle-aged males in particular, and persons living elsewhere in the state likewise have unusually long life spans. Whether the cause is genetic or environmental, sound stock or clear air and healthful water, researchers do not yet know.

Nebraskans are so closely attached to the land that the changing of the seasons, the cycles of the year, are important to them. Their lives are tuned to the greening of the spring, the heat of summer, the glories of autumn, and the exhilaration of winter blizzards; they find beauty, pleasure, and rejuvenation in watching the cottonwoods change from delicate green to full shimmering green to pure gold to leaflessness, for these symbolize all growing things. The heart of Nebraska is in her soil and its productivity.

2

The Original Inhabitants

*F*OR thousands of years man has inhabited the land that is now Nebraska. And even as the land itself has changed, through eons of ice and snow, glacial recessions, floods and droughts, high winds and erosion, so too have the people. The soil that Nebraskans till gives up fragments which tell of civilizations long past, clues to the relationship of man with the land.

The first known inhabitants were paleo-Indians who ranged the area some ten thousand years ago. They used their fluted stone weapons to hunt giant bison, mastodon, ground sloth, elephants, mammoths, and other enormous animals that inhabited the region, successors to the dinosaurs of an even earlier age. What happened to both man and animal of the Folsom age, nobody knows; perhaps the lakes and streams created by melting glaciers of an earlier age began to dry up, for the vegetation became less luxuriant and trees disappeared.

The next known people on the Plains were potterymakers; the archeologists who call them Woodland people believe they may have come from forested areas far east of the Missouri, spreading over much of the area during the years from A.D. 400 to A.D. 600 or later and living primarily by hunting. They were less nomadic than their predecessors, for they lived in primitive dwellings, partly dug out from the earth, probably roofed with skins or mats supported by light poles.

The next settlers were more sedentary people who lived in

unfortified villages and began tilling the soil, growing maize and beans rather than gathering all their vegetables from the wild. They lived between A.D. 1200 and A.D. 1450, and, because of the relative peace existing then, they did not have to expend energy on fighting, but could devote time to their newly discovered farming pursuits. They produced not only more elaborate pottery than that of their predecessors but a wide variety of stone, bone, horn, and shell tools and ornaments as well. A prolonged drought throughout the Great Plains during the latter part of the fifteenth century and fantastic dust storms that buried many of the village sites under a heavy layer of dust may have forced them out of the territory entirely.

By the time the first white men came into the Plains—Coronado from the Spanish southwest in 1541, and Père Marquette from the French in the north in 1683, the Pawnee were well established in Nebraska, occupying villages in an area generally centering around the Platte, hunting over a much wider area. They were Caddoans, part of a large linguistic family that ranged from Oklahoma to the Dakotas. Four bands settled in the area now known as Nebraska: the Chaui, the Kitkekahki, the Pitahauerat, and the Skidi, who wore distinctive scalp locks. From their earliest days in Nebraska, they apparently lived in villages, at first small ones with rectangular earthen lodges spread far apart, later in larger settlements of round earthen lodges made of poles covered with brush and dirt.

They were farmers; the Skidi band on certain occasions sacrificed a maiden to the Morning Star, and all the groups had other religious ceremonies aimed at assuaging the gods to guarantee a good corn crop. In the spring the women went to the fields, small plots of land not necessarily adjacent to the village, located where the soil was loose and fertile, and there they planted the seed—dark-colored red, blue, or brown kernels of corn, and beans, squash, melon, placing the seed in hills. They occasionally gathered a kind of wild potato. Their implements were made of buffalo bone, the shoulder blade, especially, making an effective hoe. After the second hoeing was finished in mid-June, the villagers left for the three-month summer hunt for meat, returning in September to harvest the crops. They picked and husked the corn—Indian corn had ears ranging from four to eight inches long—and boiled it, cut the kernels from the cob, and dried them in the sun, then placed them in leather bags called parfleches to store for later use. Drying was the only means of preservation they knew. Although the Pawnees ate elk, deer, bear, beaver, raccoon, badger, dog, rabbit, and squirrel for their meat, their staple was buffalo, which provided not only meat but also hide for shelter and clothing, hair for weaving and braiding, sinew for cord, thread, and bowstrings, bone for tools and implements, and horn and hooves for ornaments.

For their two great hunts, one in midsummer, the other in autumn, the Pawnees left the village, packing their skin tipis, which provided portable housing, and their other necessary gear onto travoises or frames made of two parallel poles harnessed to dogs that dragged the freight across the prairie; the Indians had no knowledge of the wheel. The tribesmen walked, ranging sometimes as far as five hundred miles, to the area between the Republican and the Arkansas rivers, in their search for buffalo. The earliest buffalo hunters had no weapons other than spears or bolos to launch rocks from a string swung around and around for momentum; later they used bows and flint-tipped arrows. Their most effective hunting ploy was to spook the buffalo into a stampede over a bluff when they could, sometimes by setting fire to the prairie to scare them, and when the animals, sometimes hundreds of them, lay piled up at the bottom of the bluff, the hunters would then approach and slaughter them with their finely honed flint knives. A successful hunt was a time of feasting and rejoicing. The villagers gorged on fresh meat, and what they could not eat they cut into strips, which they dried in the sun or over fires to form jerky, a hard, tough food. Later in the season hunting parties carried pemmican, a highly concentrated food composed of jerky, suet, marrow, and dried cherries—pits and all, which they pounded with a stone maul into fine paste, providing a high degree of nutrition.

The Pawnees were mystical, living in close communion with the land, believing in the personification of the spirits of animals or natural things. Their principal deities were Tirawa, or the Morning Star, the male or dominant force whose rays brought growth and harvest, and Atira, or the Evening Star, the female or submissive force whose cycles symbolized the changing seasons; they were not unlike the yin and yang of the Orientals. Although priestly positions were hereditary, the priests had to undergo special instruction and testing; on occasion, individual tribesmen could go into solitude, fasting in sweat lodges to seek visions from the spirits. Each band or village had its sacred bundle, holy pieces which symbolized the leadership and spirit of the group. The Pawnees had a complex mythology involving celestial objects as well as animals, and believed in a hereafter, reincarnation in the form of stars.

Before the white man came, bringing horses and metal goods, both of which completely altered the Indian pattern of living, the Pawnees developed artistic skill in pottery making and in creating tools and ornaments from stone and bone: arrow points, knives, scrapers, needles, and awls.

With no written language the Pawnees as well as other tribal groups on the Plains relied on official storytellers as their historians, men who had memorized the traditions handed down orally from one generation to the next, adding pertinent information about significant tribal happenings during their own lifetimes. The Indians also used petroglyphs, or stylized drawings, to record their group experiences, Pawnees scratching them into cliffs near Dakota City, for instance, where they are still visible, or painting pictographs onto buffalo skins, using dyes boiled from roots or berries as their paint and fluffed-out willow twigs as brushes.

By the middle of the seventeenth century, sedentary Siouan tribes—Omaha, Ponca, Oto, and Iowa—were located along the Missouri River, having moved, over a period of several centuries, from an area east of the Alleghenies in search of food and to escape their enemies. Although theirs was a patrilineal social structure—assuming kinship from the father's family—rather than the matrilineal one of the Pawnee, and their customs and tribal taboos were likewise different from the Pawnee, yet they followed much the same general patterns of living as the larger Pawnee group. They, too, were farmers, living in earthen lodges along the river and tilling the soil half the year, following the buffalo the rest of the year, living in skin tipis while on the hunt. The Omaha and Ponca were closely related in language and social culture, part of the Dhegiha branch of the

Sioux, and are believed to have lived together at one time, prior to the white man's association with them; neither group was large.

The Oto, Iowa, and Missouria, part of the Chiwere family of the Sioux, were smaller groups, part of a common Winnebago heritage, wanderers from an area now part of Wisconsin.

In the western and northern reaches of what is now Nebraska, other peoples were living in the days preceding the white man's knowledge of the region. The only ones whose identities are known are the Padoucas, or Plains Apaches. Their villages in the Sandhills of Nebraska about 1700 have been designated as the Dismal River archeological culture. The nomadic tribes were in constant motion, moving in bands or communities from one place to another, pushed from behind by warring enemy tribes, pulled in front by the need for food, both the buffalo and wild vegetation, migrating, drifting, always westerly. Even the so-called sedentary tribes were not permanently located, for they seem to have changed location every generation or two.

In historic times, however, the western and northern regions were the home of the nomadic Dakota Sioux, primarily the Brule and Oglala bands of the Teton Sioux, linguistically related to the farmers along the Missouri River but far, far removed from them in cultural patterns. The Dakota probably arrived in Nebraska after the mid-1700s, driven out of their wooded habitat in the east by the Chippewas. They were a proud warrior group, highly mobile, scorning farming and disdaining permanent homes, living in highly decorated skin tipis and gathering their food where they found it, meat from the hunt and wild turnips and berries from the prairies. Their social structure was complex, each band divided into societies more or less according to their tasks; some were warrior societies, some hunters, some priests, some police, and most of the societies had animal names—the Dog Society, for instance.

Constantly moving, always wary of danger from other tribes, the Dakota evolved a stylized pattern of family and community living, the good of the tribe more important than that of the individual; from birth, youngsters were taught never to cry, for a baby's wail could reveal the hiding place of the group. The Dakota, in common with many other Indian tribes, practiced birth control, through abstinence; they were scornful of the woman who had a new baby before the next older one was capable of walking and taking care of himself. In a highly nomadic society where mobility was necessary for survival, the community could not be burdened with large numbers of help-less babies.

Family and community were intertwined, social patterns in-volving taboos and strict regulations; a man, for instance, could never directly address his mother-in-law, and young boys were trained by uncles rather than by fathers. To lose one's temper and strike another in anger was a disgrace. Many community activities centered around religion, dances and festivals to ap-pease the various spirits who controlled nature; tautly stretched skin drums and gourd rattles provided rhythm; reed flutes and the singing and chanting of the women, sometimes of the men, provided the melody for the involved ceremonies invoking the blessings of the gods.

Sioux women were expert at working leather, chewing and scraping the hides of buffalo or other animals until they were soft and pliable, creating geometric designs on them with dyed porcupine quills, animal teeth, or shells.

By the time the white men came into contact with the Dakota Sioux, the lives of the Plainsmen revolved around their horses, descendants of animals that had strayed or stampeded from the Spanish settlements during the sixteenth century. The nomadic Indian and his horse were as one; a man's wealth was counted in horses, and his mobility was the speed and endurance of his horse, which provided him the means to roam over tremendous reaches. When no battle with another tribe was imminent, no buffalo hunt in sight, tribesmen could set forth on a horse-raiding expedition to capture strings of animals belonging to other groups.

The bravery of a warrior was accounted for by "counting coup," touching an enemy, alive or dead, with a lance, the more daring the deed the more important the coup; to his coup stick, then, the tribesman could tie another feather.

Other nomadic tribes in the western part of what became Nebraska included Cheyenne and Arapaho, members of the Algonquin family who had migrated from the eastern regions centuries earlier. There were Comanches and Kiowas, too. Although the details of the living patterns of these Indians were different from those of the Pawnee, in general their culture was strikingly similar to that of the Dakota, based on rigid codes of behavior within the group and on mobility. Their territorial lines were fluid, changing sometimes from month to month, always extending over a vast area of the prairie.

These bronze-skinned people were the original inhabitants of the land that was to become Nebraska, markedly unlike the palefaces who were to follow.

Who were the first white men to see Nebraska? Nobody knows. The Spanish were the first to try. From the south in 1541, almost eighty years before the *Mayflower* landed in New England, Francisco Vasquez Coronado and his armor-clad conquistadores traveled across the dry, treeless plain so much like their native Spain that they commented on it in their records, Coronado writing that "the country itself is the best I have ever seen for producing all the products of Spain." But they were looking for the fabled kingdom of Quivira, where everything was made of gold, not "little villages, and in many of these they do not plant anything and do not have any houses except of skins and sticks, and they wander around with the cows," Coronado wrote to the King of Spain.[1] Those cows were really bison, misnamed buffalo, whom Cortez in Mexico had earlier described as having "the hump like the camel and hair like a lion." [2] Before Coronado and his men reached what is now Nebraska, they turned around and went back to the Rio Grande. They were interested in gold, not farmland.

Half a century later the French landed in Canada, and for the next two hundred years Spain and France vied with each other for land in the New World. Not until 1700 did they know what was in the area that lay midway between the seas, midway between the Gulf of Mexico and the Arctic, separated from the east by the Missouri River and the west by the Rockies. The

1. George Parker Winship, "The Coronado Expedition, 1540–1542," *Fourteenth Annual Report of the Bureau of Ethnology,* Part 1, pp. 329–613.
2. Mari Sandoz, *The Buffalo Hunters* (New York: Hastings House, 1954) p. ix.

land was known to exist, for maps dating back to the 1500s
show the landmass, but nobody knew what was really there.
Rumors flew that the great passage to the western sea—and to
the riches of Cathay beyond—lay in that area. The Spanish,
who had discovered Florida in 1512 and conquered Mexico in
1520, wanted all the land in between. The French, who had established Quebec in 1608 and Biloxi in 1699, began exploring
from both north and south into the Mississippi River. The two
groups were aiming for the same land and were determined that
the other one would not gain possession of it.

Most of the recorded activity of the French and Spanish in
Nebraska took place in the eighteenth century. Etienne Veniard
de Bourgmont, a *coureur de bois,* was the first Frenchman to
write of the area. He had deserted his post as commandant of
Fort Detroit, married an Indian girl, and lived among the tribes
along the Missouri Valley; in 1714 he wrote of the existence of
a shallow river and made the first known reference to the name
that later was used for the region. "Higher up the river," he
wrote of the lower Missouri, "one finds the large river, called
Nibraskier by the French and Indians," [3] an obvious acknowl-
edgement that French trappers were already in the area, using
the vast network of waterways to glean the silken beaver and
other fur-bearing animals that inhabited the land to the west.
But although the French trappers knew every landmark in the
countryside, sometimes even becoming members of the Indian
tribes, more Indian than Gallic, they were chary about writing
anything down. Some were illiterate, others were avoiding the
law; they did not put anything on paper.

Eventually Bourgmont established Fort Orleans on the Missouri, visited with Indian tribes, and took some Indians with
him to Paris; he could have laid the foundations for a successful
French settlement in the area, but officialdom in France did not
follow through; the French muffed the opportunity.

In the meantime the Spanish learned through an Indian war
party, which had raided a Pawnee village and captured French
carbines and powder flasks, that the French were in the northern
plains, so in 1720 they mounted an expedition with Lieutenant

3. Quoted by Olson, *History of Nebraska,* p. 31.

Colonel Pedro de Villasur in command. He set out from Santa
Fe on June 16 with forty-five Spanish soldiers, sixty Apaches, a
priest, and an interpreter. When they reached the Platte, they
came upon a large Pawnee village. At daybreak on Tuesday,
August 13, while the Spanish slept, the Pawnees attacked; Villasur was killed, as were most of his men, and the Apaches fled;
only thirteen survivors straggled back to Sante Fe.

The French won the next round, when the brothers Mallett,
Pierre and Paul, went overland seeking a trade route to Santa Fe
in 1739; even though the Spanish forbade trading between their
people and the French, a thriving commercial traffic in con-
traband developed. To reach Santa Fe, the Mallett brothers followed the sandy-bottom river part of the way through Nebraska
and named it *la Platte;* the name stuck. The Spanish had already
named some of the rivers—their name for the Platte was *Rio de
Jesus Maria,* and for the Loup, *Rio de San Lorenzo.* Many of
the present geographic names in Nebraska were French-
inspired.

For several decades nobody really knew who owned the
land—the French, the Spanish, or even the British, who were
pushing westward to Ohio and beyond. But events taking place
far away had an effect, for by 1763 the French were officially
out of North America. The signing of the Treaty of Paris, which
concluded the Seven Years War in Europe and its New World
skirmishes known as the French and Indian War, made all the
land west of the Mississippi River Spanish, that land east of the
Mississippi, English. The French fur traders remained where
they were, floating their furs down the icy mountain streams of
the Rockies into the main thoroughfares through Nebraska. The
mouth of the Platte became known as the "Equator of the Missouri," differentiating the upper Missouri from the lower part,
and St. Louis, farther downstream at the junction of the Missouri with the Mississippi, became a significant fur-trading center, no matter which flag flew. The trappers were casual about
their nationality, swearing whatever allegiance was necessary to
get them into the land of swift-running streams and luxuriant
pelts. A man named Truteau, obviously not a Spaniard, did
exploring for the Spanish, for instance, and was replaced by a
Scotsman named Mackay; to the bearded, buckskinned trappers,

nationality was far less important than the chance to live in the untamed wilderness.

The Spanish did not have time to consolidate their gains in the Mississippi Valley, for the secret Treaty of San Ildefonso, signed on October 1, 1800, ceded Louisiana back to France, and before many of the people in the New World were aware of the change in their nationality, Napoleon agreed to sell the land to raise money for his expansion in Europe. On April 30, 1803, the United States purchased from France almost a million square miles of land through the center of the continent, paying four cents an acre for the Louisiana Purchase.

By the time the United States took over the ownership of the land lying between the Mississippi River and the Rockies, from the Gulf of Mexico to Canada, the lives of the original inhabitants in the area had already started to change through association with the fur men from an alien civilization. By this time, the nomadic Indians had learned to depend upon the horse for their livelihood. Their speed and range increased manyfold when they mounted their horses; the Indians could kill far more buffalo than before; they adapted their long bows to adjust to their mounted positions. The traders, when they came in, brought guns and powder to swap for beaver, otter, and fox pelts, and deer and buffalo skins. With firepower the Indians could kill even more buffalo, and with more skins to tan and work, a warrior needed more wives. Polygamy became more common.

The traders brought metal goods—pots and pans, metal arrow tips, axes, knives, and the Indians gave up making pottery bowls, chipping flint for arrowheads and scrapers. The traders brought glass beads, steel needles, calico and other fabrics, and even blankets; the Indian women forgot their quilling and sewed beads onto fabric, and their men wore blankets. The traders brought sugar—the sweetness few Indians had ever tasted before, and the Indians developed such a taste for it that they would drink ten or twelve cups of highly sweetened coffee in a sitting, and beg sugar from white men later on.

But most of all, the traders brought whiskey—a rot-gut composed of a gallon of raw alcohol, three gallons of water, and a pound of chewing tobacco—and for the firewater, the Indians would trade their choicest pelts, their finest furs. Then they would drink themselves into a blind stupor. In their own culture the Indians had never learned about fermentation, certainly not distillation, and the potent firewater hit them with violence; many were immoderate in their consumption. Although the United States government later enacted regulations constraining the use of alcoholic spirits in dealings with the Indians, and some bands refused to accept whiskey, most traders used firewater as a tool in negotiating with the Indians for their furs. But some trappers realized that their relationship with the Indians was one of mutual dependence, and those white men and the Indians they dealt with developed a respect and understanding as they exchanged not only goods but ideas as well.

The most powerful of the Indian chiefs of the fur-trading days in Nebraska was a canny Omaha who quickly picked up the sharpest tactics of the traders and adapted them to his own use, both in his dealings with his fellow Indians and with the traders as well. Black Bird was autocratic, a despot over the traders as well as over his own tribesmen. He raised his tribe to a warlike nation and by use of threats was able to control which other tribes the traders talked to; within his own band, he ruled with complete control. He had the traders bring their goods to him, in his own dwelling, and he took what he wanted as his bounty—tobacco, powder and lead, knives, hatchets, kettles, red and blue flannel cloth, beads, whiskey, and even guns; then he sent for his tribesmen and their furs and sold the goods to them himself, at prices high enough to make a profit of at least five times more than he had paid the traders. Those tribesmen who objected to his heavy-handed methods mysteriously fell ill; one legend says that a trader gave Black Bird a good supply of poison—arsenic, maybe—with which the chief became a prophet, foretelling the death of anyone who opposed him— even to the exact date. He was a tyrant, even with his own. But in the end, it was another one of the importations of the traders that killed him.

Unwittingly, the traders brought to the Indians a destructive force that was even more direct than whiskey: the white man's diseases. And the Indians had no immunity to them. Although syphillis brought misery, and cholera and children's diseases brought death to the Indians, it was smallpox that decimated them. In 1800, after Black Bird saw two-thirds of his tribesmen die of the spotted disease, he, too, fell ill and died. On a high hill that overlooked the Missouri River, he is said to have been buried on his standing horse, with sod and soil piled around them in a great mound, and a pole on top with his chief's pipe, fringed tobacco pouch, scalp-trimmed shield, and flag fluttering in the wind. The smallpox did not stop. By 1804 the Ponca had lost three-fourths of their population to the disease, the Oto such a large number that the tribe never recovered; in the 1830s, smallpox swept through most of the tribes of the Great Plains.

The fur trade that had been established during the eighteenth century was intensified during the first third of the next century, after the land officially became part of the United States of America, not so much because of changes in political geography as because of increased demand for furs. By the dozens the trappers came, moving westward, at first meeting with the Indians along the Missouri River, then farther inland and, as the furs became scarcer, moving to the rendezvous grounds in the high Rockies to meet the Indians, trading whiskey, beads, and blankets for the pelts that brought increasingly greater prices in this country as well as in Europe.

Some fur-trading posts were located along the Missouri River. Manuel Lisa, who knew more of furs and Indians and the territory than probably any other white man of his era, became a dominant figure in the fur-trade industry, establishing the first post on the upper Missouri in 1807, and several others later. The one named Bellevue, near Council Bluff, was the most thriving. According to legend, the name came when Lisa, the Spanish fur trader, stood on a hill overlooking the silvery ribbon of river below and exclaimed, in French, *"La Belle Vue!"* [4] His Missouri Fur Company established a trading post there in 1810, and in 1823, John Dougherty, the Indian agent, moved the agency for the Omaha, Oto, Missouria, and Pawnee there from Fort Atkinson. A few years later the post was turned over to the

4. A. T. Andreas, *History of the State of Nebraska* (Chicago: The Western Historical Company, 1882), p. 1361.

American Fur Company, operated by Peter Sarpy, and the settlement on the Missouri became a gathering point for Indians, traders, and travelers alike. Other traders had other, smaller posts, some near the mouth of the Platte on the Missouri, others far west on the Platte or the Niobrara. But most of the fur-trade movement in the nineteenth century in what is now Nebraska was transient; Nebraska was merely the highway which the traders traveled to reach the more desirable beaver grounds farther west.

The traders and trappers were the first white men most of the Indians knew. A few were men of learning, most were men whose knowledge came only from nature. Some were harsh in their dealings with the Indians, but then, they were not necessarily kind to their own, either, as the story of Hiram Scott indicates. He was left for dead by his fellow trappers in the upper Platte valley in 1827, without food, ammunition, or boat, and he crawled forty miles before he died; his skeleton was found the next spring.[5] Many of the traders devoted their time to drinking, gambling, squawing, and carousing, making huge fortunes almost overnight and losing them even more rapidly.

Without intending to, the traders and trappers furthered the change in the centuries-old life patterns of the Plains Indians.

5. Through the years, the Hiram Scott story took many forms. Various versions are given in Merrill J. Mattes, *The Great Platte River Road* (Lincoln: Nebraska State Historical Society, 1969), pp. 426–435.

3

The White Man Comes

ALTHOUGH the Indians who lived there, and the fur trappers who were moving in, knew what was in the Louisiana Territory, the vast new acquisition of the United States, the rest of the world did not. Thomas Jefferson, the president who had authorized the Louisiana Purchase on April 30, 1803, sent out explorers to study the land; he had long been intrigued with the vast unknown lands to the west.

In late summer of 1803, Meriwether Lewis and William Clark began their expedition, commissioned to ascend the Missouri, cross the mountains, and descend by the most practicable river to the Pacific, while making peace with the Indians and recording geographic and scientific observations. A year later, in July 1804, they reached the mouth of the Little Nemaha, their first camp in what later became Nebraska, and a week after that they came to the mouth of the Platte. For almost two months they followed the Missouri River along the eastern border of the region, reporting on the "great quantities of grapes, plums of two kinds, wild cherries of two kinds, hazelnuts, and gooseberries" they saw, commenting on what a great place Council Bluff would be for a fortification or trading establishment.[1]

They saw only a small part of what later became Nebraska Territory, that adjacent to the river, but they proved that it was possible to cross the new country, its flat plains and rugged

1. *The Journals of the Lewis and Clark Expedition,* edited by Nicholas Biddle, with an introduction by John Bakeless (New York: The Heritage Press, 1962), p. 16.

mountains, by water. The fabled Northwest Passage to the western sea was a fiction, they learned, but the chain of rivers provided an inland waterway of sorts, no matter how tortuous, to take them in a circuitous route to the Pacific.

Their comments on the numbers of fur traders they saw floating goods on the Missouri—eight on their outbound trip in 1804, eleven on their return two years later—were prescient; one of the striking results of their expedition was that it opened the region to the new flood of fur traders who would rush in during the next few decades and reap the harvest of beaver and other furs from the interior reaches of the country.

As the fur trade boomed and the wealth poured in, the area west of the Missouri River became of more political significance than before. The War of 1812 against the British was over, but the Treaty of Ghent in 1815 hadn't really settled the situation in which the British were covertly trying to prevent American expansion in the west; it was possible that the British were still trying to arm the Indians and agitate them against the Americans. To protect the fur traders and to counteract any remaining British influence, the federal government proposed to establish a series of military posts along the Mississippi and Missouri rivers. On the Missouri, posts were to be constructed at the Council Bluff, at the Mandan villages in what was to become Dakota Territory, and possibly at the mouth of the Yellowstone in what later became Montana.

In 1819 two groups arrived, Colonel Henry M. Atkinson's military force, which spent the winter battling disease at Camp Missouri in the bottoms below Council Bluff, and Major Stephen H. Long's scientific party at Engineer Cantonment, five miles downriver. These were the first American military forces in what later became Nebraska. The Long group spent only a winter there, leaving in the spring to make an overland survey of the west. But the Atkinson group moved to higher quarters and built a permanent camp, renaming it Fort Atkinson in 1821.

There seemed to be little military duty necessary for protecting the fur trade, and the camp became a farming area, the infantrymen and civilian hangers-on of more than one thousand persons busily growing corn and other crops on the 504-acre farm of Missouri River bottomland, to the disgust of a military inspector. In a report in October 1826, George Croghan called it the weakest fort with the worst trained garrison he had ever seen.

He wrote:

> The present system is destroying military spirit and making the officers of the base overseers of a troop of awkward plowmen. Let the soldier be one. Let him no longer boast of his skill as a tiller of the soil but as a soldier. They can raise a garden, but do not let them boast of proficiency as farmers   [2]

Fort Atkinson was abandoned the next year. Few of the other forts were ever constructed.

Twenty years later other military forts were to be established in what became Nebraska, but for a different purpose. By that time the beaver trade in the mountains was dying and the English threat in the Great Plains area was over. This time the forts were needed to protect the overland travelers who moved in increasing numbers across the Indian lands.

In the meantime, however, the settlement at Bellevue, a few miles downriver, flourished. And shortly the missionaries came. Stories of the growing moral deterioration among the Indians had begun to drift back to New England, and when the Flathead Indians, father west, sent a delegation to St. Louis in 1831, requesting "a Bible and a Black Robe," church groups heard the call to action. The news was spread in religious publications, and although the appeal was obviously for Catholic priests, Protestant congregations in New England called for volunteers and funds. It was a time of renewed Protestant missionary zeal in New England to save the souls of the heathen— Congregationalists had gone out to the Sandwich Islands, later named Hawaii, in 1820—and the possibility of service to the Indians presented an exciting new challenge.

Baptist Moses Merrill and his wife, accompanied by Miss Cynthia Brown and Ira D. Blanchard, arrived at Bellevue on November 8, 1833, and seven days later Mrs. Merrill had classes going for Indian children. Merrill translated a prayerbook and a hymnal, reducing the oral language to writing, but

---

2. Edgar Bruce Wesley, "Life at Fort Atkinson," *Nebraska History* 30, 4 (December 1949):349.

was only partially successful in diverting the Indians from fire-water and the other debaucheries the traders had brought.

The next year two Presbyterians, John Dunbar and Samuel Allis, arrived in Bellevue in October to minister to the Pawnee, intending to remain there. When Annuity Day came and the Pawnee arrived at the agency to pick up their tribal allotments, each tribe wanted to take a missionary back home. After prayer-ful deliberation on the subject, according to an old letter, the men separated, Dunbar going with the Grand Pawnee and Allis with the Loup; both of the men were treated with kindness and consideration by the Indians who felt that the missionaries brought them good fortune. In 1841 the men established a mis-sion among the Tappages on Plum Creek, not far from the present town of Fullerton, but although forty-one lodges were set up in the area, the mission failed to prosper and was aban-doned in 1846.

That same year the Presbyterians sent Mr. and Mrs. Edward McKinney to establish a mission for the Omaha in Bellevue; they opened a school the next year, and despite opposition from many sources, the mission prospered. The Rev. William Hamil-ton, always called Father Hamilton by his devoted charges, took charge in 1853 and served for the next two decades.

Other missionaries came and went. Methodist Jason Lee came through the area with a trapping caravan in 1834, en route to Oregon; Presbyterians Samuel Parker and Dr. Marcus Whit-man came through in 1835 on their way west and back. Dr. Whitman and his bride Narcissa returned in 1836. They re-mained in Bellevue long enough to minister to victims of a viru-lent plague of "spasmodic cholera" raging in the area and to suggest that the village, then located in the lowlands adjoining the river, be moved to the bluffs high above its muddy banks. During the 1830s, too, Father Pierre Jean De Smet, a Jesuit priest, came into the region to begin his life of service among the Indians, principally farther west in the Rockies.

Most of the time the traders and the missionaries were at odds with each other, the traders continuing to dispense liquor to the Indians and to take advantage of them, unwittingly providing many of the tools for their self-destruction—the missionaries trying to save the souls of the Indians, as they saw it, to counteract the influence of the traders, and to promote Indian welfare, without realizing that in superimposing their own particular culture on an already existing one, they were being destructive too. Historians generally agree that the effects of both traders and missionaries were harmful, although in different ways. As James C. Olson said, ''While the trader was merely indifferent to the Indian's culture, the missionary saw in it something that must be changed. Both contributed to its ultimate dissolution.'' [3]

Perhaps the most lasting contributions of the missionaries were their explorations to Oregon, proving that overland passage was possible to the western sea, and their enthusiasm in opening up that area to American settlement.

Before the westward movement could gain much momentum, Congress passed the Indian Intercourse Act of 1834, and the land was known informally for the next score of years as Indian Country. Until then, the vast central regions of the country had been known vaguely as Louisiana Territory or simply Part of the North American Continent.

For years Congress had worried about what to do with the Indians and, from 1820 on, had passed various laws to remove them to the Plains west of the Mississippi River. These laws opened up the fertile lands of Indiana and Illinois to white settlement, and concurrently provided the Indians a haven free from further white encroachment. The Act of 1834 forbade whites without license from the government to trespass on Indian lands and provided for the administration of the Indian country. But almost as soon as the ink was dry on the document, the boundary began to move westward to the Missouri River, where it stayed for twenty years. Although white men could not settle beyond the river in what became Nebraska, they could move across it, and within a few years a stream of travelers in covered wagons flowed across the heart of the Indian Country. From then on, little by little, the government whittled away at the lands, negotiating treaty after treaty, moving first one Indian tribe, then another, onto reservations.

3. Olson, *History of Nebraska*, p. 53.

The flood of travelers shortly became so overwhelming that the federal government established new military forts to provide protection against the Indians. Old Fort Kearny, in the southeastern part of the state where Nebraska City is now located, was in existence from 1846 to 1847. When the army discovered that the heavy overland traffic was in the Platte River valley, it established a new Fort Kearny, in 1848, at the bend of the river near the junction of the Oregon Trail, Mormon Trail, and California Trail. For a score of years this fort served as an oasis, milestone, shopping and communications center for tens of thousands of overland travelers. To provide military strength farther west, the army, in 1849, purchased Fort Laramie from the American Fur Trading Company, which had operated a trading post there since 1834. Two years later, in 1851, in a conference at Horse Creek, near present-day Lyman, Nebraska, with representatives from Indian tribes and officials from Washington, the government agreed to pay the various tribes an annuity for fifty years in exchange for letting the white man travel without harassment along the Holy Road, as the Indians themselves called the Overland Trail. But later the Senate reduced the annuity term to ten years, and sometimes the Indian agents were late with the payments and the goods given in payment were rotten.

Although the land still belonged to the Indian, the white man had come to Nebraska. Except for the military, who were stationed there on a temporary basis, the white man could not live there, but by the tens of thousands he moved across the land.

4

The Great Highway

$\mathscr{F}$OR a quarter of a century the land that was to become Nebraska was a vast highway. Long lines of great white-canvas-covered wagons—prairie schooners, they were called, in a sea of grass—creaked and swayed across the prairie, dusty columns headed west along the broad, flat valley of the Platte, one of the world's great natural highways. To Oregon at first, and later to Utah and California, tens of thousands of eager pilgrims headed westward on the combined highways of the Oregon Trail, the California Trail, the Mormon Trail, which stretched in a broad ribbon across the breadth of Nebraska. Between 1841 and 1866 an estimated 350,000 emigrants passed by, always moving westward.

One historian described the Platte Valley as "the funnel through which America literally spilled over into the West." [1] Nebraska was not the goal; she was the means to an end.

In earlier years fur traders had gone by water, using the Missouri River to lead them to the fur-bearing regions in the mountains, beyond what was to become Nebraska Territory; they floated back the furs in light pirogues, river to river. In certain seasons water passage was possible for light vessels, with considerable portage here and there, but it was impossible for heavy freight at any time.

Intermittently through the years occasional explorers had

1. Olson, *History of Nebraska,* p. 54.

gone overland following the broad Platte River valley; in 1830, the party of Jedediah Smith, David Jackson, and William Sublette, with twelve vehicles, reached Wind River in Wyoming by traveling the overland route; other traders used the Platte River road to go to the rendezvous with the Indians in the high Rockies. The discovery of South Pass, on the Sweetwater beyond the North Platte in Wyoming was the key to the route to the northwest, for it provided an easy crossing of the Rocky Mountains.

The missionaries who traveled overland in 1834 to tend the Indians in Oregon had sent back such glowing reports of the fertility and beauty of the land that almost overnight Oregon became a magnet, attracting settlers to the new country. After Narcissa Whitman and Eliza Spaulding went through South Pass with their husbands in 1836, proving that women could make the journey, the public knew that the route was fit for immigration. Negotiations between England and the United States in 1818, and later in 1843, had failed to settle the boundary between Canada and the United States and had left the Columbia River valley in joint tenancy between the two countries, a fretful situation to expansion-minded Americans. The motives of the first settlers were both missionary and patriotic; Marcus Whitman wanted to settle Oregon with Protestant Americans, others wanted to settle it with enough Americans of any kind to push out the British and possess the land. The panic of 1837 in the East added economic motivations as well for settlers to seek new lands similar to the ones they left—humid, wooded, arable.

In May 1841 the first band of eighty emigrants set out across Nebraska for the Northwest; and in 1843 a group of almost a thousand persons with all their gear in one hundred twenty wagons, trailing five thousand cattle, made the first large-scale migration to Oregon, reaching the Willamette Valley eight months later. Dr. Whitman was the guide, as Methodist Jason Lee had been for the 1841 expedition. The Oregon boundary line—subject of the "Fifty-four forty or fight" campaign cry of the Whigs during the presidential election of 1844—was settled in 1846 along the 49th parallel, and the United States had sole title to the land. Emigrants by the thousands surged across Nebraska, through South Pass, and on to the new lands.

Before long, Oregon was not the only goal. In 1847 Brigham

Young led a band of Mormons across the Plains and into Utah to establish a Promised Land for the Latter Day Saints; hundreds of others followed, in well-organized expeditions.

A year later, in 1848, California was the magnet, a gold rush erupting when news spread around the world about the gold nugget discovered by James Marshall, a farmer, at Sutter's Fort near Sacramento; California was now American land, since the settlement of the War with Mexico, and by the tens of thousands the gold seekers rushed to her shores, by sailing vessel around South America, by portaging over the isthmus of Panama, but mostly by the Overland Trail.

The Platte Valley was a superb natural highway, the best in the world, many of the travelers said. One man described the road as averaging thirty feet wide, the track as smooth and hard as "a brickyard pave." [2] General William T. Sherman, a man of few words, summed it up in 1866 when he said that it had three cardinal virtues: it was dry, it was level, and it went in exactly the right direction. [3] The great Platte River road was so well worn that even now, one hundred twenty-five years after the wagons left it, deep ruts still remain in the areas that are not an interstate highway.

The outfitting point for most of the Oregon-bound travelers was Independence, Missouri, or some other town along the river, which the immigrants could reach by boat, gathering there to form into wagon trains for the long journey ahead. Sometimes several families from the same general neighborhood back home traveled together; usually, however, they were total strangers, meeting in Independence and committing themselves to spend the next half year together, hoping their fellow travelers were sober, dependable souls, reliable with a gun to shoot game or Indians.

The travelers who formed a wagon train organized an association with a constitution and bylaws outlining the officers, camping regulations, duties, and moral concerns—gambling and drinking of alcoholic spirits, except for medicinal purposes, were forbidden. They elected a wagon master who was chief of

2. C. M. Clark, *A Trip to Pike's Peak*, quoted in Mattes, *The Great Platte River Road*, p. 10.

3. Mattes, *The Great Platte River Road*, p. 9.

the caravan, one of his functions being to assign daily tasks of hunting, guarding, cooking, driving cattle. Some of the wagon trains were joint stock ventures, everybody ante-ing up a given amount for outfitting expenses. A few of the bigger outfits had high-flown names, and one particularly sophisticated train even had uniforms for its own militia, which drilled vigorously in Independence and for the first couple of days on the trail. The trains varied in size from three or four wagons to as many as a hundred. Through experience, outfitters learned that fifteen to twenty-five wagons made a manageable group to travel as a unit.

The wagons were sturdy wooden affairs with white canvas wired up and over them to cover the loads of foodstuffs, tools, guns, furniture, clothing, crates of chickens—the supplies the emigrants thought they would need along the way and in their homes Out West. Slow-moving oxen, two or three yokes or more, depending on the weight of the wagon, provided motive power, although occasionally teams of horses or mules were used. Spare riding stock was tied on behind, and cattle straggled along somewhere in the middle of the line, their slow, meandering pace limiting the daily speed of the train.

The Oregon-bound travelers traveled west from Independence, into what is now Kansas, and then followed the Little Blue River northward into what was to become the southwest corner of Gage County, Nebraska. The trail followed the Little Blue for a hundred miles, then struck off overland across Adams County to the Coasts of Nebraska, the specific name for the gently rolling, sandy hills lying along the Platte River there, the first glimpse most Oregon-bound travelers had of the broad Platte Valley. From there westward for two-hundred-fifty miles, they followed the Platte, taking the south fork about a hundred miles past the junction of the two branches, then crossing it and going overland to meet the north fork, following it past Courthouse Rock and Jail Rock, Chimney Rock—the most famous landmark on the trail because it could be seen for miles in the rarified Nebraska air—and past Scotts Bluff, named for the abandoned trapper whose skeleton had been found there. From there the trail led into the land that later became Wyoming and, far beyond the flatlands there, crossed South Pass and then divided, one branch going northwest into Oregon, the other into Utah or California.

The Mormons used a different access to the Platte, for they had spent the winter of 1846 at Winter Quarters, now the Florence area of north Omaha. The new religion had been founded in 1830 by Joseph Smith in New York state; its followers had been hounded from one place to another including Illinois, where their Nauvoo was the largest town in the state, and they decided to go West to establish their communal organization where there was not a single Gentile, or non-Mormon. By 1846 they had reached the Iowa side of the Missouri River, preparatory to crossing into Nebraska. The federal government was then embroiled with the Mexican War in California and New Mexico, and asked the Mormons to supply five hundred men to the army in return for permission to camp the rest of the Mormons temporarily on Indian lands across the river in Nebraska. More than three thousand Mormons camped that winter in wagons, dugouts, or in cottonwood log cabins; six hundred of them perished of sickness, cold, or starvation.

The first group of 148 pilgrims left there early in 1847 to go overland to Zion, now known as Salt Lake City, following the north side of the Platte through Nebraska. Their trail led across the quicksand of the Loup River, past Lone Tree, the single giant cottonwood at what is now Central City, along the Platte, through the state. During the rest of that year and through 1860, when the Mormon migration largely ceased, a total of more than seven thousand Saints made their way across the prairies.

The Mormons were by far the best organized of the wagon trains. With a common purpose, the establishing of a religious colony, they had a cohesiveness and discipline that many other units lacked. They were formed into Tens, Fifties, Hundreds; and each person was clearly identified with a specific train from start to finish; in other westward-bound groups, wagons would occasionally drop out of one line to join a completely different train, but the Mormons stayed where they were assigned. Since the various trails followed a common route for the first eight or nine hundred miles west of the Missouri River, after 1848 many of the wagon trains were composed of some emigrants going to California and some to Oregon; after they crossed South Pass,

they branched off. But the Mormons did not choose to be ecu-
menical; they stayed by themselves. Conversely, the other emigrants seldom wanted them; they considered the Mormons religious fanatics, almost as undesirable as Indians. Mormons
traveled with Mormons.

By the time the California rush began in 1848, perhaps as
many as twelve thousand persons had already traveled the great
Platte Valley Road west, either to Oregon or to Utah. Most of
the earlier travelers were settlers, intending to establish homes
in the new country. Although in the California rush there were
also family groups planning for permanence in the West, there
were also numbers of con artists and get-rich-quick devotees.
By early spring of 1849 at the embarkation points of Missouri
and Iowa, more than twenty thousand persons were forming car-
avans to go claim the gold of California, following the trails
through Nebraska that others before them had already established. They included family parties, farmers, doctors, lawyers, ministers, gamblers, prostitutes, roustabouts. In 1849 a
total of thirty thousand persons plodded through Nebraska; in
1850, the peak year, more than fifty-five thousand crossed the
rippling grasslands.

When the wagons started out, fresh and new and neatly
packed, they held not only supplies for the trip but also the
housewares the emigrants wanted for their new homes in the
West. But as the jolting, plodding travel went on day after day,
the travelers began to lighten their loads. Sometimes it was necessary; wagons broke down and after being repaired could not
carry as much weight, draft animals weakened and couldn't pull
as much. Sometimes it was simply a matter of choice; as the
hot, windy days wore on, families began to assess what material
goods were really vital to their lives. Through Nebraska, particularly from Fort Kearny westward, the prairie was littered with
why-did-we-ever-bring-these things—a heavy walnut dresser,
for instance, or a square rosewood piano, or a set of crockery,
complete except for the few plates and cups the wife kept out to
use along the way. Some of the travelers tried to sell their
surplus goods at Fort Kearny, others simply left them at the
campsite, to be picked up later by Indians or by other passersby.
And how the Indians enjoyed these prairie offerings, donning

the ludicrous frock coats and plumed Sunday bonnets, waving the curtains or ribbons or bolts of silks in the air as trophies as they galloped across the plains.

Women's clothing, especially, was expendable, for the dusty, weathered women soon realized that the elaborate bombazine or serge gowns they had so carefully packed back in Massachusetts or Ohio were completely superfluous here. In fact, in their journals, some of the ladies shamefacedly confess that they have lost all sense of modesty and for the sake of comfort are wearing trousers! They were bloomers, voluminous Turkish pantaloons invented by Amelia Bloomer of Council Bluffs, so popular that four unattached young ladies in one train had complete wardrobes of bloomers.

The slow-moving columns of dusty wagons lumbered along ten miles or so a day, starting at daybreak, resting at noon, stopping in late afternoon to form a circle for the night, with guards posted to protect against marauders, either human or animal. The hunters of the day went out on horseback to find fresh meat—buffalo, perhaps, or deer or prairie chicken; the cooks began to prepare supper; the drovers herded the cattle into the center of the ring to keep the Indians from them, and milked the cows that were fresh. The next day on the trail the milk that had not been drunk was churned into butter by the joggling, constant motion of the wagons.

Although their maps were usually inaccurate and their guides often inadequate, the travelers were optimistic and enthusiastic about their adventures; they left messages at the log cabin at Spring Ranche for those who would come after them, scratched their initials into the trunk of the single cottonwood at Lone Tree, and exulted when they saw the gangling spire at Chimney Rock and the formation at Scott's Bluff, the most dramatic landmarks along the trail.

So slowly did they move that they noticed all manner of things along the way. Prairie dogs, for instance, sleek, shy rodents, larger than rats but smaller than rabbits. They lived in towns, hundreds of holes with mounds of dirt beside them from the deep, intricate burrows underground. Left alone, the animals would sit upright on their hind legs, their front legs extended in front like arms, and they would chatter or bark sociably to the others in the community, perhaps thousands of animals in one area. But at the approach of man, they would suddenly dart into the ground and out of sight. Prairie-dog holes were a hazard; they were small and deep, and a horse could step into one and break a leg.

When the travelers camped for the night and went away from the trail to search for fuel or water, they could see wildflowers, pink and lavender asters, yellow sunflowers and goldenrod, low-growing pink wild roses, prairie bluebells, the white wild carrot they called Queen Anne's lace. Along the trail itself, these were gone after the first week of traffic in the spring, flowers and native grasses powdered into dust by the heavy wagon wheels and ponderous hooves that ground away the vegetation and dug deep troughs into the prairie, but away from the traffic, they bloomed in profusion.

In the broad flat reaches of the prairies the wagons spread out, eight or even twelve abreast, to avoid the dust of the wagons in front. In narrow defiles, they went singly. At Ash Hollow, approaching the North Platte, the crews rigged pulleys to let the heavily loaded wagons over the bluff they called Windlass Hill.

Travelers went on both sides of the Platte, so many of them during the peak years that a caravan stopping for the night could often see the twinkling camp fires of other groups who were also bedding down for the night. The travelers knew that those fires, like theirs, were fueled with buffalo chips, dried dung, for there was no firewood available in the treeless plain; women and children collected them in their aprons as soon as the train stopped for the night. During the peak years, as many as five hundred wagons a day would lumber past the new Fort Kearny.

Neither birth nor death could stop the westward rush, a frantic almost compulsive movement. Babies were born along the way—journals indicate that 1864 must have been a fruitful year—and if the mothers died in childbirth, there was usually a nursing mother in another train to feed the child. "This is a great country for babies," one traveler wrote in a letter. "Almost every train has had one and almost every one you meet expects to have one. It beats all!" [4]

4. William Larkin, letter of June 27, 1864, *Pacific Historian* 2 (February 1958): 2–4.

Cholera was the great scourge of the trail, in 1848, 1850, and 1852, especially, when thousands died, particularly between the Missouri River and Fort Laramie, the area of present-day Nebraska. At some campsites, whole families died, and there were instances where as many as seventeen cholera-infected bodies were buried in a common grave with no coffins to shelter them; all the wagon tailgates and other possible pieces of wood had already been used for coffins. One emigrant in 1850 estimated an average of four deaths from cholera per mile of travel across Nebraska, but he traveled midseason and there were many more deaths before winter that year. Some trains had doctors along, but not even their dosages of laudanum, camphor, or ammonia would help; almost all trains had barrels of whiskey, doled out carefully and mixed with molasses and creek water for medicinal purposes. Neither doctors nor medicine could prevent the deaths.

"I had intended to notice in my journal every grave and burying place that we passed, but I have abandoned this part of my plan . . . Graves are so numerous, that to notice them all would make my narrative tedious," another writer noted in his diary.[5]

Others died from accidents, were drowned in river fordings, kicked to death by horses or mules, shot by accidental gun discharge, run over by the wheels of the heavy wagon. A few were executed, for frontier justice was swift; when survival of all depended upon teamwork and co-operation, there was no room for a villain. At the Narrows of the Little Blue, for instance, a hot-tempered wagon master, irate over the slowness with which his teen-aged hostler responded to an order, swung and killed him with an axe handle. The rest of the party held speedy court and shortly strung him up to a wagon tongue; the two bodies were buried together. But the vast majority of emigrants behaved admirably, even under the extremes which tested the limit of their endurance and fortitude.

Occasionally graves were marked with wooden slabs, ripped from furniture in the wagons, or with pieces of buffalo horn, but most of those who died were buried in unmarked graves,

5. Franklin Langworthy, *Scenery of the Plains, Mountains and Mines,* edited by Paul C. Phillips (Princeton: Princeton University Press, 1932), pp. 37–38.

wrapped in the clothing they wore. More than one out of every seventeen persons who started the trail died en route.

Perhaps the most astonishing expeditions of all were those of the handcarts to Zion, when almost three thousand Mormons, men, women and children, walked thirteen hundred miles from the Missouri River to Salt Lake City, trudging across prairie and mountains, pushing their belongings in two-wheeled wooden handcarts. The new religion was bursting with converts intent on going to the Promised Land, and proselyting missionaries in England and Europe were gaining new members by the day; Brigham Young's Perpetual Emigration Fund coffers were so badly strained by earlier expeditions that they could no longer outfit wagon trains to Deseret, the original name for what was to become the state of Utah. In 1855 he organized the handcart companies, designing the two-wheeled vehicles himself and having them made in Iowa City; on July 20, 1856, the first company of 274 persons set out on foot from Florence, pushing fifty-two handcarts. Two months later, on September 26, they trundled into Salt Lake City, a brass band and dignitaries coming out to meet them. There were four more expeditions that year, two the next, one in 1859, and two in 1860, a total of ten expeditions in which almost three thousand persons, with 653 handcarts, stumbled across the breadth of Nebraska, most of Wyoming, and into Zion. Of those who started, two hundred fifty perished en route, most of them in snows in Wyoming in November 1856.

"The carts were generally drawn by one man and three women each, although some carts were drawn by women alone. There were about three women to one man, and two-thirds of the women were single. It was the most motley crew I ever beheld," an observer of the day wrote.

> The road was lined for a mile behind the train with the lame, halt, sick, and needy. Many were quite aged, and would be going slowly along, supported by a son or daughter. Some were on crutches; now and then a mother with a child in her arms and two or three hanging hold of her, with a forlorn appearance, would pass slowly along. . . .[6]

6. William A. Linn, *The Story of the Mormons* (New York: The Macmillan Company, 1902), pp. 422–423.

Others had walked the trail, to be sure, vigorous men and adolescent boys tramping beside the loaded wagons to guide the teams, but they did not pull their own supplies nor did they maintain the pace of the handcart expeditions. For as Brigham Young had predicted, the Saints—even with the very young, very old, and weak among them, on foot—made far better time trudging across the prairie than the lumbering ox-drawn wagon trains.

Although thousands of travelers continued to roll along the great Platte River highway, their numbers dwindled after the peak year of 1850, until the discovery of gold in Colorado in 1859 whetted renewed interest in western traffic, attracting especially those who had been too young for the California gold rush a decade earlier. The tally for 1859, marked at Fort Kearny along the Platte, showed 30,000 individuals moving westward over the trail.

And almost concurrently came the advent of commercial traffic, passenger, freight, and mail, to supply the communities of Colorado, Utah, Montana, eastern California, and other areas inaccessible to the sea routes of the Pacific coast. Ben Holladay's was an early-day coach line through Nebraska; so was the Western Stage Company.

As the stagecoach companies enlarged their routes, stage stations or ranches sprang up every dozen miles or so to provide the swaying Concord coaches with fresh horses, fresh drivers, and sometimes food for the passengers. Those established by the stage companies were called stations—swing stations if they supplied only horses, dinner or home stations if they supplied new drivers and food. Mark Twain, in *Roughing It,* described the victuals as incdible, slabs of bread "as good as Nicholson pavement," condemned army bacon and slumgullion which "pretended to be tea, but there was too much dish-rag, and sand, and old bacon-rind in it to deceive the intelligent traveler." [7] Other stations, called ranches, were set up independently, sometimes as hostelries, grocery stores, or saloons, some of them operated by squaw men, whites married to Indian women. More than fifty stations dotted the Nebraska coun-

7. Mark Twain, *Roughing It* (New York: Harper and Brothers, 1872), p. 26.

tryside during the days of the trail, although not all of them were in operation at one time. Some served double duty, supplying the glamorous but short-lived Pony Express with fresh, fleet horses for the mail service that took only ten days between St. Joseph, Missouri, and Sacramento.

Freighting was big business, the standard "bull outfit" being a self-contained unit consisting of twenty-five heavy freight wagons and a mess wagon, three hundred or more head of oxen—for each Murphy wagon could carry seven thousand pounds of freight and required from six to twelve yoke, with fresh animals along to take over the pulling—and a minimum crew of thirty men. Although there were a score or more freighting companies in Nebraska, Russell, Majors and Waddell was the biggest in the late 1850s, establishing its base in Nebraska City, site of the original Fort Kearny along the Missouri River, to handle a military contract to Utah. Freighting outfits carried all manner of supplies, including foodstuffs, mining machinery, and building materials, but military contracts were their lifeblood. Russell, Majors and Waddell invested $300,000 in its operation in Nebraska City, creating a thriving community out of a deserted fort-village, and in 1860 built its own road from Nebraska City to Fort Kearny on the Platte for quicker access to the great Platte River road. Although that company did not survive into the middle 1860s, others were in operation through the state for decades later.

Mail service to Utah and later to Sacramento was established as early as 1850, but was spasmodic at best, and in 1860 Senator William Gwin of California persuaded William Russell, of the Russell, Majors and Waddell Company, to start a fast, dependable mail service. The Pony Express has gone down in American legend as the epitome of the West. The dedicated young riders, supposedly carrying Bibles in their pouches, galloped their fast ponies across the prairies and mountains between April 3, 1860, and October, 24, 1861, through pelting rain and thundering snow, making the 1,500-mile trip in ten days, missing their schedule only once. But when the transcontinental telegraph was connected, the need for the costly relays of horses and riders was gone, and the stalwart young riders hung up their saddles.

The great Platte River road, which Samuel Bowles, a Massachusetts editor, described in 1865 as "the natural highway across the Continent . . . on the line of our great cities and our great industries . . ." [8] served the nation well.

In the quarter-century that emigrants trudged along the great Overland Trail, significant events were happening in the land they crossed. When the first caravan went through to Oregon in 1841, the land was Indian country. Other wagon trains were moving through in 1854, when Nebraska became a territory, created by politicians in Washington during the maneuvering and infighting that eventually led to the Civil War. And while homesteaders rushed in to claim land in the newly opened regions, particularly along the Missouri River, pilgrims continued to stream through, many of them stopping to outfit at the raw new river towns—Omaha, especially, and Nebraska City, Bellevue, Brownville—before they headed their oxen toward the westward trail. Even through the years of the Civil War, while their brothers were fighting at Gettysburg and Antietam, they moved along the trail, a few stopping in Nebraska to live but most moving on to the Pacific.

The Overland Trail provided in part the instrument whereby the United States fulfilled what its people saw as its Manifest Destiny, extending its boundaries from sea to sea.

8. Samuel Bowles, *Across the Continent* (Springfield, Mass: no publisher listed, 1865), p. 22.

5

The Territory

$\mathcal{B}$Y the mid-1840s, the fate of the wild, unknown country of the Platte became a matter of importance to politicians, and for ten years the question of Nebraska Territory was tangled up with debates about the transcontinental railroad, slavery, states' rights, Indians, and expansionist politics in general. Historians agree that the Kansas-Nebraska Act became one of the most controversial and far-reaching measures to come before Congress in the nineteenth century.

Since the days of settlement along the eastern seaboard, as Americans had learned of the lands that lay beyond, they pushed the frontier inexorably westward. Mobility, adventure, independence, aloneness—these were part of the essence of America; Daniel Boone had said earlier that when he could hear the report of his neighbor's gun, it was too crowded in that area, time to move on; the fictional Lucketts in Conrad Richter's trilogy, *The Trees,* moved westward whenever they saw other people in the region. For possession of land and independence of action were integral parts of the American spirit.

Added to the westering, wandering proclivities of individual Americans were political realities, for as the individuals went, so followed government.

True, the land of the Platte was still Indian territory, and according to the Indian Intercourse Act of 1834, settlers were forbidden in the area, liable to being removed by military force if necessary. The Indians assumed that the law provided a perma-

nent Indian boundary. But already the frontier had moved westward from the Mississippi River to the Missouri, for Iowa had
become a territory in 1838. And so many restless Americans
had moved across the Indian country to the new western lands
beyond, that by 1850 California achieved statehood; and
Oregon, New Mexico, and Utah gained territorial status. Indian
country was not outside the United States; it was right in the
middle, a wide barrier that had to be removed.

In the East, new steam-powered railroads were proving their
practicability in transporting goods and passengers. Even before
the end of the Mexican War in 1848, which brought California
into American possession, businessmen and politicians were
discussing a railroad to connect the Atlantic to the Pacific, to
join the three-thousand-mile width of the United States together.

It was as a railroad issue that the subject of Nebraska Territory was first broached in Congress. As early as 1844, Stephen
A. Douglas of Illinois introduced into the House of Representatives bills to organize a strip of territory sufficiently wide to
make a good state, a continuous line of settlements from the
Mississippi to the Pacific, and a chain of railroads to the Pacific
constructed with the aid of federal land grants to the territories.
For the next ten years various factions debated the location of
the railroad—a northern route to Oregon, a route straight west
out of Missouri, a more southerly route along the 35th parallel,
or the Gila River route along the 32nd parallel. In the midst of
them all was Douglas, the indomitable Little Giant of Congress,
at first in the House, later in the Senate as chairman of the Committee on Territories, who wanted the railroad established along
the great Platte River route so that Chicago, his constituency,
could become the railroad center of the nation. For ten years he
maneuvered and cajoled, although he did not introduce any
Nebraska Territory legislation himself after 1848.

Before long, another, completely alien topic was brought into
the question of creating the new territory, and suddenly the
Nebraska issue became one of the extension of slavery: all else
was forgotten in the heat of the moment. When the new southwestern lands, acquired at the end of the Mexican War, were
organized under the Compromise of 1850, California was admitted as a free state because its constitution already prohibited

slavery, and the territories of Utah and New Mexico were organized with the understanding that when they applied for admission as states, their status would be governed by their constitutions. Because their desertlike reaches obviously could not support a slave economy, it was assumed that they would eventually be free states. The South was bitter, because according to the Missouri Compromise of 1820, Missouri was admitted as a slave state only if all remaining territory of the Louisiana Purchase north of 36°30' were to remain forever free. At that point there were as many slave states as free states. The Compromise of 1850 had left the score lopsided; now the new territory on the Platte would also be created as a free state. The South wanted the Missouri Compromise repealed.

For four years the battle over Nebraska Territory raged, in Congress, on street corners in the North, on plantations in the South, among Abolitionists and proslavery advocates, the arguments about whether the new territory should be admitted as free or slave. The railroad promoters were still talking, their stands depending on which route they were endorsing; the Nebraska Boomers were enthusiastic, businessmen in Iowa and Missouri who could foresee tremendous financial advantages to having a Nebraska territory opening up for settlement. But most of the loud vehement discussion was about Nebraska and slavery.

Early in 1853 a bill to organize Nebraska Territory was introduced into Congress, passed in the House but blocked in the Senate. On December 14, 1853, a new Nebraska Territory bill was introduced, delineating the area as extending from 36°30' in the south to 43°30' in the north, lying between the Missouri River and the summit of the Rocky Mountains. The bill made no reference to slavery.

By the time the bill came up for the vote on January 4, 1854, the wording was completely different. In the frantic intervening weeks, politicians had chiseled away at it, making so many compromises to assure its passage that it bore slight resemblance to the original one.

Whereas all of the discussion had been about creating Nebraska Territory, the act which was passed created two territories, the new one named after the Kansas River and lying between the 37th and 40th parallels; all the rest, lying between the 40th and 49th parallels—farther north than the original bill provided—to the Canadian border was Nebraska. Both stretched from the Missouri River to the crest of the Rockies. Furthermore, the law provided "That all questions pertaining to slavery in the Territories, and in the new States to be formed therefrom, are to be left to the decision of the people residing therein, through their appropriate representatives" and that "the eighth section of the act preparatory to the admission of Missouri into the Union, approved March 6, 1820, . . . is declared inoperative." [1] That meant that the Missouri Compromise was repealed.

Although this act was a compromise, intended to head off controversy on the floor of Congress, there was immediate uproar, but with Douglas working valiantly to keep the Democrats together through the "popular sovereignty" appeal, the bill squeaked through Congress, the House passing it on March 3 and the Senate on May 25. President Franklin Pierce signed it into law on May 30, 1854. The repercussions then were immediate, violent, and related to the slavery issue.

The turbulence that erupted in Kansas earned that territory the epithet "Bleeding Kansas," as abolitionists and proslavers alike rushed across the Missouri border into the area, brandishing and using guns and clubs and other instruments of persuasion for the elections that were to follow. But Nebraska Territory had little resident population at the time and was not contiguous to the Missouri border, source of the furor, so that it escaped the violence which rent its neighbor to the south.

The net result of the Kansas-Nebraska Act nationally was divisiveness, strife, and sectional battle. The raw emotions turned loose during the Congressional battle and in the physical combat afterward in Kansas helped lead the nation unalterably into the Civil War.

A by-product of the Kansas-Nebraska Act was the formation of a new political party. Antislavery Whigs and anti-Nebraska Democrats opposed to the repeal of the Missouri Compromise united to form the Republican party, favoring the organization

1. Text of the Organic Act, reprinted in Andreas, *History of Nebraska*, pp. 103–106.

of both Kansas and Nebraska as free territories. Although the Whig party limped along for a few more years, its effectiveness was diminished; many of its strongest leaders had left its ranks because of the slavery issue in the Kansas-Nebraska bill.

Most American history books refer to the Kansas-Nebraska Act as a slavery issue, and at the time, it was. But the bill had other long-range effects not widely understood at the moment. For the Kansas-Nebraska Act, which opened up for white settlement the vast tract of land in the middle of the continent—more than a third of a million square miles—in reality signaled the end of dreams of a separate Indian country. Although the lands designated as Indian country in 1834 had been whittled away in the intervening years, and although tracts were still left to the Indians after 1854, to be chipped and shaved away in the next few decades, it was the Kansas-Nebraska Act which opened up to white settlement what was left of the Louisiana Purchase. From that time onward, Indians of the Great Plains became strangers in their own land.

Even before the bill was signed, ambitious entrepreneurs were drawing plans for the towns and businesses they would establish in the new Nebraska Territory, which covered all of what is now Nebraska, and large parts of what became North and South Dakota, Wyoming, most of Montana, and part of Colorado. Each town, of course, was to be the capital city.

At the beginning of 1854, except for the military forces at Fort Kearny along the Platte and at Fort Laramie, there were only smatterings of white settlers in the region, perhaps fifty at the unorganized community of fur traders and missionaries at Bellevue along the Missouri River; a handful of rip-roaring opportunists at the squalid sod-house community of Dobytown, just outside Fort Kearny, which provided extra-legal services for soldiers and for travelers along the Oregon Trail; and a few who utilized the Table Creek post office which had been established in 1852 on the site of the original Fort Kearny on the Missouri River. A few others were scattered through the region, some in the Half-Breed Tract in what became Richardson County, a refuge for whites married to Indians but not part of the tribal culture. There were three ferries across the Missouri for the convenience of the westward travelers.

At Bellevue, Peter A. Sarpy, the leathery trader at the post there since 1824, got into action; most of the time he conducted his business from the Iowa side of the river, at St. Mary's, but on February 9, 1854, he and some friends organized the Bellevue Town Company, and by July 15, published a newspaper, *The Nebraska Palladium,* which announced in its first issue that "Within the last month a large city upon a grand scale has been laid out, with a view of the location of the capital of Nebraska, at this point, and with a view of making it the center of commerce, and the halfway house between the Atlantic and Pacific Oceans . . ." [2] The settlement already had the first post office in the territory, established in 1850, and the first school, organized in 1848 for Indian children.

Other businessmen on the Iowa side of the Missouri River began to organize communities on the Nebraska side, reckoning that they could strengthen their own positions by having sister towns across the river. Under the Federal Townsites Act, they could stake out three hundred twenty acres of land for a town; they could pre-empt other land, and, by selling lots could make a financial killing in the new territory while boosting their own situations at home.

James C. Mitchell, formerly of Council Bluffs, Iowa, across the river, was the driving force behind the establishment of Florence, site of the Mormons' old Winter Quarters, renamed for Mitchell's adopted daughter. He chose his site because "the river here is something less than three hundred yards wide with a solid ROCK BOTTOM!!" [3] his advertisement of September 29, 1854, said; those advantages would provide unsurpassed footings for the bridge that would indubitably cross the river there. A bridge company was formed in February 1855, but it was to be ninety-eight years before the bridge was built; it was dedicated in May 1953.

Three men who had operated a ferry service at Table Creek

2. Olson, *History of Nebraska,* pp. 79–80.
3. *Omaha Arrow,* September 29, 1854.

were the organizers of what became Nebraska City; John Boulware and his son John B., who had been postmaster, and Hiram P. Downs, who had been caretaker of the abandoned Fort Kearny there, were joined by several men from Sidney, Iowa, who came across the river on Boulware's ferryboat to help Downs plat the city they were sure would become the territorial capital. But when settlers began to arrive months later, the Boulwares left for the wilderness farther west; they didn't like the congestion.

Another ferryboat operator, Samuel Martin, a profane, alcoholic old trapper married to an Otoe, was responsible for starting Plattsmouth, located at the junction of the Platte with the Missouri. He had secured a permit the year before for squatter's rights and had skidded the logs from his old place in Iowa across the river ice in midwinter, using them to build a two-story house to accommodate the public; a couple of enterprising Iowans from Glenwood helped him with that and another, smaller one-story building. They were ready when the bill was signed making Nebraska a territory, and so, too, were scores of would-be settlers on the Iowa side of the river, waiting for Martin's ferry to take them across; some two hundred fifty of them had already pencilled their names on claim stakes within the limits of what is now Cass County before the legal organization of the territory. At the time of the first territorial census in 1855, many of the persons listed as Plattsmouth residents actually lived in Iowa and never did cross the river to live. In fact, even some of the early legislators did not live in Nebraska.

The village of Brownville, established on August 29, 1854, was named for a Richard Brown, who didn't live there long; it had hopes of being the capital city. Instead it achieved fame as the landing place of boats plying between St. Louis and Omaha, as many as forty or fifty steamers plying the Missouri River trade regularly.

Fontanelle was another community established that year, situated inland on the Elkhorn River. Its settlers, a group from Quincy, Illinois, arrived in Bellevue looking for land and asked Logan Fontenelle, an Omaha chief, to help them. He was the son of a French father and an Omaha mother, educated in St. Louis, conversant with both Indian and white cultures and knew all of eastern Nebraska. He directed the group to the spot they chose, and the newcomers named the settlement in his honor, but somehow misspelled his name. They established a university there in 1858, but neither the town nor the university thrived, and by 1873 the university was closed and the town of five hundred persons had dwindled to a crossroads village.

The first two-story house in Nebraska was originally located at Saratoga, another short-lived river community, which aspired vainly to be the terminus of the transcontinental railroad. The house was built by Erastus Beadle, publisher of dime novels, who sought to save the life of his wife by sending her west to breathe the pure prairie air; it was built in sections in Pittsburgh and shipped down the Ohio and up the Mississippi and Missouri rivers to Omaha, where it was put together again. Whether Mrs. Beadle ever lived in it, whether the fresh air of the plains cured her, nobody now knows; when the entire town of Saratoga decided to relocate further south, the house was moved by ox-team to a location which is now Fourteenth and Howard in Omaha. Saratoga had another distinction in that on February 11, 1857, the territorial legislature in its first session granted a charter to the University of Nebraska to be located at Saratoga; the university didn't get as far as the village did in its organization.

The laying out of the town of Omaha was a rollicking affair, part of it jumping the gun on the legal opening of the territory by several months. William D. Brown had operated a ferry across the river since 1850, and three years later some Council Bluffs men approached him, ostensibly to form a ferry company but really to have a town-site company ready when the land became a territory. There had been a settlement at Council Bluffs, on the Iowa side—first named Miller's Hollow, then Kanesville—since the Mormon expedition of 1846–1847, and the town had become an important emigrant outfitting point for the California gold rush, having a population of 2,000. With an established community on the Nebraska side of the river too, the men figured, surely the area would attract the transcontinental railroad; the Iowans had been eyeing the land across the muddy river for the most advantageous town site.

In November 1853, they launched Brown's leaky scow into

the water, with one man to row, one to bail out the water, and Brown to pilot around the sandbar. They landed in tall, stiff grass much higher than their heads, slogged through it around a slough and across the river bottom and up to the tableland, startling a flock of wild turkeys. The next morning they pounded stakes to mark the claims they would file the minute the land was legal. In May, three weeks before President Pierce signed the Kansas-Nebraska bill, Iowa Congressman Bernhart Henn got a postmaster appointed for Omaha, and by May 28, 1854, A. D. Jones's log cabin was built, a wide shingle with the words POSTOFFICE BY A. D. JONES pencilled on it, nailed to the shanty.

As soon as the territory was organized, Postmaster Jones—who kept the mail in his hat, later in a bushel basket—began surveying the town, laying out 320 blocks with streets one hundred feet wide, except for Capitol Avenue, which was 120 feet wide. Carpenters began chopping down trees along the riverbank to erect log cabins, a saloon keeper set up a tent, and the town was started. The two convivial masons who laid up bricks for what the entrepreneurs confidently called the Capitol Building, the first brick structure in town, decided that the occasion was such an historic one that they laid their pint bottle of bourbon, not yet finished, in the wall for posterity. (Twenty years later they resurrected it and discovered the statehouse whiskey to be as good as ever.)

On July 4, the community held a picnic on the town site, with the firing of an anvil brought over from Council Bluffs having to substitute for cannon fire, a common stunt for later Fourth-of-July celebrations throughout the region. The powder, too, came from Council Bluffs. There was the usual political oratory, for a former congressman from Ohio was in the area and made the customary patriotic speech even though he wasn't running for office. Not long afterward, the first Omaha newspaper, the *Arrow,* a weekly printed in Council Bluffs, was distributed. By the end of the year Omaha City had some twenty houses, saloons, and stores, and two shacks, which served as hotels. The Douglas House, the more pretentious of the two, had no floor in the dining room; the table was made by driving poles into the ground for stakes with rough cottonwood boards used for the top; the sides were open, and often the table was covered with snow while the boarders were trying to thaw their frozen food. Sleeping arrangements were not so luxurious as the dining details.

By the time Nebraska Territory was officially organized, Omaha City had a population of probably one hundred persons and was by far the most thriving of settlements. It was a muddy, dusty town, depending on the weather. Neither streets nor walks were paved, and when the hot sun would come out after a rainstorm, the mud would be baked into a desert of dust, and when the winds were from the south, dust storms would rage for days. But when they were over, a delightful calm would fall over the community.

So eager were the developers to establish communities that the first Nebraska legislature, meeting on January 16, 1855, granted charters to seventeen towns, most of them with "City" in their names, but most of them existed only on paper and never were realized.

Rough, raucous men, full of gusto and imagination, some of them out to make a quick dollar and then go on to the next newly opening area, others firmly intending to settle and live in the new land of promise, the first community fathers in Nebraska were a breed apart. Perhaps half of them stayed on in the towns they promoted; the others went on to greener, or at least different, fields.

Farmers, too, were securing acreage. As soon as the Indian title to the land was extinguished, the land was part of the public domain and available to private individuals. The Pre-Emption Act of 1841 was still in effect, allowing an individual to file a claim on one hundred sixty acres, live on it a year, and acquire title by paying $1.25 per acre at the time the land was put up for sale. Or he could purchase it with military bounty land warrants, or buy it directly, on or after the date that the land was put up for public auction. Military bounty land warrants were given to veterans of United States military service, Mexican War veterans by then, and allowed the holders to acquire title to the land immediately, without residence requirements; they had cash value, for a congressional act of 1852

allowed them to be assigned to other individuals, and speculators often sought out destitute veterans or their widows to purchase the documents, usually for fifty cents an acre.

Because the tide of immigration and land speculation ran
ahead of the surveyors, an act of March 27, 1854, allowed the
settlers to live on unsurveyed land and as soon as the surveys
were made to choose the hundred sixty acres whose surveyed
lines corresponded most closely to the land they were on. Even
before the land was open, adventurous spirits were spying out
the land and noting choice locations, and as soon as the news of
the passage of the Kansas-Nebraska bill reached the frontier,
hundreds of settlers rushed into the territory to put up their
claim cabins, shanties mostly, to hold the land.

To protect their presurvey claims, the settlers organized claim
clubs, similar to ones established on earlier frontiers. One of the
first public meetings in Nebraska Territory was under the "Lone
Tree" on the riverfront of Omaha, near the ferry landing, on
July 22, 1854, when the Omaha Township Claim Association
set up twenty "laws" about marking claims and protecting
them. The Belleview Settlers' Club, organized October 28,
1854, said that its limits extended to the Platte River on the
south, the Missouri on the east, north to the Omaha limits, and
west fifteen miles. By the time the first townships were sub-
divided, claim law was in force for about one hundred miles
along the Missouri River.

It was to be three years before the surveys were finished in
the eastern part of the state, and five years before the first public
sale of lands. In the meantime, the claim clubs gained strength,
enforcing the rights of their members, watching to see that no
usurper took over a claim already established, using guns or
ropes if necessary to persuade claim jumpers to clear out of the
area.

One of the policies of the claim clubs was that free homesteads should be available; they proposed that every pioneer in
Nebraska should have three hundred twenty acres of land and
that when latecomers arrived, the original pioneers could sell
one hundred sixty acres apiece and use the cash to pay the pre-
emption fee for the other hur.dred sixty. The first territorial

legislature passed an act recognizing claim clubs and defining their authority, even though the land belonged to the federal government and the organic act creating the territory required that the primary disposition of the land should be under federal law. By the time the surveys were completed and land offices established, however, the need for the claim clubs was past and they quietly passed out of existence.

The first sale of lands was held in 1859; one hundred thousand acres were purchased with cash, and seven hundred thousand acres with land warrants, most of those purchased by speculators.

While the opportunists on the prairies were platting towns, the president and the Senate in Washington were lining up the territorial government. They offered the governorship first to William O. Butler of Kentucky, who declined, and then to Francis Burt, a forty-seven-year-old Pendleton, South Carolina, editor and lawyer who had had a distinguished career in governmental service. He accepted, leaving his home on September 11 for the four-week journey by private conveyance, railroad, stagecoach, steamboat, and wagon to Bellevue, the only really established community in the territory. When he arrived on October 7, he was so ill he went to bed immediately in Father Hamilton's log cabin adjacent to the Mission House, which was intended to be the site of the first territorial government. On October 16 he took the oath of office from his bed, and two days later, on October 18, he died.

Thomas B. Cuming, secretary of state, became acting governor and ordered that the census be taken, as required by the organic act creating the territory, to determine territorial representation. The line between Kansas and Nebraska had not yet been surveyed—in fact, it was two years before the base line was surveyed as far as one hundred miles westward—and the permanence of almost every white settler was questionable. Military personnel were not included, and whether white traders in the areas still set aside for Indians were to be included was never very clear. The seven deputy marshals reported on November 28 that there were 2,732 inhabitants in the area—351,558 square miles, the size of France and the British Isles combined; 1,818 lived south of the Platte and 914 north of the Platte.

With figures in hand, Cuming then assigned the north-of-the-Platte section seven councilmen and fourteen representatives—but only six councilmen and twelve representatives to the area south of the Platte, despite the fact that the south part had twice the population. The dissension his action caused is still reflected, in many ways, to the present day; seldom does the South Platte United Chambers of Commerce, for instance, agree with its counterpart on the north side.

The Platte River flows through the middle of the state from west to east, "too shallow to be ferried, too wide to be forded, and people too poor to bridge it," according to the old settler saying. Although in dry seasons during arid years, men and animals can walk across bone-dry parts of its broad, sandy riverbed, until the state was sufficiently solvent to build bridges across it, it was an effective natural boundary.

Early in 1855, amid uproar from embittered south-of-the-Platters, Cuming and the legislature moved the state capital to the upstart north-of-the-Platte community of Omaha. "There seems to be little doubt but that Bellevue might have obtained the capital if inducements of a substantial character had been held out to certain influential men by the Board of Missions," a Nebraska historian wrote cryptically in 1882.[4] Cuming reportedly studied Omaha, Plattsmouth, Florence, and Nebraska City before settling on Omaha, and the legislature voted with him. An Iowan, he was accused of promoting the fortunes of Omaha to help the development of Council Bluffs across the river. Omaha had already started constructing the capitol building, a two-story brick building, thirty-three by seventy-five feet, which was provided by the Council Bluffs and Nebraska Ferry Company "without a cost of a single dollar to the government."[5] It was the only brick building in town, and its windows were curtained with red-and-green calico.

So incensed were the losers that they spent most of the first

4. Andreas, *History of Nebraska*, p. 109.
5. Andreas, *History of Nebraska*, p. 686.

legislative session investigating charges of bribery; the battle carried on through the fourth legislative session, when J. Sterling Morton, later to become a distinguished Nebraska statesman, agitated to have the southerners secede to Kansas; the dissidents held their own legislative sessions in Florence for a while. Peace eventually was restored, and thirteen years later the capital was removed to the new town of Lincoln, south of the Platte, amid angry accusations that this maneuver was as shady as the move from Bellevue to Omaha had been.

Although the first legislature was charged with much work to fulfill the legal requirements of setting up the territory, it spent much of its time bickering over procedural matters. Many of its frontiersmen members were inexperienced in creating law, most of them were caught up in the factionalism that surrounded the location of the capital. A *New York Times* correspondent described what he called a typical session of the territorial legislature of the 1855–1857 session:

> It is a decidedly rich treat to visit the General Assembly of Nebraska. You see a motley crowd inside of a railing in a small room crowded to overflowing, some behind their little schoolboy desks, some seated on the top of the desks, some with their feet perched on the top of their neighbor's chair or desk, some whittling—half a dozen walking about in what little space there is left. The fireman, doorkeeper, sergeant-at-arms, last year's members, and almost anyone else, become principal characters inside the bar, selecting good seats and making themselves generally at home, no matter how much they may discommode the members . . . A row starts up in the secretary's room, or somewhere about the building, and away goes the honorable body to see the fun . . . then a thirsty member moves an adjournment and in a few minutes the drinking saloons are well patronized. . . .[6]

The territorial legislature bumbled along, usually taking care of essential routine matters but seldom initiating any startling legislative actions, probably performing no better and no worse than many others in like circumstances in other new territories.

---

6. J. W. Pattison, quoted in Addison E. Sheldon, *Nebraska: The Land and the People*, 3 vols. (Chicago: Lewis Publishing Company, 1931), 1:277.

It was the United States Congress which set in motion the forces that brought about the great explosion that was to occur in Nebraska after the Civil War.

Within a six-week period in mid-1862, Congress passed two bills which had been long in the making and which brought about far-reaching changes in Nebraska, accelerating the settlement of the land.

The first was the Homestead Act, which President Abraham Lincoln signed into law on May 20. The second was the act of July 1 granting a charter to the Pacific Railroad to cross the Plains. The law also provided grants of ten—later twenty—alternate sections per mile of the public domain, and it was the seven million acres of Nebraska land eventually granted to the railroads by Congress that caused the lines themselves to become powerful promoters of settlement.

The Pre-Emption Act of 1841 hadn't worked out well in Nebraska. The rich were getting the land and not farming it, the poor were working themselves to a frazzle and losing it. After the land sales in 1859, it turned out that most of the Nebraska land for sixty or seventy miles west of the Missouri went to speculators who bought it with warrants—usually paying fifty cents an acre for them—or who later foreclosed on the farmers' mortgages, which carried interest rates as high as forty percent. The farmers had paid $1.25 an acre for their land, a quarter-section of pre-empted land costing two hundred dollars, an impossible sum for farmers, particularly after the bad years of 1857 and 1858. The farmers had taken the lands, gambling that they could produce enough to pay for it within the twelve months allotted by law, and they had lost.

At the beginning of the public domain in 1785, the United States had considered public land a commodity to be disposed of, selling it for what it would bring and using the money to pay debts and meet the expenses of the new United States. But the settlers moving westward for new farmlands began to object, claiming they had rights to land in return for their labor. Several early efforts at legislation for free lands upon the public domain were turned down in Congress or by presidential veto, but the Republican Congress of 1862 finally passed the law which provided that "any person who is the head of a family, or who has arrived at the age of twenty-one years, and is a citizen of the United States, or who shall have filed his declaration of intention to become such . . . and who has never borne arms against the United States government or given aid and comfort to its enemies" could file a claim upon one hundred sixty acres for a fee of ten dollars, and after living on the land or cultivating it for five years could receive a patent.[7]

A Nebraskan, Daniel Freeman, always considered himself the first homesteader in the United States. According to legend, he was a soldier in the Union Army on furlough when he spotted a piece of land he wanted, on Cub Creek near the present town of Beatrice. The Homestead Act did not go into effect until January 1, 1863, the day he had to be back at his army post in Kansas, and he said he persuaded the registrar of the land office in Brownville to unlock the office right after midnight to record his entry. The Homestead National Monument is located on his land now, its 195 acres larger than Freeman's original holding. Although the Homestead Act of 1862 and the acts that followed turned out to be somewhat less than ideal—wheeler-dealers even then could find loopholes to circumvent the law—still the acts were the impetus to the almost overnight settling of the new territory along the Platte.

7. Sheldon, *Nebraska: The Land and the People*, 1:318.

6

The Railroad

NEBRASKA was born as the great railroad era began to develop in the United States. Because of the railroad Nebraska became a territory, because of it she thrived. Under its aegis, farmers settled, towns began.

From the time that the first steam locomotive, the Tom Thumb, chugged along the Baltimore and Ohio tracks in 1830, Americans had been intrigued with the potential of rails in breaching the vast spaces of the United States. Each year new lines were added, narrow-gauge ones, wide-gauge ones, and in-between ones, and by changing lines every hundred miles or so, a traveler could span great distances by rail in the East. With the opening of California, Americans began to dream of a transcontinental railroad to unite the whole United States, and it was to secure a route favorable to his constituent town of Chicago that Stephen A. Douglas had promoted the organization of Nebraska as a territory.

When Congress chartered the transcontinental railroad in 1862, to encourage the prohibitively expensive construction it gave the Union Pacific all odd-numbered sections of land within the first ten, then later twenty miles, on each side of the proposed line westward from the Missouri River, a total of twenty sections for each mile of road constructed. Later on, when the Burlington and Missouri River Railroad moved across the southern part of the state, it too was given alternate sections extending forty miles along its right-of-way, the two lines owning more than seven million acres of Nebraska farmland, fifteen percent of the state. In addition, the Union Pacific was given a loan of $16,000 for each mile constructed on the plains, $32,000 for each mile in the foothills, and $48,000 for each mile in the mountains, the rails to connect with the Central Pacific, which started in Sacramento and moved eastward, to forge a line extending across the breadth of the country.

Construction on the Union Pacific began at the end of the Civil War, in 1865. War veterans, immigrants, anybody who could wield an axe or a hammer rushed into Omaha, recruited to build the line into the wilderness. Crews ranged all along the Missouri River, as far as one hundred fifty miles north of Omaha and sixty miles south, felling cedar, oak, and walnut trees for railroad ties, denuding the wooded banks of the Missouri. When those were gone, the railroad ordered more lumber from Wisconsin and Minnesota. The railroad used 2,640 ties for every mile laid. When only cottonwood logs were available, the soft posts were "burnetized," dipped in zinc chloride to make them more durable.

Until 1867, when the Chicago and North Western Railway reached Council Bluffs, all supplies had to be shipped to Omaha by steamboat, up from St. Joe, and even after that, everything had to be ferried across the Missouri, for the railroad bridge was not built across the Missouri until 1871. Summertime, that was fine; wintertime, when the river was frozen, materials could be skidded across the ice or sent on a temporary bridge built on pilings driven into the ice. In the in-between times, when the ice was too thin to hold much weight, or was broken off in floes floating downriver with the pilings, supplying material was a gamble.

The surveyors went out first to locate the right-of-way, crews of eighteen to twenty-five men including civil engineers, rodmen, flagmen, chainmen, axemen, teamsters, herders, and cooks, with white duck tents for sleeping quarters and large quantities of arms and ammunition. Out in the field where the crews were expected to live off the land, a hunter was assigned to each crew to bring in wild game. While the surveying crew was at work, the battery of helpers struck camp, loaded up, and had it located at nightfall close to the scene of that day's operations; surveyors could cover as much as three or four miles a day. Beyond Fort Kearny, surveying crews had military escorts and always slept with their guns beside them for instant action; from time to time a surveyor was killed by Indians.

Then came the grading crews, private individuals or companies under contract and supplying their own horse-drawn plows and scrapers, shovels and wheelbarrows, each crew working its assigned section, as many as three thousand men at a time working at top speed. All supplies, often including water, had to be hauled in, sometimes from hundreds of miles away, brought in by ox-drawn freighters. At the height of construction through Nebraska, as many as three hundred freighters plodded back and forth, carrying commissary supplies as well as building materials; the cost of hauling freight was more than that of the actual grading process. Grading crews worked as much as two to three hundred miles ahead of the rail-laying gangs, and when the terrain was level could grade a hundred miles of line in thirty days. They lived in hastily constructed dugouts or soddies along the way.

The rail-laying crews were the elite, as many as four or five hundred men working at a time, with the locomotive inching its way behind them. The men worked in a smooth, pendulumlike motion, laying a mile of track or more a day, putting down ties, then chairs, then the rails, four men to a pair of rails swaying backward and forward lifting, turning, placing the rails, their motions governing the movements of the whole crew. The contractors, Brigadier General John Casement and his brother Dan from Painesville, Ohio, evolved an almost militarylike precision in unloading the flatcars of supplies, forty rails and the exact number of ties and chairs for them on each car, enough for a mile of track.

Rail-laying crews were housed on the train that chugged along behind them, a movable village which crawled along the newly laid rails. The front car carried the rail supplies, then came the engine and tender, and the provision car, kitchen and bakery cars, dining car, washroom, eighty-foot sleeping cars, and finally the granary with feed for the ox-teams that supplied extra services. The rail-laying crews worked from early morning until about five o'clock, with an hour at noon for a heavy dinner, and spent the evening hours playing horseshoes or cards, singing Irish ditties about railroad work, or in other relaxation before bedtime at dark; they were paid $2.50 per day.

Along the way, end-of-the-rail communities sprang up about every hundred miles, moving along as the crews themselves moved. These were colonies of tents and portable frame buildings put up by the railroad, surrounded by a floating population of saloon keepers, prostitutes, gamblers, and sharpers of all kinds, the community known popularly as "hell-on-wheels," although the railroad called it a terminus. As soon as the rail-laying crew caught up and passed, the terminus would be moved another hundred miles westward, there to set up its same facilities. Kearney was the first in Nebraska, the old Dobytown outside Fort Kearny (the town had added an *e* to its name); perhaps some of the girls from Dirty Woman's Ranch stayed on for the railroad crews.

The rail gang reached Columbus on a Sunday, pushing hard to make up for delays earlier, and laid two miles of track that day with the whole town watching, seventy-five men, women, and children missing Sabbath services to see the progress of the rail crews. Later, when the first commercial freight came along the tracks, the Union Pacific superintendent donated a load of pine lumber from it to the Congregational Church, possibly in atonement.

Across the flat, desolate plains the iron ribbon moved, a mile at a time, the workers putting the rails in place in a rhythmic sort of ballet. Ahead of them the grading crews dug and scraped, the bridge crews built bridges across the streams, everybody preparing for the rails; behind them the locomotive chugged back and forth from Omaha bringing supplies.

By October 5, 1866, the rails were laid past Cozad, a year ahead of schedule, and to celebrate the occasion the Union Pacific sponsored a grand excursion for members of Congress, territorial officials, financiers, society figures, and a scattering of European nobility, some of whom brought their servants. The nine-car excursion train, pulled by two locomotives, left Omaha on October 23, and went as far as Columbus the first day. That night the excursionists disembarked for a lavish meal served in a tent in the brightly lighted encampment and shortly theraiter found themselves in the middle of a moonlight war dance performed by Pawnees from the nearby reservation. The next morning at dawn the terror-stricken travelers were awakened by a mock battle, in which the same Indians were being attacked by other Indians dressed as Sioux.

The second day the train passed Silver Creek, Lone Tree, Grand Island, Wood River, Kearney, Elm Creek, Plum Creek, and Willow Island, arriving at what later became Cozad, 279 miles west of Omaha, before nightfall. There were speeches, fireworks, a concert, a specially printed newspaper struck for the occasion; the next morning while some of the men left the train to go on a guided buffalo-hunting excursion, others rode on to the end of the line thirty miles ahead. On the way back to Omaha two days later, stopping en route to look at prairie .dog villages and other phenomena, the group saw a prairie fire, which Thomas Durant, vice-president of the Union Pacific and manager of the excursion, had ordered lighted after dark to give the travelers excitement. The *New York Times* reporter who was one of the guests reported the whole jaunt in fulsome detail.

By November 1866 the rails were laid through to North Platte, and winter was setting in. Within three weeks there was a town of a thousand people on the prairie, a prefabricated town, the warehouse, bunkhouse, mess hall, and general store brought from Omaha, each part of each building numbered for ease in putting everything together on the site and then taking it down later and moving on to the next town. This was the first winter headquarters for the rail-laying crews—and around it were the tents and shacks for the extracurricular crews: whiskey peddlers, gamblers, cribhouses. The winter was intensely cold, the only warmth was that provided by booze and broads. By Christmas, the rails stretched three hundred miles west of Omaha; the men had laid 265 miles in nine months, in one of those months a total of 65 miles of track. In one single muscle-straining day, they had spiked down three miles of track.

When Nebraska became a state, on March 1, 1867, the railroad stretched completely across the state. On May 10, 1869, the golden spike was driven at Promontory Point, Utah, uniting the rails of the Union Pacific with those of the Central

Pacific from California; the transcontinental railroad was completed, and passengers at last could travel by train from one sea to the other across the United States.

The construction of the Union Pacific was one of the most dramatic single accomplishments of the era in the United States. It was the first railroad across the barren plains, the pioneer, the long-dreamed-of link across the country, the challenge of man against geography. It was a race against time, for Congress had set a deadline and the Union Pacific was competing against the Central Pacific out of California for miles and subsidies; in places it was a battle against Indians, although certainly not to the extent that the breathless newspapers of the day reported. It had all the elements of drama which appealed to the American public. Added to the natural suspense of the enterprise were the colorful personalities of the men in charge who stage-managed the construction into a theatrical production; they were not railroaders at all but speculators accustomed to grand gestures with plenty of press coverage. Thomas Durant, former physician, now vice-president in charge of construction, was interested in the financial gains the railroad would bring him and his friends. George Francis Train, Durant's crony, an eccentric, goateed, Mephistophelian-appearing man who was always called by all three names, manipulated the labyrinthine organization of the Credit Mobilier and Credit Foncier, cover institutions for financing the railroad and handling land sales. Both men were free-wheeling, imaginative, unfettered souls, as were also their associates. General Grenville M. Dodge, who became chief engineer of the project midway, was a military man, not a railroader.

The undertaking was awesome, one that could not have been accomplished by timid men; building a ribbon of steel across the uninhabited land with no labor save that which was imported, no materials save those which were hauled in, called for a special breed of gamblers. The lures, of course, were the subsidies which the federal government paid for each mile of track constructed and the possible profits from the sales of lands also contributed by the federal government, for without them no one would have even considered the venture. Whatever their mo-

tives, whatever their gains, these flamboyant financiers succeeded in the physical union of the West with the East, speeding
the development of the country.

Other railroads were eager to get into the act. The Burlington
and Missouri River, which had built and operated railroads
through Illinois and Iowa since the 1850s, became the second
trunk line into the state, beginning construction late in 1869 on
a southerly route west out of Plattsmouth. The line, stretching
westward two hundred miles to join the Union Pacific mainline
at Kearny Junction (no extra *e* this time), was completed in
1873, and the Burlington later extended its mainline on to
Denver and laid a network of interconnecting rails covering a
large part of the state. But the building of the Burlington had
little of the drama of the Union Pacific.

In the first place, it was not then a transcontinental railroad,
although it later made connections that made through travel possible to California. Nor was its construction the first dramatic
plunge into the barren new country; by now, railroad building
was old hat to the public. Nor was it pushing, straining against a
deadline; its work could be more leisurely. It was merely an already existing railroad extending its lines in a businesslike way
without fanfare. Although the construction processes of the two
railroads were separated by only five years in time and sometimes only a few miles in space, they were worlds apart, as different as possible in procedures, tactics, intent, and lasting influence.

True, the country had changed tremendously in those five
years, settlers swarming in by the ten of thousands; a railroad
had already been built so that there was no suspense about it.
When the Burlington had a promotional excursion to celebrate
the completion of its first fifty miles of track, from Plattsmouth
to within a mile of Lincoln, it was not a top-drawer social event
nor was its guest list worthy of publication. It was free, open to
the public, and the public came. The Burlington did not have
enough passenger cars in Nebraska yet—they had to be ferried
across the river at Plattsmouth—so the rolling stock consisted of
flatcars equipped with benches. Uprights at the corners held
slats overhead; freshly cut cottonwood branches nailed to the
slats protected the passengers from the wind, smoke, and the

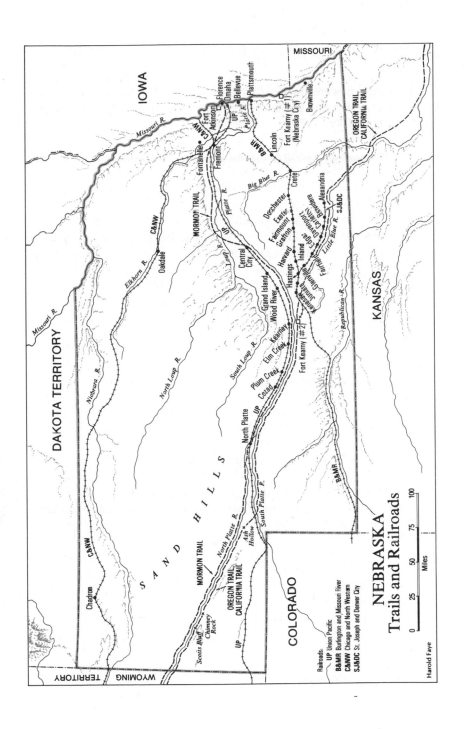

NEBRASKA
Trails and Railroads

Railroads:
UP Union Pacific
B&MR Burlington and Missouri River
C&NW Chicago and North Western
SJ&DC St. Joseph and Denver City

Miles
0   25   50   75   100

Harold Faye

hot sun. The excursionists rode from Plattsmouth to Lincoln and back; there were no lavish meals, no staged Indian forays nor prairie fires—just a bumpy, cindery ride on freight cars on the Fourth of July, 1870.

While the Burlington did not have the subsidy that Congress had made available to the Union Pacific for construction of the rails, it did have the same land grants; since in some places the lines were close enough together that there would be overlapping of land, the Nebraska court allowed the Burlington to take its complement of land in other parts of the state where necessary. As the rails were being built, the Burlington concentrated its efforts on colonization, both in this country and abroad, to sell its lands and create markets for the services of the railroad. By the end of 1873, the Burlington had 240 miles of mainline built and had organized communities the entire length of it, including its alphabet towns west of Lincoln: Crete, Dorchester, Exeter, Fairmont, Grafton, Harvard, Inland, Juniata, Kenesaw and Lowell, the towns about ten miles apart so that a man with a team could go to town and back in a single day. These were planned, permanent settlements, not the end-of-the-track temporary villages that sprang up, willy-nilly, along the Union Pacific for construction workers. Burlington town-site officials platted villages, helped settlers dig town wells, and provided other services for the new young villages, and the company spent a half-million dollars in 1872 to promote foreign immigration, in addition to its already large expenditure to stimulate domestic migration to the area. At the end of 1873 its record of three years' sales showed that the Burlington had sold more than a quarter-million acres of Nebraska land for more than two million dollars.

Although through the Credit Foncier, its land company, the Union Pacific also promoted immigration, sold land, and developed town sites, the proportion of its income derived from these sources was less than that of the Burlington, which, though smaller in size, concentrated its efforts on site development.

A third trunk-line railroad, which served the northern tier of counties in the Niobrara Valley, was the Chicago and North Western, which reached Chadron in the rugged butte country of northwestern Nebraska in July 1884, after the Sioux had been removed to reservations in South Dakota. Although it did not have federal land subsidies, the line received fifty-five thousand acres of land from the state. It too was interested in promoting settlers in the area.

With all the land that the various railroads had to sell and with their need to develop markets for future railroad traffic, they launched a promotional campaign hitherto unknown in American business. They distributed millions of glowing brochures, sponsored agricultural fairs in Chicago and elsewhere to demonstrate how big the pumpkins and squash grew in the fertile Nebraska soil, and established immigration societies in Eastern cities as well as in centers of northern Europe, touting the marvels of the lush new land. They had special immigrant tariffs for farm implements and nursery stock, to encourage permanent settlers. The Burlington's slogan was "A farm on every eighty," for the railroad did not realize that, in most parts of Nebraska, an eighty-acre farm was not large enough for subsistence.

"You have only to tickle it (the land) with a plow and it will laugh a harvest that will gladden your hearts and make joyous your homes," the Pagett and Stinchcomb brochure for the Burlington said rhapsodically. "The bright sky, pure water, and clear, life-inspiring atmosphere of this region give to men and animals the vitality and inspirations of youth . . . the paradise of invalids . . . anti-bilious, anti-consumptive and anti-dyspeptic. Old men and women grow young. . . ." [1]

Perhaps it was the embellishments of the railroads, even more than the lure of free homestead land, that brought about the rapid settlement of Nebraska.

1. Pagett and Stinchcomb, *A Descriptive Review of Adams County, Nebraska, showing the Resources, Climate, Water, Timber, Grasses, Grains, Towns and People* (Omaha: no publisher listed, 1879), p. 9.

7

The White Man and the Indians

AS the flood of immigration swept over the land and the white men put up permanent buildings, built fences, slaughtered the buffalo and left the carcasses to rot on the prairie, the Indians became more and more alarmed.

Big Elk, an Omaha chief, had long before told his tribe:

> A great flood is coming, will soon be here. I am old and near the grave. I may be gone before it comes but I am sure it will come. The wild animals which God has given us for sustenance will disappear, even the birds will find no resting place; some of you may not understand my meaning but if you do, prepare yourselves, take what steps would be best for the people.[1]

Perhaps as a result of his advice, but more likely because their mode of living was more amenable to reservation life and they had adjusted more gradually to the white man's customs, the semisedentary tribes along the Missouri River acquiesced to federal regulations generally without a struggle. But not so the nomadic Indians of the West, who swore to make a last-ditch stand to retain their historic lands; the story of their confrontation with some white men is one of violence and bloodshed.

The Oto and Missouria had gone peaceably into reservations in the 1830s and were finally moved to the Indian Territory in

---

1. Norma Kidd Green, *Iron Eye's Family: The Children of Joseph La Flesche* (Lincoln: Johnson Publishing Company, 1969), p. 8.

Oklahoma. In 1854 the Omaha were settled in reservations along the river, where they are still.

The Ponca did not fare so well. After four successive treaties, each one ceding more land, in 1865 they were settled on a reservation in northeast Nebraska where the Niobrara flows into the Missouri; there they planted their crops on the land allotted to them. In 1876, the United States government ordered them to move to Indian Territory in Oklahoma; when the tribe objected, federal officials sent ten chiefs to Oklahoma to look over the situation. The Indians were wholly dissatisfied with what they saw, the stony land, the hot climate, and the ague or malaria that had sickened many of the other Indians who had been removed earlier to the area. But the federal agents would not let them return to Nebraska to tell their fellow tribesmen. In midwinter the chiefs started back home on foot, fifty days without rations, picking corn from cornfields and pounding it between stones for food, sleeping on the prairie, leaving bloody footprints in the snow. When they finally returned to their community to report to their tribesmen, the tribe voted not to go south. But the following year an Indian agent with a command of United States soldiers arrived to escort the tribe to northern Oklahoma; along the way many died, and when the tribe arrived on the reservation, there were no houses, no shelter, no food.

Less than two years later, almost a third of them were dead and the survivors ill with malaria or malnutrition. Chief Standing Bear determined to return to Nebraska to bury the body of his son, and with his own family and friends, a party of thirty persons in three wagons drawn by ponies, made the ten-week journey without permission of the federal government. A detachment of United States soldiers arrested the fugitives and marched them back to Fort Omaha en route back to Oklahoma. There T. H. Tibbles, assistant editor of the *Omaha Herald,* heard the story and publicized it all over the country; Susette LaFlesche, an Omaha who later became his wife, made speeches in New York, Boston, Philadelphia, Washington and elsewhere, achieving fame under her Indian name of Bright Eyes, and drawing attention to the plight of the Indians. Two prominent lawyers in Omaha, Andrew J. Poppleton and John L. Webster, took the case to court, and in a celebrated ruling on their petition for a writ of habeas corpus, Federal Judge Elmer J. Dundy declared that "an Indian is a person within the meaning of the law," one of the first legal acknowledgements that an Indian was a person.[2]

"If a white man had land, and someone should swindle him, that man would try to get back, and you would not blame him. Look on me. Take pity on me, and help me to save the lives of the women and children. My brothers, a power which I cannot resist, crowds me down to the ground. I need help," Standing Bear said at his trial.[3] The chief was freed and allowed to return to northeastern Nebraska, where he lived out his life. The following year an Indian commission studied the case of the Ponca and finally allowed those who wanted to return to Nebraska to do so; about one-third of the surviving 833 members of the tribe went back to their homeland.

The semisedentary Pawnee, largest tribe in Nebraska, signed three separate treaties with the federal government between 1833 and 1857, ceding their lands, finally ending with a fifteen-by-thirty-mile tract along the Loup River in the central part of the state, although they continued to roam outside the reservation; they generally were the ones who plundered and stole from the emigrants along the Overland Trail. The Pawnees were subject to incursions from their traditional enemies, the Sioux, and after a Pawnee hunting party was massacred near present-day Trenton in 1873 by Oglala and Brule Sioux, they requested permission to move to Indian territory; three years later their reservation in Nebraska was formally exchanged for land in Oklahoma.

Although the nomadic Sioux lived up to the terms of the treaty they signed at Fort Laramie in 1851, which allowed the white man to travel the Holy Road, or Overland Trail, without molestation, they were nonetheless unhappy at the growing numbers of persons who disturbed the land and upset their age-

2. Olson, *History of Nebraska*, p. 131.
3. Sheldon, *Nebraska: The Land and the People*, 1:117.

old tribal patterns of living. An incident stemming from a misunderstanding brought about the first in a series of skirmishes which erupted into the Indian Wars of 1864.

On August 17, 1854, a lame cow belonging to a Mormon wagon train wandered into a camp of Brule Sioux who were waiting along the North Platte, east of Fort Laramie, for the issue of goods guaranteed them by the Treaty of 1851. They slaughtered and ate the cow; the Mormons found out about it and complained to the commandant at Fort Laramie, and Lieutenant John Grattan, fresh out of West Point and full of contempt for Indians, went forth to battle. He disregarded the Indian chief's offer to bring to justice the offending braves and opened fire on the camp with his two cannon, killing Bear, the chief. In retaliation, the Indians went on a rampage, killing Grattan's group and frightening other whites in the area.

The following year the Dakota Sioux terrorized travelers on the trail, and in August 1855 General William S. Harney set out from Fort Leavenworth, Kansas, with twelve hundred men to settle the Indians. On September 3, at Blue Water Creek near Ash Hollow, Harney struck, killing 135 Sioux men, women, and children, old and young alike, earning the sobriquet Squaw Killer. He captured all the rest and forced them to march in chains to Fort Laramie as an example to all Plains Indians, one being a pregnant squaw whose unborn baby was bayonetted. She was forcibly marched until she died. The show of strength on the part of the United States military forces put down Sioux raids for a while. There were military expeditions against the Cheyennes in Nebraska and Kansas in 1856.

For the next several years, the Sioux watched in alarm as more and more whites came into the area, many of them settling there. The talking wires, the telegraph, began to cross the state, then the iron rails and the steam horses of the white man's railroad. Indian chiefs who had been to white men's meetings realized the numbers and might of the white men and cautioned their tribes to peace, but on Sunday, August 7, 1864, the Indians struck in concerted action. Cheyenne, Brule, and Oglala Sioux and some Arapaho united, swooping across the Plains from Julesburg in the South Platte in western Nebraska through to the Little Blue in the southeastern part of Nebraska, attacking stagecoaches, emigrant trains, freight wagons, stations, and ranches throughout the breadth of the territory.

The first attack was on an emigrant train just beyond Plum Creek, now Lexington, in the Platte Valley; when people at the ranch saw flames of the burning wagons, they telegraphed the warning all along the line, alerting other ranches. As a result, the eleven who were killed there were the only white casualties along the Platte. But in the Little Blue, there was no telegraph, and upwards of one hundred persons were killed and scalped, others wounded, and two women taken into captivity, sixteen-year-old Laura Roper and Mrs. Eubanks, whose nursing baby the Indians later tomahawked. Eyewitness accounts said that as many as four hundred Indians were involved in the depredations along the Little Blue.

The First Nebraska Cavalry was ordered to Fort Kearny to protect stagecoaches and freight wagons, and Fort Plum Creek was established as an intermediate station between Fort Kearny and Fort McPherson, farther west. The Indians, impressed with this display of military might, made no further concerted attacks against the whites but conducted small, sporadic raids on isolated points. The situation was tense. On all sides the Indians saw examples of the forked tongue of the white men; Indians who had accepted reservation status were cheated with issue goods that were to repay them for the loss of their hunting grounds. While some federal officials promised the Indians that they could keep their lands "so long as the grass shall grow," others were opening roads through the land, to Montana, and later on, to the sacred hunting grounds in the Black Hills of Dakota. Indians who assembled in peace to surrender, Black Kettle's Cheyennes at Sand Creek, just over the Colorado line, were massacred on November 29, 1864, by troops commanded by Colonel J. M. Chivington, a former presiding elder of the Nebraska Methodist Conference.

Congress established a Peace Commission in 1866 to try to remove the causes of the Indian wars and to persuade the Indians to give up their nomadic ways and accept reservation status; as a result of a conference at Fort Laramie in 1867 some bands did go into reservations, the Brules under Spotted Tail, the Oglalas under Red Cloud. But young Indians were in no mood for peace; they saw the perfidy of the white man and the total destruction of their own way of life.

For the next ten years western Nebraska and the lands northwest were in a state of warfare. The Indians wiped out the command of W. J. Fetterman on the Bozeman Road on December 21, 1866, and destroyed large numbers of soldiers in the battle at Beecher Island on September 17, 1869; the War Department established new camps in the area, including Camp Sheridan and Fort Robinson near the reservations, Fort Sidney in the west to protect Union Pacific construction crews, and Fort Hartsuff in central Nebraska to protect settlers in the Loup Valley. In the meantime, the Indians were having to accept more and more cessions of their lands. When they refused to give up their sacred grounds in the Black Hills, the United States government declared on December 6, 1875, that all Indians had to be on reservations within two months, an impossibly short length of time, and on January 31, 1876, the entire Sioux Nation was turned over to the War Department to crush the hostiles by force.

A band of Sioux under Crazy Horse, the mystical leader of the Oglalas, engaged General George Crook's troops in a bloody battle at the Rosebud on June 17, and a week later, on June 25, 1876, the main body of Sioux annihilated General George Custer's command at the Little Big Horn in Montana, a battle celebrated in yellow journalism as Custer's Last Stand. For several months after that, the United States Army searched for the elusive Indians, and in October, General Nelson A. Miles forced about three thousand of them to surrender; others later came in to accept reservation status. The next spring Crazy Horse brought in two thousand of his followers; he was killed at Fort Robinson on September 7, 1877, bayonetted with the excuse that he was trying to foment another war.

In the meantime, the Northern Cheyennes who had participated in the Battle of the Little Big Horn had been captured and sent to Indian territory in Oklahoma. In 1878 a small band under Dull Knife broke away from the reservation and made their way back to their homeland, eluding thousands of United States cavalrymen as they trudged, barefoot and starving, across the snowy reaches of Kansas and Nebraska, six hundred miles in the dead of winter. They were captured near Fort Robinson, close to the South Dakota line, and were confined there, and when on the night of January 9, 1879, they tried to escape, most of them were killed.

The last Indian resistance was crushed. Their great leaders were dead or broken in spirit. The Plains tribes went into reservations, the Pine Ridge and the Rosebud in South Dakota, just over the Nebraska boundary, leaving the nomadic ways of their ancestors and accepting the ways of the white man, trying to farm the barren lands of western South Dakota. United States troops at two forts, Robinson in the west and Niobrara in the east, kept them under surveillance.

In 1890 the broken Sioux began to prepare for the Ghost Dance, a ritual to propitiate Wovoka, prophet of the Great Spirit, to bring the buffalo back to the Plains. Frightened settlers called military forces; General Miles came out from Chicago, and the Nebraska National Guard was ordered to the northwestern part of the state. Sitting Bull was killed in a melee growing out of an attempt to arrest him at Standing Rock. When the remnants of the Sioux at Wounded Knee, just beyond the Nebraska line into South Dakota, staged their Ghost Dance, an entire band was slaughtered, men, women and children alike. From then on, Nebraska belonged to the white man.

8

The State

N 1867, Nebraska became a state. By then portions of the territories of Colorado, Dakota, and Idaho had been carved from her, and her size had been reduced from the 355,000 square miles of her earliest territorial days to substantially the same size she has been since, 77,000 square miles. The transcontinental railroad crossed her breadth, homesteads and villages were located throughout the area, no matter how sparsely, and her population was more than fifty thousand persons.

For nine years, ever since 1858, people had talked about statehood, but the topic had become so involved with the politics of the Civil War and Reconstruction that nothing was done. The territory had been created in 1854 by a Democratic administration, and the early officials were Democrats. In the intervening years the Republican party, successor to the old Whig party and splinters of the original Democratic party, had developed, its principles opposing slavery and proposing homesteading appealing to the Northerners who settled Nebraska. As the area began to fill up with Union veterans, most of them members of the new Republican party of Abraham Lincoln, timing became significant in deciding when Nebraska would ask to become a state; politicians wanted to secure for their own party the offices that would be filled as a result of statehood.

In 1864 the territorial legislature secured from Congress the enabling legislation that authorized Nebraskans to draw up a state government. But although the territory was obviously ready to apply for statehood, politics got in the way: whichever political party was in control at the moment Nebraska became a state would have all the political plums, appointments to various offices. So long as the Republicans were in power, the Democrats would not agree to statehood; if the Democrats were in control, the Republicans would not. Since it had been a Republican legislature that had made the first move toward statehood, the Democrats stalled, pointing out to the voters in 1864 that statehood would likely cost them money, for the settlers would have to pay more in taxes than they had been paying, to cover the amount that the federal government was then supplying the territory. The voters appreciated economy; to the constitutional convention in Omaha in July, they sent delegates who promptly voted to adjourn.

But the governor and the legislature were unwilling to let the matter stand. In February 1866, they assembled a voluntary committee that met in secret to draft a constitution which was then pushed through the legislature without being printed, without allowing amendments, and without giving legislators a chance to read it; most of them had no knowledge of what was in it. Then the legislators submitted the constitution to the public to vote on it at a special election, at the same time voting for state officers who would take office if the constitution were approved. It was a close election, some votes not being counted, others being challenged—sometimes, elections were determined by those who counted the ballots more than by those who cast them. The Republicans, then in power, won, the constitution was approved, and Nebraska had both state and territorial legislatures, the territorial ones already in office and the state ones elected to take office.

When the constitution was forwarded to Washington for approval, Congress discovered that one of the articles said that only free white males could vote, a provision that was an anathema to the post-Civil War Republican Congress. For nine months, Congress argued, finally passing the bill to admit Nebraska to statehood on condition that ''there shall be no abridgement of the exercise of the elective franchise or of any other right to any person by reason of race or color, excepting Indians

not taxed." [1] President Andrew Johnson, already at odds with
Congress over the same issue in the defeated Southern states,
vetoed the bill; on February 9, Congress overrode his veto, and
the act was submitted to the state and territorial legislatures,
who met in joint session on February 20–21 to make the necessary change. On March 1, 1867, President Johnson reluctantly
signed a proclamation admitting Nebraska as the thirty-seventh
state of the Union.

By that time, Nebraska had two governors and two legislatures in office at the same time. Alvin Saunders was the territorial governor, David Butler the state governor. The state legislature had met on July 4, 1866, to elect two United States
senators, and in February 1867, to change the "fundamental
conditions" for statehood, so that when the state legislature met
on May 16, 1867, for the first time since statehood, it was in its
third session.

In achieving territorial status in 1854, Nebraska had been a
cause celebre; although the difficulties in achieving statehood
had not been so far-reaching, even so her admission to statehood had caused uproar and dissension again on the national
scene.

One of the first items of business was the location of the capital. Although the new territorial capitol building, constructed in
1857–1858, was in good shape, the south-of-the-Platte contin-
gent was still annoyed that the capitol was in Omaha, so it voted
a new site, a section of land inland in Seward, Saunders, Butler,
and Lancaster counties, to be called Capitol City. To block the
vote, an Omaha legislator suggested naming it Lincoln, assuming that no right-minded Democrat would vote for that hateful
name—but the bill passed anyhow. Lincoln was established as
the location for the capital, the state university and the state agricultural college as a unit, and the state penitentiary, most of
the plums of the brand-new state.

The capital commission reported that an area near the salt
flats in Lancaster county had natural beauty and commercial
possibilities as well; it was to be donated by its owners, even

1. Sheldon, *Nebraska: The Land and the People,* 1:364.

though the legislative act governing the removal of the capital had directed that the city be located on state lands assigned by the federal government. The area was platted, with twelve-acre sections reserved for the capitol, the state university, and a city park, with lots saved for ten different churches, the Lancaster county courthouse, a city hall and market place, a state historical library association, public schools, the Independent Order of Good Templars (a temperance organization), the Independent Order of Odd Fellows, and the Ancient Free ànd Accepted Masons. Sale of other lots was to pay for building the new capitol.

But nobody bought any lots. While the Omahans gleefully predicted that with "no river, no railroad, no steam wagon, nothing," [2] the town was destined for isolation and ultimate oblivion, and an Omaha newspaper prophesied that "nobody will ever go to Lincoln who does not go to the legislature, the lunatic asylum, the penitentiary, or some of the state institutions," [3] the commissioners frantically tried to sell the lots. It took some financial shenanigans to do it, but by the end of three weeks, they'd sold about fifty thousand dollars' worth, at prices ranging from forty to one hundred forty dollars each. Then they set out to construct the state capitol, knowing that if the building was not ready for the legislature by January 1869, it was likely that no legislature would ever meet in Lincoln.

The commissioners advertised in Omaha newspapers for architects; nobody replied. They advertised in Chicago newspapers; one lone architect submitted a plan. It wasn't quite what they had in mind, but they accepted it and started advertising for bids. One single bid came in—they accepted it, and then started searching for materials. A limestone quarry near Beatrice produced stone of satisfactory quality, and all the teams that could be hired were put on the road to haul the stone to Lincoln; by December 1, 1868, the capitol was ready for occupancy. It had cost $75,000—almost twice the estimate of $40,000, and it began to fall apart almost as soon as the doors were opened—it had to be replaced only twelve years later—but it was ready.

---

2. *Omaha Republican,* quoted by Olson, *History of Nebraska,* p. 147.
3. *Omaha Republican,* quoted by Olson, *History of Nebraska,* p. 147.

In its first session in its new quarters, the legislature chartered the University of Nebraska on February 15, 1869. Its development at first was as slow and uncertain as that of the capitol; the State Teachers Association thought that establishing a university was impracticable when preparatory subordinate schools were needed more, and the other communities which had already planned universities thought it hoggish of one town to claim both the capitol and the state-supported university. But in the fall of 1871 the university building was finished, and the faculty of five opened classes.

The Burlington and Missouri River Railroad connection from the river reached Lincoln in 1870, and by the end of the year, the town had a population of twenty-five hundred people. Before long, three church-related colleges—Nebraska Wesleyan, Cotner, and Union—were started, and the town basked in discussion clubs, literary societies and meetings of its thirteen temperance groups.

But the affairs of state did not go smoothly. Even while Governor Butler was being elected to a third term in 1870, the legislature was talking about the bribes he accepted, that he hadn't abided by the law in picking out the land for the town, had let the contract for the insane asylum for more money than the legislature had appropriated and to a builder who could not give bond, and had even lent school funds to friends, as a personal favor, without security. It certainly was true that the state capitol and the insane asylum, hastily built, were already beginning to fall part, and that nobody could trace many of the state funds which seemed to bounce from one personal bank account to another.

On March 6, 1871, the legislature approved eleven articles of impeachment against the first governor of the state of Nebraska. Butler was convicted on one count—of appropriating school funds from the federal government for his own use—and was removed from office. He was not otherwise punished; the state confiscated some of his personal property to cover the missing funds, but later he tried to get an appropriation to reimburse him for his losses. He returned to Lincoln later as a state senator, and within a few more years was a candidate for governor again.

The state auditor was impeached but not convicted, and the state treasurer was severely criticized; he and his deputy had put state funds in their own bank but did not carry them in a separate account so there was no way of checking on what had happened to them.

It was an awesome record for the first officials of a brand-new state.

Nonetheless, the state government did accomplish some positive action in its early years, despite its preoccupation with the off-hand business practices and outright venality of some of its members. On February 12, 1869, for instance, the legislature passed a law exempting from taxation the lands which had been planted to trees, a one-hundred-dollar exemption for every acre planted in forest trees, and a fifty-dollar exemption for every acre planted in fruit trees. The next year it enacted a law obliging every city, town, and village to plant trees; and two years later, on April 10, 1872, observed the first Arbor Day, one of Nebraska's unique contributions to the nation. J. Sterling Morton, an ardent Democrat, and Governor Robert W. Furnas, an equally ardent Republican, both of them distinguished horticulturalists, overlooked their political differences when it came to the promoting of tree planting in Nebraska.

The legislature also passed a herd law requiring farmers to fence in their livestock, a law that was to pose problems later when large-scale ranching developed in the western part of the state. By 1870, however, prairie settlers outnumbered the ranchers; many of them were too poor to fence in their fields, and wandering livestock often destroyed their crops. Townspeople realized that if Nebraska was to grow in population and agricultural production, the crops of the farmers must be protected by law.

Not so successful was an effort to promote a new state constitution in 1871; it was not until 1875 that a well-worked-out constitution was voted by the electorate, superseding the one of 1866, which had been passed hastily and almost furtively.

In the next few years, as villages were platted and county governments organized, many other public officials were charged with gross inefficiencies in office, some of the difficulties the result of ignorance and ineptness, others brought about by outright dishonesty. By 1900, a large number of the counties had been involved in county-seat fights, ballots from elections burned, wafted away by the prairie breeze, or otherwise unaccountably lost. And a number of the counties had had at least one treasurer charged with shortages.

Even the supreme court was not above suspicion, allegedly agreeable to making decisions in terms of cash. A legend goes that Judge William Gaslin, seeing a body dangling from a Hangin' Tree, convicted by lynch law, commented, "Well, that's one decision the supreme court can't overturn!" He was particularly bitter because one of his decisions had been reversed, according to an unverifiable legend, with the payment of enough cattle to fill a two-locomotive train.

The growing pains were difficult. The state was exploding with population, its problems multiplying; many of its new residents were inexperienced in positions of responsibility. But such was the resilience of the new state on the prairie that it survived.

9

The Homesteaders

BY the hundreds and then the thousands, the homesteaders came, spreading out from the wooded lands along the Missouri into the broad, flat, treeless reaches of the prairies. The first waves of settlers were young veterans mustered out of the Union army, full of ginger and itching for adventure, with no taste to go back to the home-place, in Ohio or Illinois or New York state.

In wagons they came at first, following the Overland Trail part of the way until it was time to turn off to head for the land they wanted. Later they came on the Union Pacific or the Burlington. Even before the rails were finished through the area, ebullient young settlers would ride to the end of the line, wherever that was at the time, and would get off and walk, perhaps twenty, thirty, forty miles beyond, carrying their worldly goods with them, looking for the place they wanted to homestead, fertile soil, close to water, not yet claimed.

"I was a young businessman in Michigan, about the time many Civil War veterans were moving from Michigan to Nebraska, where they could secure free homesteads," Adjutant General A. V. Cole wrote, many years later. "I crossed the Missouri River at Plattsmouth on a flatboat. The Burlington was running mixed trains as far west as School Creek. We rode to that point, then started to walk to Juniata," a distance of some forty miles. He stopped in one settlement of four houses that night, walked a dozen miles to another four-house community, both of them railroad towns, and passed a shanty farther on, where the pre-emptor was sitting in the sun carving up buffalo meat. From then on, "there was not a tree or living thing in sight, just burnt prairie," he wrote.[1] It was not an auspicious introduction to the area, but it apparently did not squelch his enthusiasm, for he staked out a claim, somehow survived until he could get shelter built, and lived there for the next forty years.

Wherever the newcomers had come from, there had been building materials of some kind available, whether trees to be chopped down and made into logs, or rocks to be gathered and mortared. But on the Nebraska prairies, there was nothing. The only building material was the dirt the settlers stood on.

In hillsides or in areas abutting streams—for many small waterways course the state—the homesteaders could dig into the bank and create dugouts, lateral caves, shoring up the sandy soil overhead as best they could. Often the crust of soil that formed the roof was so flimsy or weakened by rain that it gave way under the pounding hooves of horses or stampeding buffalo. Startled homesteaders in their dugouts sometimes woke from a sound sleep to find the thrashing hooves of a horse and perhaps the booted legs of the rider dangling over them, having punched through the roof of the dugout in the blackness of night.

But on the level ground, where there were no embankments to carve into for a dugout, no trees to rest under, there was no shelter. Those settlers who had arrived in wagons could live in them until they had time to build; those who were on foot or had come on the railroad cars had nothing to protect them from the crisp highland nighttime temperatures nor the predators of the plains. In later years, when there were homestead shanties of sorts every few miles, the newcomers could share a bed or sleep on the dirt floor—for there are no strangers on the prairie, then or now—but the earliest settlers had to toss their blankets wherever they could, away from such obvious hazards as rattlesnakes, and sleep under the stars. The next day they began to build of sod.

Who built the first soddy? Nobody knows, but it was some-

---

1. A. V. Cole, "Early Experiences in Adams County," *Nebraska Pioneer Reminiscences* (Lincoln: Nebraska Society of the Daughters of the American Revolution, 1916), pp. 18–22.

one who had learned from an Indian trader how the Pawnees on
the Loup and Elkhorn rivers banded dirt around their round
lodges made of saplings, or how the Mandans up in Dakota
built houses of dirt. For generations the semisedentary Plains Indians had utilized the soil as building material for their lodges.
Settlers in Kansas, who predated the Nebraskans by a decade,
had already developed sod-house construction and refined it,
contriving a special implement called a grasshopper plow,
which cut the sod deep and square, keeping the wiry roots intact.

Old-timers say that when they shoved the grasshopper plow
into the ground to make the first break into the tough virgin sod,
the soil gave a sort of sigh, as if it knew that the old days were
gone forever. Sod-busting was hard work, not a job for strip-
lings.

The best sod came from a lagoon in the late summer when the
fine roots were solidly meshed together, the thick mat having
developed during the growing season. With the grasshopper, the
sodbuster plowed strips a foot wide, cut them two feet long, and
put them onto a skid or platform to be moved without breaking
to the building site. There they were laid up like giant bricks,
the blocks nestling together snugly without mortar. There was
an art to soddy building, and a skilled craftsman was in great
demand.

"To build a sod house would require about three weeks'
work for a man and a team," wrote Walter Croft, who was such
an artisan in mid-Nebraska.

> The first thing was to clear a place the size of a house, which would
> usually be about 16 by 24 feet. The walls would then be built inside
> the clearing and would be about two feet thick. The door and the
> front window were made in one opening . . . The ridge pole at the
> top was generally about ten inches in diameter and quite often brush
> would be used in place of rafters, and then the sod laid over them.[2]

Not everyone was as precise nor as skilled as Croft, however.
Fifteen men arrived in Boone County to homestead, for instance,
and although none of them had ever seen a sod house nor had a

2. Walter Croft in *Past and Present of Adams County*, edited by J. J. Lewis and
William H. Burton (Chicago: S. J. Clarke Company, 1916), p. 328.

clue as to how it should be built, they wanted it finished by nightfall. They began, with fifteen definite ideas about procedures; the only thing they all agreed on was that in laying the sod the hair side should be on top. By the end of the first day, they had the wall up five feet tall, but by morning it had fallen flat on the ground. The next day after arguing about who was to blame they built it back up and braced the wall by tipping the breaking plow against it; there was no roof yet. During the night a northwester roared in and blew off everything loose—it took three months to find the wagon cover, they said—and for three days the men huddled in a nearby draw under a shelter of tall prairie grass. Finally the wind stopped and they got the soddy built; the 14-x-18-foot structure housed the fifteen men until they could get other houses built. Probably most soddies were built with procedures less professional than Croft's but more so than those of the fifteen gormless Irishmen of Boone County.

The thick walls of the soddy provided insulation to make it cool in summer, warm in winter, and cozy generally, but always ill-ventilated. The house was dark because it did not have many openings—the first windows had no glass and seldom had even oiled-paper—and the walls were so thick that whatever light filtered through the single window was considerably reduced by the time it got into the room. Many stories are told of families who finally achieved the financial stability to build a wooden house, only to discover that sunlight hurt their eyes.

After the first rush of building the soddy, the family would sometimes calcimine or plaster the walls, the white surface helping lighten the room. The old newspapers other families used to paper the walls took away some of the roughness of the dirt wall.

Window ledges, two or sometimes three feet wide, were favorite places for color-loving pioneer women to set the potted geraniums and begonias they had brought with them, as slips, from their homes back East. Often the low-pitched roofs of soddies blossomed with wildflowers that had been interspersed with the native grasses in the lagoon, purplish-red buffalo peas or yellow butter-and-eggs waving in the prairie breeze. Mark

Twain, seeing a sod house in western Nebraska, commented, "It was the first time we had ever seen a man's front yard on top of his house." [3]

There were advantages to soddies, for in addition to their built-in insulation, they were low and hugged the ground; during tornadoes and other high winds on the Plains, soddies stayed in place while flimsily built wooden houses took off across the sky. In fact, soddies could be insured; their premiums were far less than those for frame houses because they were better risks against wind and lightning damage; Samuel Harpham insured his place near Kenesaw for $650 in 1890, the premium for five years costing $19.50.

When melting snowbanks eroded part of the wall, it could be repaired easily, just for the trouble of going to the lagoon for more material. Soddies were small, seldom more than two rooms big; when there was need for privacy, someone would nail up a blanket to curtain off part of the house. The walls were so thick and hard that they held nails readily; the family shotgun was usually hung on hooks over the front door, out of the way of the youngsters but easily available for shooting game or scaring off marauding Indians; the occasional piece of lumber the family acquired could be used for shelving for the few pieces of crockery—often Queensware—which the family had brought from back East.

There were disadvantages, though, as well. Unlike the adobe of the southwest, which is sun-dried to bricklike consistency before it is used in building, the sods were taken from the earth and laid into place directly, still damp from the earth, taking along the small wildlife of the soil. Unless the holes were carefully chinked on the inside, occasionally mice and sometimes even snakes would slither from their burrows into the house, or would crawl down from the bushy roof. Many an early-day pioneer yarn tells about the mother—always the mother—seeing a rattler dangling down from the ceiling, hovering over the baby's cradle, although no snakebite deaths were recorded among infants.

The roof usually leaked, and few of the soddies had floors

3. Mark Twain, *Roughing It*, p. 23.

other than of tamped earth, and from time to time the floor was
a muddy mire. Otherwise, however, the floor required no more
sweeping with the homemade broom than the sophisticated one
of wide boards that every soddy-living woman dreamed of having. Somehow or other, bedbugs were the scourge of sod-house
living; they were not endemic to the soil but apparently travelers
passing through and stopping overnight in the only house in
sight dropped them off. Old-timers who told of their days in
soddies always began to scratch, a reflex action closely associated with the past.

With the broad humor the settlers developed, they referred to
their building material as Nebraska marble, and they used it for
barns, chicken houses, even schools. Sod houses of considerable size were built, including the famed two-story Haumont
house in Custer County, which only recently was bulldozed
back to the soil from whence it came.

Shelter the settlers had, and food as well: prairie chickens,
mallards and brants, antelope and deer, and the peculiar long-
eared, high-rumped hare they called the jackass rabbit, its name
later abbreviated by the ladies to simply jack rabbit. Game was
available to anyone with a gun. The buffalo which had been the
staple of the Indians for generations past had largely disappeared from the Plains by the time the main body of homesteaders arrived, millions of the dim-sighted animals having
been killed by the buffalo hunters in the period between 1867
and 1883.

There were wild fruits in the brush along the streams—small,
oval, bluish-orange plums, mouth-puckering, shiny black
chokecherries, yellow and red currants, clusters of tiny purple
grapes, and in the short grass in the uplands of the Sandhills,
buffalo berries and sand cherries. There were greens as well, in
wild lettuce, lamb's quarter, watercress, wild asparagus, all
available just for the plucking.

The settlers brought with them supplies of staples, including
cornmeal, molasses, the "starter" for flapjacks or biscuits, and
salt pork, which provided seasoning for greens, lard for spreading on bread, and fat which the housewives mixed with camp-
fire ashes to make soap, boiling it in huge black cast-iron kettles

in the yard outside the house. For fuel in this treeless country they used buffalo chips, later cow chips—they called them Nebraska coal—and a few converted their stoves to accommodate twists of prairie hay which made a hot, too-fast fire. Some families even bought hay-burning stoves out of the Monkey Ward catalog. In later years the homesteaders used corncobs as fuel.

Shelter they could contrive, food they could locate somewhere, fuel they could manage. The big problem on the wide open prairies was water. The earliest settlers claimed land close to water, along streams or springs; later homesteaders had to take upland tracts, carrying their water by the bucketsful, sometimes six or eight miles from the creek, for their own uses and for their livestock until they could dig their own wells.

Although some people used dowsers, men with forked branches of peachwood or willow, to locate the the most favorable spot for water, it was possible to find quantities of water in almost every part of the state just by digging, although it might be several hundred feet down. The digging was done by hand; some of the early wells were so broad at the top that there were steps part way down, but most of the homesteaders were in such a hurry for water they did not bother with such foolishness. They simply dug and dug and dug with their spades, and when they finally reached water, they cleaned out the bucket, made sure the knot was secure on the rope, and had the people on top pull up the first draught of water.

They used whatever materials were at hand for well-casing—sometimes planks, sometimes bricks or rocks, sometimes even stovepiping metal, anything that would keep the walls of the shaft from collapsing; if the soil was firm, they used no casing at all.

Seeing the first well on the tableland was an emotional experience, for it signified permanence to the settlers, that they had achieved a degree of stability and affluence. But the wells were not without hazards. Many a collection of old-timers' reminiscences tells of unwary settlers stumbling into them in the dark of night and of their struggles to get out, clawing their way up far enough in the shaft to call for help. F. W. Carlin, for instance, who sprained his ankle and bruised his body on the way down, spent two days and three nights digging his way out of a 143-foot well with a penknife; others lived to be excavated from the wells, only to die later of their injuries. Two well diggers in Holt county were in a cave-in; they died after two days and it was another day before their bodies could be recovered.

Before long a new kind of workmen evolved—well drillers who used horsepower and drills, rather than manpower and spades, to drill wells. And the settlers turned to a more efficient means of drawing water up out of the ground after the well was dug.

Just as the dirt they stood on was the most plentiful building material, so the constantly blowing wind was the most plentiful source of power. The prairie dwellers turned to windmills. Although for centuries windmills had been used in various parts of the world, it was the farmers on the prairies who adapted them to commonplace use, reducing the towers to simple framework, the sails to circles of small vanes set at oblique angles to catch the wind most effectively.

Sometimes the windmills were store-bought, Dempsters, maybe, from the company in Beatrice which had been established in 1878 to sell them, later to make them from its own design. Sometimes they were handmade affairs, constructed of scrap iron, bits of wood, and anything that was loose, with perhaps two or three dollars' worth of new mechanisms.

By 1900 the Nebraska landscape was dotted with tens of thousands of round wood wheels, or sometimes metal, on spindly towers, creaking away in the breezes, pumping water for man and beast alike; the windmill became the symbol of the Plains, in villages as well as on farms. Until only recently, the town of Axtell, for instance, had as many neat, tidy, well-oiled windmills as it had newly painted white houses.

But the wind that could provide benefits could switch, in a moment, into an agent of destruction, for it fanned the prairie fires that were the scourge of the Plains. In the hot, dry weeks of late summer and early fall, when native grasses were tinder-dry, any spark could set them afire, and with no natural barriers to stop them, the flames would sweep across miles of plains, a blistering inferno that destroyed everything in its way.

In generations past, before the Indians had acquired guns and ammunition from white traders, they had used fire for their buffalo hunts; they chose a time and place when the winds and the terrain were right and set fire to the prairie grass to send the buffalo into a stampede over a bluff, where the hunters could slaughter them for food, hides, sinews, and bones. The Indians had respect for prairie fires, and when they started the flames themselves they knew what natural terrain would stop them. It was the Indians who advised the earliest settlers how to combat prairie fires: they said that man should not try to outrun the fast-moving flames but should take to the nearest bare ground, either sand or dirt without grass, digging down, if possible to escape the intense heat.

Sometimes it was lightning that started a prairie fire; sometimes it was an improperly tended camp fire along the trail; in later years, when the tall-stacked coal-burning locomotives chugged through the state, it was often a stray cinder that set the prairie ablaze. But no matter what caused the fire, the alarm "Prairie Fire!" alerted the countryside to action. Men hitched their teams to plows and rushed frantically to plow firebreaks, strips of bare ground twenty or thirty feet wide, around their houses; if there was time, others set back fires to burn off the land, to starve off the rushing wall of flame, with men standing by with wet gunnysacks or blankets to slap out the new, lifesaving flames. The most difficult part of controlling a prairie fire was the flying, windblown cow-chip ember. Light in weight, easily flammable, a blazing chip could be blown to remote areas, there to set fire to a new area of dry grass long after the original fire was contained.

A bad loss of life from prairie fire came in October 1873, when the wind swept the smoke of a great fire toward a country schoolhouse in Saline county. Against the teacher's objections one of the mothers took some of the children and started home, running across the prairie from the flames. The blackened, scorched bodies of ten children and the mother were found later; those who had stayed with the teacher took refuge in a piece of bare ground and were saved. One of the most extensive prairie fires in memory of man was one which was set deliberately in October 1864, to control the Indians. The cavalry put the torch to a four-hundred-mile stretch, from Fort Kearny to the Colorado line, utilizing the scorched-earth tactic that soldiers from Julius Caesar onward have known about; the flames stretched across southwest Nebraska into western Kansas and eastern Colorado, and down into the Texas Panhandle, where they finally died.

As soon as the settlers had broken the sod and planted the seed—either seed they had brought from back East or bought at the outfitting store or even borrowed from an obliging neighbor—they needed to fence in the field to protect it from stray cattle, horses, or even marauding wildlife. The problem was what to do for fencing when there was neither timber nor rock available.

In the eastern parts of the state, early farmers planted osage orange trees in the hopes that the bushy tough-wooded trees would provide a fence of sorts while they were growing; the wood was hard as ironwood, and the milky sap made it impervious to rotting. But in the rest of the state, the high, windswept prairie where every tree that was planted had to be watered by carrying buckets of water to it by hand every week or so, that was no answer; fences were needed now.

If a farmer had only one or two pigs, he could make a dugout pen for them, digging a hole in the ground big enough that they could not crawl out. The cow was staked out to grass by tying the end of a long rope around her horns and securing the other end by driving an iron picket pin into the ground; the tether pin was moved to a new place every day so that the cow could have a chance to graze. Some of the farmers turned to the same building material they used for their houses, and built elaborate fences of sod, thick, sturdy walls that took time to put up, used lots of space and were not movable at all; the ordinary farmer had neither the time nor the strength to put up a sod wall around his place.

In 1873 in Illinois, an inventor named Joseph Glidden twisted some wires together, put in some barbs to discourage anyone or anything from leaning against the wires, and in less than ten years had revolutionized farming on the Nebraska farm. Barbed wire provided cheap fencing with a minimum of posts; it also caused settlers' wars, crystalized the differences between home-steader and cattleman, and brought about the end of the open range for cattle. The third element in the new prairie culture had been added—sod houses, windmills, and now barbed wire.

Except for moments of crisis, the homesteaders of northern, central, and western Nebraska were alone, separated by miles from their nearest neighbors. A writer, a chance passerby, sensed the isolation, the loneliness, the bleakness of the lives of the early Nebraska sod-house settlers. "We were at sea," Robert Louis Stevenson wrote of his journey through Nebraska in 1869:

—there is no other adequate expression—on the plains of Nebraska. It was a world almost without a feature; an empty sky, and empty earth. The green plain ran till it touched the skirts of heaven. It is the settlers at whom we have the right to marvel. Upon what food (do they) subsist, what livelihood can repay the human creature for a life spent in this huge sameness? He is cut off from books, from news, from company, from all that can relieve existence. He may walk five miles and see nothing; ten, and it is as though he had not moved; twenty, and still he is in the midst of the same great level.[4]

The sameness of the prairie that Stevenson noted was one of the treacheries of the new country; there were few trees, no landmarks or lines of demarcation: the unending expanse of prairie all looked alike. When the sun was shining—which is often, in Nebraska—a man could distinguish east from west, but on a cloudy day or starless night it was easy to become confused and lost. One pioneer yarn tells of a country doctor near Exeter becoming lost on his way home from a country call and wandering most of the night on the prairie only a short distance from his home; neither he nor his horse knew where they were.

Some of the settlers were bachelors, a very few were spinsters, usually young women taking claims in their own names adjoining land being pre-empted by their parents. But most of the homesteaders were family groups, usually strong young farm couples with young children, hundreds of miles and a civi-

4. Robert Louis Stevenson, *Across the Plains* (New York: C. Scribner's Sons, 1903), pp. 49–50.

lization away from their families, living in a harsh land of sky and grass and lonesomeness. Hard physical labor, disappointments, privation—all of these the resilient pioneers could stand; it was the loneliness that was the hardest of all to bear. And it was the women who suffered most.

Although the families were isolated, men occasionally had opportunities to see other, non-family people, either at times of crisis, such as a prairie fire, or in communal work, such as helping with haying or threshing, or in perhaps occasional trips to the nearest town, a day's ride away, to file papers at the courthouse, borrow money at the bank, or buy supplies of goods that couldn't be raised on the farm. But the women stayed at home and hungered for the sight of other adults, other women to socialize with.

In the summertime, when most of their activity was out of doors, women could tolerate the solitude for they were busy hoeing the garden, cooking in the big black pot over the camp fire to preserve foods for winter, feeding chickens, and in many cases helping their men in the fields. But in the winter, when the farm work was finished and the icy winds kept everyone inside the dark, reeking soddy day after day, the women suffered. A. V. Cole, telling later of his homesteading years, said that his wife spent most of her early years in Nebraska crying of homesickness. "My heart went out to Mrs. Cole," he wrote of his bride who had arrived in Nebraska after a prairie fire, nineteen years old and a thousand miles from her people. "The wind blew more fiercely than now and she made me promise that if the house ever blew down I would take her back to Michigan." During a violent storm later, he said "Mrs. Cole almost prayed that the house would go down so she could go back East." [5] Others did not have as indulgent husbands, nor the money for a return trip, so that the possibilities of escape for them were nonexistent.

Some did not survive; there were suicides, desperate women drinking lye, hanging themselves if there was a ridge pole high enough, slitting themselves with a butcher knife—but almost never using a gun, for ammunition was dear. Others lapsed into

5. Cole, "Early Experiences," p. 22.

depression and in some cases violent insanity, which resulted in the woman's being taken away, for as early as 1864 officials realized the need for an insane asylum and made arrangements for Nebraskans to be sheltered in Iowa institutions until Nebraska herself could build an asylum five years later. Overworked, poorly nourished, continuously child-bearing, with no one to talk to except the family members she was responsible for day after day, the pioneer woman had to learn to live with loneliness.

Many of the women arrived as brides, their wedding trips the joggling, jolting trip overland to the new country. Some, too, came to be brides, mail-order wives of bachelors who advertised in lonely-hearts publications and sent tickets to the pretty girls pictured there. Often the girl who arrived on the train or the coach bore slight resemblance to the picture, but the man who met her did not seem to be the one described in the letter, either. Strangers, they wed and lived together alone on the prairie, far removed from other human beings. When immigrants from Europe flocked to the Nebraska prairies, the women seldom had a chance to learn the new language; their isolation was complete for even when they saw other people they could not converse.

When they could, settlers took homesteads in the vicinity of people they already knew. In many cases, colonies of farmers would travel together—the Monroe group from Allen's Grove, Wisconsin, for instance, who settled near Trumbull, or the Lenawee County, Michigan, colony near Juniata—and would acquire land as near as possible to friends, even though they realized the distances were so great they might not see each other frequently; just knowing that friends were somewhere in the neighborhood was comforting. Sometimes the groups were centered around a particular church—the Friends or Dunkards or Mennonites. Newcomers from Europe were especially eager to be close to fellow countrymen, and colonies of Swedes, Danes, or Germans sprang up on the prairie. There was a cluster of Negro homesteaders in the Sandhills. Those who wished to acquire land contiguous to friends usually had to buy railroad lands, for the homestead lands were claimed so quickly there was little choice of location.

Almost every year brought some natural catastrophe that

tested the settlers' power of survival. In 1872 it was a raging blizzard in the western part of the state; it was still buffalo-hunting time and hunters were caught out on the prairies, many of them greenhorns who did not know how to take cover. No one knows how many perished, but dozens of bodies were found later, and surgeons at army posts—Cottonwood Springs, then known as Fort McPherson, and Fort Laramie—were busy afterward amputating frozen hands and feet, even gangrenous legs, of survivors.

The next year in the southern part of Nebraska it was the Easter Sunday blizzard, which started on April 13 with a dust storm, then a tornado, and finally a four-day blizzard which completely immobilized the area. Many newcomers were still living in their wagons; they took refuge with families already established in soddies, as many as twenty-three in one small place in Kenesaw, and seven adults and two half-frozen horses in a shanty near Inland, the horses trying to eat through the rough pine scantlings all the time they were inside. Several persons took shelter in a small, low, sod chicken house, and when they were rescued four days later could not stand up, having been hunkered down for such a long time.

The winter of 1880–1881 was a bad one, for from October 15, when four inches of snow fell, through April 10, when two inches fell, there was not a single day that the ground was entirely free of snow, and the temperature was below zero for weeks at a time, falling to 32 below on January 9. The Blizzard of 1888, known as the Schoolchildren's Blizzard, hit on January 12 in midafternoon, just as youngsters were starting home from school, most of them afoot over miles of open prairie. More than two hundred persons froze to death, many of them children; some of the ones who were rescued died later after their frozen arms and legs were amputated. More would have lost their lives had not some of the prairie teachers been resourceful enough to keep the children in the one-room schoolhouses overnight, although one young teacher in Adams County was later chastised by the school board because she allowed the youngsters to play cards while they huddled around the pot-bellied stove through the night and she was docked a day's pay because she didn't hold classes the next day.

There were summertime catastrophes as well. On July 26,

1874, when the corn was coming along well and the garden vegetables were far enough along to promise a full larder for the winter, "a haze came over the sun, deepened into a gray cloud, and resolved itself into billions of gray grasshoppers sweeping down upon the earth with a roaring sound like a rushing storm. As far as the eye could reach in every direction, the air was filled with them," a contemporary historian wrote.[6] Every leaf, every stalk, was covered with the gnawing things, and when the grasshoppers finally lifted, there was nothing left but bare ground; even the carrots and turnips underground were chewed away. Spade handles were gnawed where palm grease had soaked the wood. Housewives who rushed out to cover their gardens with aprons to protect them from the insects watched helplessly as the grasshoppers methodically chewed through the aprons to get at the cabbages underneath. People who were out of doors when the insects landed were covered with stinging bites.

Old-timers, with the wry humor they had to develop in times of trouble, later insisted that the grasshoppers, devouring everything in sight that was green, even chewed up the green paint on the new schoolhouse. The fish in the streams, the chickens in the yards, ate so many grasshoppers that for days afterward their flesh was inedible; not only did the homesteaders have no vegetables, but they had no palatable meat for a while. Where there were railroads, the trains couldn't run; the grasshoppers were so thick they made the rails slick, without traction.

The grasshoppers left their eggs, and for the next three years, despite the efforts of the settlers to dowse them in kerosene, to burn them, to dispose of them in any way whatsoever, there were infestations, although none so big again as the one of 1874, which covered the Plains from Canada to Texas.

But the settlers stayed. Many of them, at least. Even through the rough year of 1890 when, during July, there were twenty days of temperatures above one hundred degrees, one of them one hundred ten, another one hundred fifteen, and the hot winds and drought shriveled the corn in the furrow. Even through 1894 when, on July 26, a furnace wind began from the south-

6. Sheldon, *Nebraska: The Land and the People*, 1:494.

east and blew for three days, drying up everything in sight. That was the year some people hired rainmakers who set off explosives to blast some rain from the sky. That didn't work; nothing could bring the rain. What was worse was that the bank panic of 1893 on Wall Street which had broken many banks reflected even out to the Nebraska prairies; nowhere was there money to borrow. This time the settlers stayed because they could not afford to leave.

But even though their lives were often bleak, the homesteaders found pleasure from simple activities, hitching up the teams and driving twenty, thirty miles if necessary for sociability. Anything was a bee—a rafter-raising bee for a neighbor's barn, when all the men in the township joined to help with the physical labor and the women gossiped as they set out the simple foods they had brought along to share; an occasional quilting bee when the women would find companionship as they sat around the quilting frame, their needles working as fast their tongues; a Friday afternoon spelling bee at the sod-house school when not only the youngsters but also the adults took their turns at the hard words, although it sometimes developed that not all the grown-ups knew their letters. There were occasional barn dances, for somewhere in the neighborhood there was bound to be a pump-organ and someone to play it, and always there was a fiddler; someone could be prevailed upon to call the square dances, and the rest of the time the parents, youngsters, blushing teen-agers and even light-footed grandparents would dance the schottische or the polka. The occasions were rare, and because of their rarity, they were precious. They were the leaven that made endurance possible.

In 1863, the year the Homestead Act went into effect, there were 349 entries made for fifty thousand acres of Nebraska land; by 1900, entries totaled nearly one hundred fifty thousand, for almost twenty million acres of land. But less than half of those homestead entries were ever completed. Many of the farmers were undercapitalized and had no reserves to fall back on during the bad years; most of the farmers had had no experience with farming in semiarid lands and some could not adapt their farming procedures to the different demands of the land. Some farmers settled on land so poor that a quarter-section could not support a family. Just because the land was free was no guarantee that it would be productive.

The Homestead Act which the farmers had hailed with such enthusiasm in 1862 when it was enacted hadn't worked out exactly according to plan. The Homestead Act itself provided one hundred sixty acres for each entrant, and the original Pre-Emption Act of 1841, which was still in force until 1891, allowed him to claim another hundred sixty for $1.25 per acre. The Timber Culture Act of 1873 permitted him to claim still another quarter-section in return for planting at first forty acres, later ten acres of it, to trees. Those who took advantage of all the possibilities could acquire three-quarters of a section of land for a relatively small expenditure of cash and a large amount of hard labor; by purchasing railroad land, they could enlarge their holdings even more.

But one provision in the Homestead Act made it possible to circumvent the spirit of the law, to get large holdings into the hands of the speculators, for one section in the law allowed settlers to file homestead claims, then after six months commute or purchase the land for a minimum price of $1.25 per acre. Speculators hired people to file claims, then paid their commutation fees, and took title to the land. Although the law limited each person to one entry, many individuals made multiple entries, usually using other names. Likewise, much of the more than a million acres of land assigned to the use of agricultural colleges, under the Morrill Act of 1862, went to private speculators, as did a large portion of the Indian lands. Nebraska was more fortunate than many other states, however, in that the agricultural school lands brought more money per acre—the proceeds were used for the endowment for the agricultural college—and were sold to a larger number of persons, than were the cases in many other states.

By the time a family was settled in its holding on the prairie, breaking the sod, battling the wind, and praying for rain, it made no difference how the land had been acquired. A homestead from the government, a tract from the railroad, a timber claim, a pre-emption—it made no difference; in any case, the payments were difficult and at times even survival was in doubt. The wonder of it all is that any of the settlers remained.

10

The Towns

AS fast as the rails moved west, new towns sprang up in their wake. And because they were organized almost simultaneously, and in many cases by the same land company officials, the towns followed the same developmental patterns, almost a monotonous similarity.

Even those towns along the Missouri River which had been established earlier, independently of one another and with no connection to the railroads, were almost duplicates of one another, for they were started at almost the same instant and underwent the same growing pains—Nebraska City, Falls City, Bellevue, Plattsmouth, Tecumseh, Brownville. The town of Omaha, with its great burst of population, was different only in numbers; the pattern was the same. They were raw, raucous communities with a touch of gentility that few other new river towns ever accomplished; after the first mad rush of opportunists into the area, a more stable, although no less enthusiastic, group of people arrived, planning less on getting rich overnight and leaving than on accumulating wealth over a period of time and living there permanently. They brought their wives with them, built homes and businesses, erected public buildings, and had an aura of respectability about them that the first get-rich-quick arrivals lacked.

Many Omaha residents came from "fine old Eastern families and were well educated, many of them college bred, the women having all the graces of Eastern refinement, and they gave to the

early life of the community a leaven not to be found in many of
Omaha's rival cities up and down the trans-Mississippi
region," [1] an Omaha historian wrote in 1916. But there was
another side to the town, too, described by another historian.
Omaha in 1870, he said,

> . . . may have had city airs, but there were also many
> characteristics which smacked of village days. Most of the streets
> were unpaved, and alternately dusty and muddy. Steamboats still
> stuck their prows in the mud at the levee . . . Innumerable
> whiskey shops with faro banks attached kept in full blast night and
> day. On Saturday nights the town was alive with open carriages
> occupied by questionable women, from the sixty-one houses of ill
> fame. Squaws and papooses begged for money and drinks on the
> streets. Strangers and fortune seekers swarmed in the hotels and
> grog shops. . . .[2]

It was a booming prairie town.

The phenomenal growth of Nebraska was an almost overnight
sprouting; everything happened at once. The settlement of the
whole Great Plains area is one of the most dramatic stories in
human history, the voluntary mass migration of several million
people to an unknown land. Perhaps in Nebraska the story is the
most clearly delineated because its development was com-
pressed into such a short span of time. In less than a quarter of a
century, the land changed from unknown Indian country to an
area of cultivated farms and populated villages. It is no wonder
that all the towns looked alike!

In the case of the towns established by the railroad land companies during the 1870s, the similarities were so great that the
traveler to the bustling little communities on the prairie had to
look at the name on the sign of the brand-new railroad station to
know exactly where he was. In each railroad town, the main
street of course paralleled the railroad tracks; other streets in the
plat were named after trees—Elm, Cedar, Pine—and United
States presidents—Lincoln, Washington, Jefferson—sometimes
the states from which most of the early residents had come—

1. Clement Chase, "Reminiscences of Early Omaha," 1916; reprinted in *Nebraska
History Magazine* 17 (July–September 1936):196.

2. Walker D. Wyman, "Omaha: Frontier Depot and Prodigy of Council Bluffs,"
Nebraska History Magazine 17 (July–September 1936):143–154.

Michigan, Wisconsin, Ohio—and sometimes other towns on the railroad system—Burlington, Chicago, Denver.

First construction in the village was the town pump, dug by the railroad company, and almost overnight an outfitting store sprang up, then a blacksmith shop, the railroad station and town site land company office, a lumber yard, sometimes a livery stable, and always a hotel. The hotel, a sleazy frame structure which the prairie wind swept through, provided a bed of sorts for newcomers to the community; sometimes it, had no more than four sleeping rooms, but each of them had several double-sized beds so that expanding numbers of people could be accommodated. The sleeping arrangements, coincidentally, provided a means of getting acquainted—nobody remained a stranger in the raw new prairie villages. When the westbound train came in, people in the hotel rooms moved closer together to allow space for the newcomers; when the eastbound train left, they could spread out a little because somebody would be going back home to get the wife and children packed up to move out to this great new land of opportunity.

Within a week or two there would be several quickly built little frame houses dotting the landscape—homes on village lots were not usually made of sod—and more going up. The houses were small, without plastering or insulation, without excavations or foundations, bald, primitive structures perched on the prairie, faint dusty or muddy trails leading to them for there were no streets marked off yet. The fragrance of the nearby wildflowers was overpowered by the resinous smell of the raw pine sawdust, the lilting song of the meadowlark drowned out by the pounding of hammers. Even before carpenters finished nailing the boards on the backs of the rough, four-square frame store buildings, merchants were selling goods out of the front part, pots and pans, hoes and spades, nails, essential groceries, all the necessaries the newcomers had to have to establish themselves in the best little town in the country. At night, the merchants themselves would sleep under the counters until they could take time off to build houses for themselves. It was a frenzied, energetic, optimistic atmosphere; everyone was in a hurry, full of hope.

Before long the first settlers were well enough established that they petitioned the governor for the right to hold elections and organize the county as a governmental structure; in some cases, there were only twenty-five or so qualified voters—males, that is—in the area when the county was formally organized. In the loosely held elections, the voters decided where the county seat would be and who would be the officers, the county commissioners, county clerk, treasurer, justice of the peace, assessor, superintendent of schools, and other officials, sometimes having to leave blank spaces in the table of organization to avoid doubling up on assignments. The election in Frontier County posed difficulties; nobody had a pen, but somebody finally located a nib point and managed to tie it with string to a piece of dry weed stalk so that the proper papers could be signed.

Whatever village became the county seat had to store the county's records and conduct its business in settlers' homes until a frame building could be pounded together for a courthouse. But that village was assured of prosperity, because people had to go there to transact business. Every village aspired to the honor, and when for one reason or another the county seat was moved from one town to another, the one which lost usually dwindled away.

Occasionally the removal of the county seat was accomplished without judicial approval; eager villagers armed with hunting guns, enthusiasm, and sometimes firewater, helped themselves to county records, often under cover of darkness, and took them back to their own town, papers floating away from the saddlebags or from the piles on the wagons. Many early-day Nebraska community records seem to have disappeared.

The controversy between Beaver City and Arapahoe in Furnas County was so bitter and the county seat changed hands so often that for years neither town would build a courthouse but rented the cheapest possible rooms for the county government; one was a shanty which was not finished on the inside and the other was a hotel room. The county jail was a dugout along Beaver Creek, the sheriff and his shotgun providing security, an arrangement that supplied the sheriff with an opponent for euchre, seven-up, and other card games; if the prisoner had funds, he bought the sheriff cigars. Knox County finally es-

tablished its county seat not in any of the towns already in existence but in a specially organized village named Center and
located in the exact center of the county; it is an exception to the
theory that the location of the county government brings progress to a community for it remains only a crossroads.

Often it was years before communities effected town incorpo-
ration and further taxation, but county organization was essential.

Among the earliest business enterprises in almost every community was the newspaper; in 1860, there were fourteen in the
territory, and in 1874, ninety-nine in the state. By 1889, the
number had increased to five hundred, with perhaps fifty or
more others being foreign-language publications to serve the immigrants from Europe who could not yet read English. The
usual Nebraska newspaper of the 1880s was a weekly with
copious quantities of boiler plate on the inside, ready-prepared
editorial material of recipes, patent medicine advertisements,
serial novels, and news from around the world, so that the inside pages of most of the papers looked alike. The front and
back pages were devoted to local news, notes about comings
and goings, paragraphs about what the town needed next in
terms of development, and a few business-card advertisements
for land-office companies, lawyers, and, later on, doctors and
barbers. Sometimes the newspapers didn't last more than three
or four issues, but while they did they were ebullient, irrepress-
ible in their visions of the future of the town. The most-needed
service, according to most of them, was a flouring mill, the fa-
cility to turn the farmers' wheat into flour, a need even greater
than that of the sugar press, where farmers could have sorghum
stalks turned into thick molasses. Whether the two burrs, or
stones, of the flouring mill would be powered by the nearby
stream or by a team of horses working around and around a
treadmill was unimportant; the existence of a flouring mill
seems to have been a status symbol for a new community even
more important than its convenience.

Saloons, too, were among the early enterprises in almost
every community, opening up for business when there were
only a few houses in the area. In Crete, on the Fourth of July in
1870, Dick Cater was selling booze before he had the roof on

his shanty-building saloon, supplying the neighborhood from the stocks of beer and barrel of whiskey he brought with him. Although almost every settlement had saloons, they often thrived in the midst of controversy. On the one hand were the thirsty souls, carpenters building houses on the prairie who wanted to settle the sawdust in their throats; farmers breaking the sod looking for relaxation from their labors; cowboys herding cattle up the trail from Texas seeking temporary oblivion; European immigrants accustomed to their daily tot. On the other hand were the narrow-lipped Prohibitionists calling for complete banning of anything alcoholic.

From her earliest days, Nebraska had had prohibition laws. The Indian Intercourse Act of 1834, even before the area was a territory, had forbidden "disposing of spiritous liquor" to the Indians, and the first territorial legislature in 1855 passed "an act to prohibit the sale and manufacture of intoxicating liquor" to anybody, but neither law was enforced. Three years later, in 1858, the legislature reversed itself and enacted a law permitting the granting of liquor licenses. From then on, the forces of Prohibition, echoing a movement that had started in New England a few decades earlier, were active in Nebraska, both territory and state, trying to get laws passed and rigidly enforced to prohibit any liquor production or consumption whatsoever. From the 1870s until the passage of the state prohibition law in 1917, the subject was a political issue as well as an emotional moral one.

In 1881, the Prohibitionists—by now an active political party—succeeded in promoting the passage of the Slocomb Act, a high license law which called for a minimum license fee of $500 for a saloon in the smallest town, with other license fees scaled upwards for larger-sized communities, the theory being that if you can't get rid of evil, at least use it for tax dollars. (When the vote was taken on the Slocomb Act in the state legislature, a number of senators weren't available; one was pretentiously eating his dinner in front of the big window at the Commercial Hotel, ostentatiously absenting himself from the vote.) But high-priced licenses did not deter saloons from opening, and only a few villages were successful in passing local ordinances keeping Demon Rum out.

Saloons there were, and along with them came gamblers, setting up games wherever there was room, particularly in settlements with a fair-sized transient population; if the saloon was large enough, the boys in the back room ran the game. In the earliest days, a greasy deck of cards was all that was necessary to start a gamblin' house, but later, as the towns gained sophistication, the establishments became ornate affairs with one-way glass in the doors, high-stake games, elaborate gambling devices, and according to local newspapers, connections with The Syndicate; who or what that was, was not ever identified.

Almost every community of any size had facilities to serve the lusty male population of the prairie, which at times outnumbered the women, particularly in the earliest days of settlement and especially in the cowboy towns of the western part of the state. The first brothels were plain and functional, housed in tents, sod houses, or in the same sort of raw pine buildings as the rest of the business buildings in town; as the towns progressed in size and economic stability, the houses of prostitution were among the first enterprises to upgrade their facilities, painting the outside walls, putting curtains at the windows and carpets on the floors. In some Nebraska towns, the first brick building reputedly was a house of joy; the indignant editor of one county newspaper in the early 1880s reported that one of the local houses of soiled doves was that very week installing fancy flocked wallpaper from Paris, France, costing $2 per roll. Local newspapers carried such frequent chatty items as to indicate that such institutions as Old Hat's in Columbus or Jack Anderson's in Grand Island where Maggie Mustard, Venus Weber, and the other girls from Dobytown were in business, might be social centers of the community; official histories of Nebraska communities never even hint of their existence.

A number of murderers were traced through brothels; several of them cut pieces of cretonne or other fabric from washstand skirts to use as masks, and when they dropped the masks at the scene of action, the fabric could be traced—possibly those were the only houses in town with curtains of any kind! The murderers of Cass Millett, a grocer in Hastings, were located through Kit Millet's house and later lynched; Sam Bass, an outlaw, was traced through a bordello in Ogallala.

While the business part of the village progressed, settlers began social organization almost as soon as they learned their neighbors' names. They organized a school district with the teacher-lady assigned to hold classes in the front room of an already built home until they could construct the schoolhouse; they established several different denominational churches, congregations clustering for Sabbath services in members' homes until they could erect the necessary buildings; they formed Masonic lodges and one or two other fraternal groups in the same patterns they had left behind in Illinois or Michigan, planning the lodge halls they would build as soon as they had time; they formed a Grand Army of the Republic post and drew up designs for the G.A.R. hall, for in many early villages the Union veterans of the Civil War were the principal settlers.

The present and the future were one; these townspeople saw not the bleakness of their windswept, treeless communities but rather the towering cities that would be there next week. They threw together their immediate buildings but they planned for permanence.

Even before they hammered together their first barnlike town halls, the villagers had cultural diversions; theatrical troups, lyceum speakers, entertainers of all sorts, boarded the railroad cars in Omaha or Denver and went from one community to the next, presenting programs in whatever facilities were available. At first, these were likely to be saloons which usually had the largest rooms in town; the saloon keeper would shove the glasses aside and cover the bottles with a blanket—to protect the sensibilities of the ladies—and the townspeople would roll in nail kegs and cover them with splintery planks to form seats for the performance. If there was a piano in town, it was moved in; otherwise a mandolin or fiddle provided necessary musical accompaniment. Candles in the front of the area set aside for the stage provided footlights for the productions of *East Lynne* or *The Queen's Lace Handkerchief* or *The Little Duke,* most of them tearful melodramas that attracted wild applause. The lecturers were usually inspirational speakers describing the evils of drink or the necessity of woman suffrage—Susan B. Anthony was an indefatigable trouper during the 1870s, appearing in many Nebraska communities—or telling of travel in the Holy

. . .

Land. Occasionally the programs would be home-grown ones, for some communities organized cornet bands or singing societies or fife-and-drum corps. Whatever the program, everyone in town attended—and clapped.

Almost concurrent with their first building, a number of communities began to plan colleges, some of them because the residents appreciated the value of education, others because they realized the prestige of a college would attract people to the new town. In the thirteen years that Nebraska was a territory, its legislature granted charters to twenty-eight colleges and universities, nine of those in 1857 alone; only five of those chartered did open, however fleetingly. An educational historian writing in 1892 attributed the eagerness of town organizers, even those of so-called paper towns, to charter institutions of higher learning to the fact that "so many young men fresh from college or seminary were among the early settlers in the territory." [3]

After statehood, from 1867 to 1900, dozens of other academies and colleges actually were started; since the state legislature did not charter anticipated colleges, only those really under way, there are no records of the near-misses. There were colleges in Fairfield, Franklin, Neligh, and Weeping Water, for instance, as well as in Bellevue, Hastings, Hebron, and Fremont; they covered most of the populated part of the state. Many of the institutions were denominational; the Christian Church started two; Methodists, five; Catholics, ten; Lutherans, four; United Brethren, one; Friends, one; Episcopalians, three; Baptists, two; Presbyterians, six; Congregationalists, six; and Seventh Day Adventists, one. In addition, there were a number of private or proprietary institutions, and the state University of Nebraska at Lincoln, which held its first classes in 1871.

Although most of the institutions of necessity had to concentrate on the academy, or preparatory school departments, because few of the high schools then in existence held full nine-month sessions or went through the twelfth grade, the academic offerings were ambitious, leaning heavily on Greek and Latin classics, didactics, and mathematics. Most of the graduates or

---

3. Howard W. Caldwell, "Introduction to Higher Education in Nebraska," *Transactions and Reports of the Nebraska State Historical Society* 3 (1892):205–206.

NEBRASKA

A photographer's essay by Joe Munroe

NEBRASKA

Photographs in Sequence

Buffalo near Valentine.
Omaha skyline and Missouri River.
Union Stockyards at Omaha.
Lincoln railyards, capitol in background.
Chimney Rock on the Oregon Trail near Bridgeport.
Aurora housewife.
High school football practice, Lincoln.
Sandhill country.
Railroad near Seward.
Platte River, east of Grand Island.
Cattle near Broken Bow.
Farm worker near Hastings.
Tumbleweed on highway near Valentine.
Ruts of the Oregon Trail near Ayr.
Irrigation near North Platte.

those who left after attending a year or two became teachers or ministers, smaller numbers, doctors or lawyers.

In the meantime public schools were established, the county superintendent being one of the first officials elected after the county government was formed. By 1880, when the population was 452,402 persons, there were 2,701 schools in Nebraska, many of them one-room country sod-house schools, the others more pretentious buildings in the towns and villages scattered throughout the state. Only seventy schools claimed to offer instruction through the twelfth grade. The county superintendents certified the teachers after testing them on spelling, reading, writing, grammar, and arithmetic and passing on their moral deportment; sometimes even in the towns teachers were no more than eighth-grade graduates who had taken the normal training class, but they attended Teachers Institutes every summer for a week or two to review; their average salaries in 1880 were $130 annually. The schoolhouse, a small hastily built frame structure, was the source of pride to the town, signifying that the town was one of substance. Although in the country, school terms sometimes lasted no more than three months of the year—the children had to work in the fields during the growing season, and sometimes didn't have shoes to wear during the coldest months—town schools were more likely to have terms of six months or more. The legislature in 1877 enacted the first compulsory school law, requiring children from eight to fourteen years of age to attend school at least twelve weeks a year; by 1889, seventy-three percent of the children actually did attend school. In 1890, there were 6,243 school districts in the state.

In the new young town, churches were important to settlers who had come from the mid-century Protestant revival in New England or been affected by it in other parts of the country. Baptists, Presbyterians, and Catholics had been the first missionaries in the state, tending to the Indians; after the territory was established, a number of other denominations were represented in the first churches established for the settlers. The Rev. W. D. Gage, for whom Gage County later was named, served as pastor of the Methodist Church in Nebraska City, established in October 1854. By 1860 there were thirty-two Methodist congregations in Nebraska; fourteen Presbyterian; and smaller numbers of Congregational, Baptist, Episcopal, Lutheran, and Christian churches; there were three Catholic churches.

Ministers saddled their horses early on Sundays to ride from one group to another, sometimes having such a large circuit to cover that they could serve individual churches only once every two or three weeks. In some towns, congregations held joint services and alternated ministers, the Congregational pastor one Sunday and the Presbyterian the next Sunday, for instance, so they could have the services of an ordained minister each week. As soon as they could, congregations erected their own plain wooden churches, the tall spires jutting into the prairie sky; in the Nebraska tradition, most of those buildings were paid for by the time they were completed, the rapidly growing towns attracting sufficient numbers of church-going residents that the congregations grew in direct proportion to the growing census of the town itself. By 1890, when the population of the state had increased thirty-seven times over that of 1860, from 28,841 to more than a million, there were 2,979 church organizations, including 738 Methodists, 387 Lutherans, 284 Baptists, 278 Presbyterians, 213 Catholics, 176 United Brethren, 141 German Evangelists, 110 Episcopalians, and 100 Disciples of Christ, congregations ranging greatly in size.

In addition to their religious function, churches provided a means of sociability for women and children especially, through missionary society and ladies aid meetings, choir practices and sewing circles, Sunday School and Christian Endeavor or Epworth League meetings, the only social outlet many families had. Week-long revivals in the fall, hymn-singing confessionals under a tent, were as much social occasions as religious experiences. Even though prairie religion was fundamentalist in doctrine and evangelistic in form, it did not break out into the emotional hysteria of primitive camp meetings in other parts of the country.

The American Sunday School Union, a nondenominational program, was particularly active in outstate Nebraska in the latter part of the nineteenth century, finding its strength in communities too small to support a variety of congregations; within its neutral confines Methodists, Baptists, Brethren, Presbyterians, and anybody else could worship ecumenically each Sunday. The Sunday School Union held elaborate parades each year and often sponsored outings by chartered train to a distant point, hundreds of hymn-singing picnickers on an eight- or ten-car Burlington train, for instance, which stopped at each town along the way to pick up passengers for the excursion to the Blue River picnic grounds near Crete or Beatrice. Representatives from denominational Sunday Schools would join the expeditions too, and brass bands accompanied the group to make the occasion a festive one.

The hellfire-and-brimstone attitude of the Protestant church of that era spilled over into some affairs of the community; from time to time particularly forceful ministers, acting through a ministerial alliance or even as individuals, would draft an embarrassed police force into action and would stage well-publicized raids on gambling houses, bordellos, and other outposts of Sin, gleefully burning poker chips, roulette wheels, and other gambling devices in public bonfires; several decades later, ministers added Sunday Movies to their catalog of Sin. Otherwise, however, the church was not an instrument of social change; its focus was on individual conversion and salvation, and membership and attendance at church services seemed to be its goals.

Although the church did not concern itself with broad sociological issues, its building was sometimes utilized for meetings dealing with social causes. In some communities the women felt so at home in church buildings—and so uncomfortable and alien in the town hall, hotel, or whatever other public building was available, where they might unwittingly rub elbows with saloon keepers, loose women, or other representatives of Sin—that they held their meetings in the church to organize budding philanthropic or humanitarian activities. Here temperance societies were started, the founding of orphan homes or hospitals discussed, the Young Women's Christian Association organized, a charity club started, none of them allied with the denomination or congregation whose building housed the meetings. Meetings of suffragettes were not held in some church buildings, however, for some congregations did not support the idea of allowing women out of the kitchen and into the polling places.

The flood of immigration from Europe into Nebraska in the 1880s changed the religious complexion of the state; from the Scandinavian countries and parts of Germany came various sects of Lutherans, and from Ireland, Bohemia, and other parts of Germany, the Catholics, each group living in self-contained seclusion within the communities where it established itself. The lives of the immigrant parishioners revolved around the church in the same way as those of the native-born church members; the Lutherans associated with Lutherans, the Catholics with Catholics.

Although the church played a significant role in the development of the state and its attitudes, probably no more than a third of the population of Nebraska in the 1870s and 1880s had church membership of any sort.

By 1880, thirteen years after statehood, twenty communities in Nebraska had populations of more than one thousand persons. They included Falls City, Nebraska City, Omaha, Plattsmouth, and Tecumseh along the Missouri River; Beatrice, Fairbury, Columbus, Fremont, Lincoln, Schuyler, Seward, Wahoo, and West Point in the eastern part; Aurora, Grand Island, Hastings, Kearney, and York in the central part; and Sidney in the far west; the settlers were covering the state.

A number of these towns, especially those that had had rapid, almost overnight growth, had had disastrous fires, the flames devouring blocks of tinder-dry raw frame buildings and the wooden sidewalks as well. The ill-equipped volunteer fire companies, many of them with only hand-pulled hose carts and unreliable sources of water, had not been able to contain the flames. As soon as the embers died, the fire-stricken communities enacted ordinances restricting business construction of wood, and the era of building for permanence began.

Although there were only a few quarries in Nebraska, mostly near Beatrice, there were many in Colorado, and trainloads of granite, sandstone, and limestone building blocks began to be brought into the state. Brickyards sprang up in areas where the soil was suitable for brick making, particularly in Hastings, Lincoln, and Endicott, and a new flurry of construction began. Business blocks, schoolhouses, churches, banks, hotels, Masonic Temples, G.A.R. halls, all sorts of fine new structures large enough to accommodate the new town populations were underway; there was a shortage of masons and skilled construction workers to handle the demands of elegant Victorian architectural designs.

The settlers who had been content earlier to live in austere little cottages had now achieved sufficient means to build more substantial, more impressive homes; immigration into the state from Europe brought skilled craftsmen who could turn out elaborate fretwork and carvings, lead the beveled glass windows which often had stained-glass panes in them, and work in stone and marble. Settled communities began to blossom with imposing residences with piazzas and verandas, turrets, bay windows and balconies, parquetry floors, all decorated with glazed tiles, turnings, and intricate woodworking dear to the Victorians' hearts. These homes were large, two or three stories tall, with curving staircases of walnut or oak rising out of the front hall; they had stables far larger than the previous homes had been; and they had neatly concealed privies in the back yards. For although some communities provided illuminating gas, later electricity, to produce light in the elegant homes, and even running water in pipes, mostly for fire hydrants, few communities had any sort of sewerage system until the 1890s. Lack of sewerage was the cause of complaints by local boards of health, who cited the garbage and offal flung into alleys as responsible for epidemics of typhoid fever, diptheria, summer complaint, and other diseases which were periodically epidemic.

Modest little frame church buildings were replaced with impressive brick-and-stone prairie Gothic structures, wooden schoolhouses with tall brick buildings which had spiraling tubular metal fire escapes bolted to the sides. Those communities which had built little square wooden courthouses ten years earlier now floated bonds to construct massive stone county buildings, monuments to the stonecutter's art; they had towers and domes and cupolas at the top, usually with clocks in the turret, romantic statues of blindfolded Justice just under the lightning rod, and impenetrable jails in the cellars.

Street-railway companies laid rails in Nebraska communities to provide public transportation by horse-drawn cars; Lincoln,

Omaha, Hastings, Fremont, Beatrice, Columbus, Nebraska City, Norfolk, Grand Island, Kearney, Red Cloud, South Sioux City, Wymore, York, and Plattsmouth residents could take the streetcar to run their errands. Some towns, in fact, had more than one line, the two competing lines in Hastings, for instance, laying their own track by day and ripping up the competitor's rails by night during the construction process. Water wagons made the rounds during the summer, sprinkling the dusty streets in front of subscribers' homes, and most towns were beginning to consider paving the main streets with brick cobblestones manufactured right here in Nebraska. It was a good thing, too, for in Fremont the streets were hog wallows after a good, hard rainstorm; one time a number of citizens were so annoyed— their carriages couldn't even pass on the muddy streets—that on one of the residential streets they launched a rowboat, labeling it the mayor's yacht, and had one of their cronies fish from it, dropping his line into an even deeper hole where he hooked a dummy dressed to resemble the mayor.

Telephones were being installed, with Omaha, Lincoln, Grand Island, Columbus, Kearney, Fremont, Plattsmouth, Beatrice, Hastings, and Nebraska City wired up by 1882, some of them served by more than one company. Subscribers to the American Bell Company (later the Nebraska Telephone Company) could not talk to persons whose lines were on the Independent Telephone Company system; merchants who wanted to do business by phone had to subscribe to both companies, listing their numbers as Blue 39 and Red 57, for instance, and a few homeowners with talkative families and heterogeneous friends also had both telephone lines running into their homes. When Hebron acquired a telephone system, the railroad station number was two-two, so that when the operator said "Number please," all the caller had to remember was "toot-toot." The first long-distance connections were between Omaha, Arlington, and Fremont, a 41-mile distance, in 1882.

With their increasing affluence and sophistication, towns all over Nebraska began building opera houses; within a ten-year span the prairie was studded with imposing stone structures with stages, dressing rooms, orchestra pits, elaborate boxes, grand stairways, expanses of gilt and heavy red plush and velour, and seating space for several hundred people. Grand Island called hers Liederkranz Hall, and Central City the Academy of Music, but Fremont, Kenesaw, Hebron, Kearney, Hastings, and others called theirs simply Opera House, although as it turned out, operas were seldom performed there. The buildings served as auditoriums for touring theatrical companies, political caucuses, high school graduations, local musical recitals, and speeches of all kinds—William Jennings Bryan was a perennial orator. Sometimes to its chagrin a church had to hold its services in the Opera House on Sunday mornings until its own splendid new structure could be finished for the congregation had already outgrown its little old building.

By 1890, thirty-seven Nebraska communities had opera houses, some less pretentious than others, to be sure, but each one identifying the town as one of stability now and high hopes for the future, a town dedicated to leaving the roughness of frontier days behind in its search for permanent, solid development. The towns ranged from Omaha, with its elaborate Boyd's Opera House, to Lincoln, from Albion, Clarks, DeWitt, Fairmont, Greeley, North Bend, Madison, St. Paul, Syracuse, to Wymore, some of the towns no more than struggling villages but all of them sharing visions of greatness. The Opera House is the symbol of the dreams and illusions of Nebraska towns of the 1880s, the vehicle for cultural growth in a raw, uncouth community which was sure it would be the commercial and aesthetic center of the whole region just any day.

And perhaps the communities weren't so pretentious, after all, in their aspirations. For the Nebraska towns of the 1880s bore slight resemblance to the brash young jerry-built communities of ten or fifteen years earlier, and in view of those changes, who knew what would happen in the next few years. Residents of Kearney fully anticipated that the nation's capitol would be moved there from Washington, D.C.

Whereas the first construction had been frenzied, unplanned and temporary, now it was on a more organized, more orderly, permanent basis, and the volume of building was greater. Town land titles had been quieted by then; almost any town of any size had had legal problems about land companies, railroad land and original homesteaders, and fancy legal footwork in the mid-

1880s was necessary to clear titles and smooth over the acrimony that grew out of disputed land ownership.

Streets were laid out neatly, four-square with the compass, brick sidewalks and spindly new trees beside them; even if the legislature hadn't required towns and villages to plant trees, they probably would have anyhow. Towns also began to develop land for parks.

New commercial buildings had three-foot thick granite foundations, elegant cornices, stamped metal ceilings, wrought ironwork on the overhangs that protected pedestrians from the summer sun. New banks were under construction; manufacturing companies for harness, headers, and other farm equipment, retail concerns, businesses of all kinds were starting; by now there was a supply of laborers to handle almost any job. Immigrants from Europe swarmed into the state, Irish and Czechs settling in the new stockyards area of Omaha, Germans from Russia in Lincoln and in other Burlington railroad towns to provide cheap, willing labor. With more ostentatious homes and buildings, more detailed work in the factories, there were more jobs to be done. The early settlers who had prospered had done exceedingly well and could now settle back to spend their money, paying somebody else to do the hard physical labor they had done themselves before.

During the 1880s, the chasm between the social classes in Nebraska towns was greater than it had been earlier or would ever be later. Victorian manners dictated social behavior. Ladies had calling cards in elegant card cases, for instance, and with their fans and bonnets and high-buttoned shoes made calls on their friends on certain afternoons, leaving on the silver salvers in the front reception halls their calling cards with corners bent appropriately to signal whether they wished the call returned; ladies were at home at elaborate tea parties on New Year's Day, newspapers publishing lists of who would be entertaining so that friends could stop by. Dinner parties in homes were heavy, many-course affairs with great displays of linen damask, crystal goblets, heavy silver pieces; in Fremont, one family had dinner settings for eighty guests. There were more catering facilities in Beatrice, Columbus, Fremont, Hastings, and other communities then than there have been since, to ac-

commodate the lavish, frequent social occasions; entertainment
was almost always done at home. In some towns, the most ostentatious families had liveried Negro hostlers for carriages,
those families perhaps having arrived in the state only a decade
earlier with barely more than a Civil War pension in hand.
There were cotillions and germans and balls of various kinds in
the splendid new ornate hotels; for smaller, more intimate occasions there were oyster suppers, high five card games. The
style of living was probably no different from that in other
towns in other parts of the United States at the time, but coming
so soon after the raw, bleak days of the prairie development, it
must have seemed ludicrous.

On the other side of town, the newcomers, largely immigrants from Europe during the 1880s, lived in the rough,
quickly built little frame houses that resembled the ones the first
families had since torn down. They worked from sun-up to dark
without stopping, as their predecessors had done, but for wages,
not for a homestead. The men worked in brickyards, in packing
plants, as common laborers; their wives took in wash, wrapped
cigars—for there were cigar factories in Fremont and Hastings—and were charwomen.

Even as the architectural styles were changing in Nebraska
towns, so the cultural level was rising. Many of the young men
who had come alone to the new country a few years earlier to
make their fortunes had by now gone back to their old homes to
claim as brides the sweethearts who had been waiting in Illinois
or Pennsylvania, many of them having attended academies in
the meantime. These women brought with them their libraries of
Greek and Latin volumes, their square rosewood pianos and
mandolins, their easels and painting kits, creating a nucleus of
artistic appreciation and accomplishment hitherto unknown on
the prairie. With large imposing homes to live in and retinues of
immigrant servants to staff them, these wives—a different breed
from the first sod-house settlers—turned to organizing book
clubs, art classes, musical groups.

In the middle 1880s a feverish land boom erupted, spreading
from east to west, from Omaha to Crete to Hastings to Kearney
and beyond, escalating rapidly. "Land Is King!" the full-page

newspaper advertisements said, and everybody agreed, hurrying to buy and sell. In Hastings from January to March 1887, transfers of land entered in the courthouse books ranged from $50,000 to $100,000 per day; a choice lot in town would sometimes be sold two or three times within a few hours, increasing in price with each sale, a lot which sold for $300 one month selling for $1,800 the next, for instance. The city limits were laid out far beyond the towns; additions were staked out into the cornfields. Every community was sure it would become a great commercial center or railroad metropolis—and who was to say them nay? Anything was possible.

Who or what was responsible for the land hysteria of that particular moment nobody has ever been able to determine. It undoubtedly was sparked by the railroad boom which had begun in the 1870s and achieved epidemic proportions in the 1880s. Every community of any size envisioned itself as a railroad metropolis, with five or ten or who-knows-how-many lines radiating from it, providing more direct routes to markets and probably forcing the hateful freight rates down through competition. Rates were so high that it cost a farmer one bushel of grain to ship another bushel to market, but all Nebraskans realized that they were dependent upon the railroads. The Covington, Columbus and Black Hills Railroad, the Omaha, Niobrara and Black Hills Railroad, the Kansas City and Wyandotte, the Grand Island and Denver City, the Chicago and Rock Island, and the Missouri Pacific—these and dozens more were planned, although no more than one out of four of the widely touted ones ever came to fruition. Even so, the miles of trackage almost trebled during the 1880s; whereas at the beginning of the decade, there were only 1,868 miles, by 1890, there were 5,144. Railroad officials went to the communities they planned to serve, promoting the sale of railroad bonds to help finance the construction. Few towns turned them down; in fact, when Cedar County enthusiastically voted $150,000 to the Covington line, and Dixon County, $87,000, and Knox County, $77,000, the state supreme court stepped in to say that no government body could bond itself more than ten percent of its valuation.

There were other causes for the land boom, too. There had been good rainfall and the crops were abundant, and there was more of everything in the land of the Platte; the decade of the 1880s brought the greatest increase in population, the establishment of more new towns, more schools, more churches, more post offices than in any other decade in Nebraska history.

The land boom was the outgrowth of the natural ebullience and optimism of persons who, finding themselves in a situation of incredible growth and change, are willing to believe that anything is possible. The land fever was contagious and spread rapidly, from family to family, community to community, land values rising to enormous heights.

Although the boom had been gathering momentum over a period of two or three years, its most frenzied activity took place between March and July 1887. Then one day it was over. Nobody knew why, any more than they knew how it all had started, but all of a sudden people were left with high-priced land on their hands and no market for it at any price. The wild time of land speculation was over.

11

The Populists

By the late 1880s, some of the good things that had happened to Nebraska turned sour. The rains stopped; the crops had dried up; the banks wouldn't loan money. In desperation, the farmers rebelled—and the Populist Revolt began. It swept over the entire state and beyond, townspeople and farmers alike, for in an agricultural economy such as Nebraska's, what affected the farmer affected everyone.

It turned out to be part of a national agrarian protest movement which was particularly strong in the Great Plains region; out of Nebraska itself came the movement's great national leader, William Jennings Bryan, the Lincoln lawyer whose speaking skills won him fame as "the boy orator of the Platte."

In the beginning, the principal target of the farmers' wrath was railroads, symbol of everything that ailed the farmers. Landlocked in the center of the country, the farmers were dependent upon the railroads for transporting goods in and produce out; they long had had the feeling that as small shippers they were being unfairly discriminated against when they sent their grain to market. They pointed to rebates, pooling, and rate-fixing as evidence. They resented the fact, too, that the railroads were not paying taxes for their lands, even the "lieu lands" which the Burlington owned in parts of the state far removed from the railroad tracks themselves. The farmers were having to pay taxes, including those to pay off bonds issued to help build new railroads. But the new roads hadn't broken the railroad monopoly at all.

Many Nebraskans felt that the two major railroads, the Union Pacific and the Burlington, controlled Nebraska politics on all levels, local as well as in Lincoln and in Washington. To make their voices heard, the farmers organized various groups; the first Nebraska chapter of the Farmers' Alliance began in 1880, and before long, the Nebraska state organization was the largest in the country. By the late 1880s, the Nebraska newspaper, the *Farmers' Alliance,* a powerful political organ, began urging that the organization take political action. Nebraska members of other groups, including some which had been founded as political parties, joined the coalition—the Greenback Party, the Anti-Monopoly League, later the Knights of Labor. In early summer 1890, a scorching hot season, the combined forces circulated petitions, and in less than thirty days, collected fifteen thousand signatures, calling for a People's State Independent convention.

Eight hundred delegates, representing seventy-nine counties, met at Bohanan's Hall in Lincoln on July 29, 1890, to organize the People's State Independent Party. (In years to come, it was to be known variously as the Independent, or People's, or Populist party.) The delegates listed their grievances against the railroads, the grain elevators, and the stockyards, against the monetary system that kept money tight, against the establishments that had allowed these ills to proliferate. And they drafted a platform that called for government ownership of railroad and telegraph lines, free coinage of silver, abolition of land monopoly, tax reform, and an eight-hour day for all except agricultural workers. They nominated as governor the president of the Nebraska Alliance, John Powers, a white-bearded man who lived in a sod house on his homestead in Hitchcock County; he headed the slate that included candidates for the state legislature as well as for Congress.

The campaign of the late summer was a gala one. The drought was so severe that farmers didn't need to go into their dried-up fields. So they hitched up their wagons, packed meager lunches in their baskets, and took their families from one rally to another—twenty thousand people in Lincoln, a thousand wagons at Wymore, sixteen hundred wagons in Hastings. "We farmers raised no crops so we'll just raise hell," they cried, and they paraded, and they sang "The Mortgage Has Taken the Farm, Mary" and "Good-Bye, Old Party, Good-Bye." [1]

When the votes were counted in November, the Populists had control of the state legislature, electing fifty-four men to the house and eighteen to the senate; they had elected two of the three new congressmen—the third was William Jennings Bryan to his first term in Washington—and they had come close to seating their man Powers as governor; he lost to an Omaha businessman, Democrat James E. Boyd.

Politically inept because of their lack of experience, the Populists in that legislative session nevertheless managed to put on the books a number of laws inspired from the Populist platform, including the use of the Australian or secret ballot, a provision for free textbooks, changes in the handling of public funds, and an eight-hour day for nonfarm workers. But although they passed and sent to the governor a bill to regulate railroads and to establish minimum rates, they could not muster the necessary three-fifths majority to override Governor Boyd's veto.

In the elections of 1892, although the voters elected the first Populist to represent Nebraska in the United States Senate, they split the votes in the state legislature so that none of the three parties—Populist, Democrat, Republican—had a majority in either house. To achieve a workable legislature, the Democrats and the Populists joined forces, the same fusion of Populists and silver Democrats which brought about the election of Fusion party governors in Nebraska in 1894, 1896, and 1898. The decade that followed saw Nebraskans prominent in a nationwide political and social effort to reinforce the rights of the individual as opposed to the might of big business.

Although as an independent third party, the Populists were never able to get complete control of the Nebraska state government, such was their strength that many of the reforms they advocated were later adopted, no matter which political party was in office. The Democratic legislature of 1897 created provisions for the use of initiative and referendum for the first time, the

---

1. Sheldon, *Nebraska: Land and the People,* 1:688–690.

means of letting the electorate vote directly on laws; that legislature also passed laws regulating stockyards and the telephone and telegraph companies. The Progressive Republican legislature of 1907 enacted laws which brought more important and permanent changes in the political structure than those of any previous session, most of them advocated by the Populists fifteen years before. Among them were those which provided for a state-wide compulsory primary election, a Child Labor Act, an Anti-Free-Pass Act to combat the bribery-by-pass which the railroads had practiced for years, especially to senators and other political leaders, a Two-Cent Passenger Fare Act, and an Anti-Discrimination Act. The legislature also created and defined the power of a state railroad commission, established a state bureau for the investigation of insect pests and plant diseases, created a board of pardons, prohibited brewers from holding any interests in saloons, and endorsed the idea of providing for the popular election of United States senators.

Even at the time of World War I, the influence of Populism and agrarian reform was felt when remnants of the old party formed a Non-Partisan League in Nebraska, following a similar organization begun in North Dakota. Rather than nationalizing the railroad and telegraph lines, the league aimed at creating state stockyards, packinghouses, cold storage plants, elevators, creameries, beet-sugar factories. Strongly supported by the Farmers Union, particularly in rural communities which were predominantly German, the League attracted the wrath of the Council of Defense and did not manage to accomplish much in Nebraska.

Although Bryan was closely allied with Populist principles, he never left the Democratic party, hoping to effect change from within. And as a result, he was defeated when he ran for the United States Senate in 1894, and he never again won an elective office, although on three different occasions he was the Democratic party's candidate for the presidency of the United States. In the campaign of 1896, running on a platform of free silver, which he helped write—"You shall not press upon the brow of labor this crown of thorns; you shall not crucify mankind upon a Cross of Gold," his most famous oration went—he was the candidate of two political parties, both the Democrats and the Populists having nominated him, even though his espousal of free silver was in direct contradiction to the gold policy of Democratic party faithfuls. Nor did he win in 1900, when he ran on a platform opposing American imperialism and the acquisition of the Philippines; nor in 1908, when his platform was based on business trust-busting.

In the presidential campaign of 1912, he was influential in bringing about the nomination of Woodrow Wilson, and as a result Bryan was made secretary of state after Wilson became president. After serving for three years, however, Bryan resigned from the cabinet rather than sign a strongly worded note to the German government that he felt would lead to war.

A man of deep personal and political integrity, Bryan was possessed of tremendous personal magnetism, the greatest orator of his time. During his 1900 campaign alone, he made more than six hundred speeches, carrying the voice of the common man throughout the country. Through his speeches, and his writing—for he was the editor of the *Omaha World Herald* from 1894 to 1896, and of *The Commoner,* a weekly published in Lincoln, after 1900—he helped push the Democratic party to absorb many of the principles which Populism espoused. He lived to see the nation, which had consistently rejected him, adopt many of the reforms he urged—the popular election of senators, income tax, requirements of publication of ownership and circulation of newspapers, the creation of the department of labor, Prohibition, and woman suffrage.

Although Populism did not ever achieve a dominant position in the American political scene, it had a profound effect upon the nation. Populism was not an institution peculiar to Nebraska—it was a movement of agrarian discontent throughout the farming regions of the West, Midwest, and South—but in Nebraska as elsewhere it was powerful enough to force change through established political parties.

12

The Cattlemen

N the wide-open, treeless spaces of the Plains, in the
region beyond the hundredth meridian, where the short
grass grew, the land was becoming cattle country. In an
almost foreordained way, the cattle and their habitat came
together.

From the 1860s onward, coming from the south to the north,
a new breed of men came onto the land—first the buffalo
hunters, then cattle drovers, and finally the cowboys on ranches,
which were sometimes as big as whole countries in Europe. Although their numbers were not great in comparison with those
of the homesteaders who were settling or of the Overland Trail
emigrants who were still moving westward, the robust men of
the west, often transient hired hands on horseback, contributed
to the development of western Nebraska. They helped make it
cattle country.

At first the land was covered with buffalo, millions of
ungainly, shaggy-coated bison in herds so large that when they
stampeded across the prairie, the earth thundered, and the horizon was black with lumbering bodies. The grazing grounds of
the Republican herd, biggest of the four main groups which
ranged from Montana to Texas, covered the western part of
Nebraska, the animals nourished on the nutritious grasses there
as they migrated northward in the spring, southward in the fall.
For generations, using bows and arrows and then the guns they

acquired from the white men, Indians had hunted the buffalo, relying on them for their subsistence, using every part of the animal; so important was the buffalo to their lives that their religion was based in part on the creature which provided them with food, shelter, and clothing.

The early white men in the area, travelers along the Overland Trail and the earliest settlers, slaughtered the animals for food, enjoying particularly the succulent hump and the tongue. The first professional hunters also killed them for meat, under contract to the United States Army to supply frontier forts, or to the railroad to furnish fresh meat for their construction gangs. Everyone assumed that the buffalo were inexhaustible, so enormous were their numbers. Mari Sandoz, in her book *The Buffalo Hunters,* said that no other animal of any size "ever grew so numerous on the whole earth as the American bison upon the Great Plains, and no animal ever adjusted to his environment more completely." [1] Yet within the space of fifteen years, white men exterminated the buffalo.

In the late 1860s, when the Indian problems were quiet, the hide hunters came, dozens, then hundreds of them, with their long-barreled guns and ammunition, their skinning knives, their pegs to stretch the hides out on the ground to dry. They wanted no meat; they wanted the hides for buffalo robes, for the tough leather that could make harness, belts, buggy tops, shoes, book bindings, furniture. When they killed the animals—forty a day, sometimes more, for each man—they skinned the buffalo where they fell and stretched the hides to dry, leaving the meat to rot and the bones to bleach in the prairie sun. With luck, each professional hunter could kill twenty-five hundred animals during the winter season, selling the hides to the buyer who stacked the bales of flints, or dried uncured hides, in huge piles at the Union Pacific freightyards at Plum Creek, Ogallala or Sidney, waiting to be shipped out to the tanners back East.

In winter the hides were prime, the coarse hair full and dark. Hunters and skinners went out together, staying two or three months at a time in primitive camps, which they moved day by day, hoping to catch fifty or a hundred animals at a time each

---

1. Mari Sandoz, *The Buffalo Hunters* (New York: Hastings House, 1954), p. ix.

day. With their field glasses they studied the countryside and on their ponies they moved to the general area, but when they approached a stand, they slipped out of the saddle and slithered along the frozen ground, downwind to keep the keen-smelling buffalo from catching their scent. They stopped, checked the sights in their long-range guns, and in one belly-flopping session killed ten or twelve animals or even more before the others fled. The hunters, their heavy winter clothing caked with dried blood and reeking of the manure they crawled through, were sometimes Civil War veterans with no other jobs; usually, however, they were the new breed of fur-trappers, young, strong, willing to work hard and risk their lives for a few months of the year in return for the high prices the hides brought. Some years the flints, the green hides, were worth two-fifty each.

By the mid-1860s there there weren't as many buffalo left as there had been ten or twenty years earlier, certainly not the twelve or fourteen million the earlier travelers had estimated. Idaho outlawed hide hunting in 1865. Dr. David Franklin Powell, assigned to Fort McPherson along the Platte, wrote in September 1873:

> Just think! over a thousand pounds of meat left to rot upon the prairies for every animal skinner, while thousands are meat-hungry or starving . . . I earnestly beg (people) to use their influence in enforcing the game laws of this State, or if none exists, see to it at once that some measure be taken to prevent such slaughter, or every buffalo will be killed or driven from our state.[2]

An earlier witness, Sir W. F. Butler, on a buffalo-hunting excursion to Fort McPherson in 1867, apologized to his host, Colonel R. I. Dodge that his group had killed more than thirty buffalo. "Never mind," said the host. "Kill every buffalo you can. Every buffalo dead is an Indian gone."[3]

The buffalo hunting continued. There weren't enough left in Nebraska for the kind of excursions the Kansas Pacific railroad ran down in Kansas, with city fellows shooting from the trains, but there were several elaborate, top-drawer buffalo hunts along

---

2. Paul D. Riley, "Dr. David Franklin Powell and Fort McPherson," *Nebraska History* 51 (Summer 1970):167.

3. Sandoz, *Buffalo Hunters,* p. 88.

the Union Pacific, wealthy adventuresome sports taking the train to North Platte and making their headquarters at Fort McPherson, where General Phil Sheridan assigned his troops to help with the hunt. One such excursion took place in 1871, when James Gordon Bennett of the *New York Herald* and other dignitaries arrived to hunt with Buffalo Bill Cody. That trip was merely a prelude to the royal party which arrived the next year, on January 12, 1872, Grand Duke Alexis of Russia and his retinue eager to hunt the monarch of the Plains, meet real-live Indians, and participate in prairie activities. The week-long buffalo hunt, complete with champagne and other necessaries, was a huge success; Spotted Tail, Brule Sioux chief, shook hands with the Grand Duke, his tribesmen gave a show of horsemanship, lance-throwing, bow-shooting, and sham battle; and the party slaughtered dozens of buffalo, although not nearly so many as the same number of dedicated buffalo hunters could have in the same amount of time.

By 1885, the buffalo were gone. In fifteen years, from 1870 to 1885, more than ten million had been exterminated, killed for their hides. In their place were miles of bleached buffalo bones, covering the prairie. For the next few years human vultures gathered them up to send to the factories back East to make phosphates and carbon; one bone-buying firm said that over a seven-year span it alone bought the bones of nearly six million skeletons. Soon even the bones were gone.

But as the buffalo hunters disappeared from the Plains, a new breed of wiry, rangy young men appeared, the cattle drovers from Texas. For with no buffalo to crop the lush prairie grass in Nebraska, there was room for cattle.

Texas had been cattle country almost from the days of its earliest settlement. The Spanish had brought in cattle that in time evolved into the Texas longhorns, which thrived in the semiarid reaches of Texas, grazing on the native grasses of the enormous spreads that the earliest landowners there had acquired. The raising of cattle in Texas was easy; in fact, many of them grew wild, living their lives in the mesquite and ironwood, far from man. The problem was not in raising cattle, but in marketing them. When railroads spread out across the country in the late

1860s, Texans began to drive their cattle overland to the tracks in the north, at first through Missouri, eastern Kansas and eastern Nebraska. But shortly towns were built up, farms established, fences installed, and the families there put up so much opposition to the drives that the Texas cattlemen had to look elsewhere. As the rails stretched to the west, the cattle drives aimed straight into Kansas, first to the Kansas Pacific at Abilene and then to the Santa Fe at Dodge City. By 1870, the Union Pacific offered rates that were so much lower than the Kansas ones that the cattle drives were extended several hundred miles northward.

Schuyler was the first end-of-the-trail town in Nebraska; in 1870 its population jumped from less than one hundred to more than six hundred as the drovers brought in 50,000 head of Texas cattle, but shortly the rails moved west and the stock pens came down. The next end-of-the-trail town was Lowell, at the end of the Burlington and Missouri railroad, a community which boasted four saloons to slake the thirst of the cowboys, gambling establishments, a hangin' tree for justice, and a Boot Hill. But after a year of glory, Lowell passed into history, for a bridge over the Platte River made easy access to Kearny Junction, the junction point of the Burlington and Union Pacific, and the town of Kearney thrived.

By 1874 the cowboys felt so at home at Kearney that when guests sitting on the front piazza of the Harrold House saw them coming, they ducked inside to escape the whizzing shots. There was so much commotion from the raunchy cowboys letting off steam that finally the townspeople organized a home guard, fortified the Burlington station as an armory, and tried to keep peace. By 1875, an uneasy truce was made between the cowboys and the settlers, but by that time Kearney was on its way out as the end-of-the-trail; the stock pens and the excitement had moved west to Ogallala.

And for the next ten years, from 1875 to 1885, Ogallala was a rip-roaring town, the toughest one on the whole drive up from Texas. Its dance halls, gambling houses and saloons—dugouts, soddies, tents and raw frame buildings—were perched on the high prairie beside the railroad tracks. For six months of the year, from the arrival of the first herd from Texas, usually about

June 10—the exact date was always the cause of betting—to November, when the cattle buyers had finished shipping their stock, it was a town with no night, "the Gomorrah of the cattle trail," Andy Adams called it.[4] Bliss, the cowboys called it, as they rushed into the monte establishments or the Cowboy's Rest saloon, where, a latter-day historian wrote:

> Gold flowed freely across the tables, liquor across the bar, and occasionally blood across the floor as a smoking gun in the hands of a jealous rival or an angered gambler brought an end to the trail of some unfortunate cowhand on the stained boards of Tuck's Saloon.[5]

During the ten years Ogallala existed as a cow town, seventeen violent deaths were recorded; the permanent population of the town was only one hundred.

The first year, between sixty thousand and seventy-five thousand cattle were driven to Ogallala, and the second year, more than one hundred thousand. From then on, each year until the end of the cattle drives, about that many more came up the hot, dusty Western Trail. The last day's journey was particularly difficult because in the thirty miles between Stinking Water Creek and the South Platte, the streams were often dried up.

The buyers were waiting in Ogallala. Some of the cattle went on up into Dakota and Montana to Indian reservations, often driven by the same cowboys who had brought them up from Texas. Most of the stock, however, was sold to Nebraska and Wyoming ranchers for their newly developing businesses; they drove the cattle to their own spreads, fed them for a year or two, and then drove them back to the railroads for shipment to Eastern markets in the April and October roundups.

The end of the cattle trail came suddenly; homesteaders were taking lands in western Kansas, fencing in their plowed lands, making the drives more and more difficult. In 1884, a virulent epidemic of Texas fever swept over Nebraska, brought with the longhorns and affecting thousands of head of cattle already on the Nebraska range. The resulting quarantine laws brought the end to the Texas cattle drives.

4. Andy Adams, *The Log of a Cowboy* (Boston: Houghton Mifflin, 1903), p. 259.
5. Norbert Mahnken, "Ogallala—Nebraska's Cowboy Capital," *Nebraska History* 27 (April–June 1947):85.

In the meantime, seventy-five miles west in the Panhandle of Nebraska, another trail was booming, for gold had been discovered in the Black Hills of South Dakota. By 1876 the Indians had been put into reservations and compelled to relinquish rights to their sacred hunting grounds there, and by the thousands the gold-seekers swarmed across the Black Hills trail. The village of Sidney, laid out nine years earlier by the Union Pacific as its rails moved westward, quadrupled almost overnight. The Camp Clarke bridge over the North Platte River opened on May 13, 1876 to accommodate the stage and freight wagons as well as the stream of private wagons leaving Sidney en route to the Hills. Six-horse mail coaches capable of making ten miles an hour were put on the route; heavy freighters—thirty yoke of oxen hauling trains of ten or twelve wagons—lumbered out each day, taking as much as a million pounds of freight at a time from the huge freight houses that had been built almost overnight; one business firm frequently shipped as many as four hundred thousand pounds on a single day. The Union Pacific was running doubleheaders, loaded with freight and passengers, into Sidney, where two lines of daily stagecoaches took them on up to the Black Hills.

Fort Sidney, established in 1868 to protect railroad construction gangs from the Indians, was still in operation; the soldiers, the freighters, the roustabouts and hangers-on made Sidney such a lawless town that at one time, according to legend, the Union Pacific refused to stop its trains there, running them right through town at high speed with the doors locked, for the protection of passengers and freight, and threatened to remove its buildings "and allow the town to die of dry rot," [6] if order was not restored immediately.

By the mid-1880s, railroad building into the Black Hills region ended the freighting business, increased technology in mining made placer and pan mining impracticable, and the lusty town of legend began to calm down. Most of the filth-encrusted, gun-toting men who had swaggered through its dusty streets were gone, moved on to more exciting towns, or else settling down to quieter, more sedate lives.

6. Nellie Snyder Yost, *The Call of the Range* (Denver: Sage Books, 1966), p. 66.

By then, the western reaches of Nebraska were prospering from a business that was to become of lasting value to Nebraska, and to the nation. Started almost by accident, the beef-cattle industry was colorful in its formative, adolescent years; it was tinged with financial bravado and peopled by vigorous, brash, often eccentric financiers from several nations; it was punctuated with shootings, congressional investigation, and presidential ire. The cattleman and the cowboy had come to Nebraska.

In the early years Nebraskans had dabbled in cattle raising—at first, oxen on road ranches along the Overland Trail, the proprietors selling or trading draft animals to immigrants whose stock was foot-sore by then, and later beef cattle in the southwestern part of the state between the Platte and Republican rivers to supply Indian agencies to the north and west. Those areas had good pasturage and were protected from the Indians by Forts Kearny, McPherson, and Laramie. These were mostly feeding operations, on a temporary basis; there was little thought of commercial production of beef cattle.

Although various ranchers in Colorado, Wyoming, and Nebraska later claimed to have been the first to see the possibilities of raising beef in the short-grass country of the Great Plains, nobody really knows who should have the credit. Probably several visionaries had the idea simultaneously; it was a logical one, for land which had sustained millions of buffalo only decades earlier certainly should be capable of feeding large numbers of cattle. The story, no matter whose name is attached to it, is that somebody left cattle, or perhaps oxen, in the area over the winter, usually inadvertently, and then discovered them the next spring in prime condition, having been nourished by the native grasses that retained their nutritional qualities in the dry winter air. The man who made the discovery began large-scale cattle raising in the area.

Among the early Nebraska ranchers in the western Platte Valley were Edward Creighton, builder of the transcontinental telegraph and Omaha pioneer millionaire, who ranged working oxen there as early as 1859, and went into the beef business eight years later when he drove three thousand head of cattle from Schuyler to the western grasses; and J. W. Iliff, who probably ranged cattle in the area from the early 1860s onward. From then on, various men went into the cattle business, including freighters whose business had been ruined by competition from the Union Pacific, eastern Nebraska farmers who discovered that grazing was more profitable and less work than farming, army scouts and military men, buffalo hunters, Easterners, and Europeans. Early ranchers in western Nebraska included R. C. Keith, who began in 1867; Coe, Carter, and Bratt, who brought in twenty-five hundred Texas cattle to the Platte Valley near Fort Kearny in 1869; John Bratt, Colonel James H. Bratt, Buffalo Bill Cody, James H. Cook, the Newman brothers, and Frank and Luther North. Two other Irishmen from Omaha followed Creighton's lead; the ranching interests of John and Mark Coad were also extensive.

Land there was, for most of it was still unclaimed. Free range, it was called. A man could appropriate government land for his own uses, build a ranch—a house, usually a soddy, a bunkhouse, some corrals and a shed or two—and be in business, letting thousand of cattle run free, grazing the grasses that needed no tending at all, getting water from any of the dozens of streams that rippled through cattle country—the pretty stream called the Dismal, the Lodgepole, Pumpkin Seed Creek, Medicine Creek, the Snake, the Calamus, or the others. All a man really needed to spend money on was the cattle.

If he wanted to, a rancher could homestead a quarter-section and buy some railroad land. Buying railroad land meant getting twice as much, for it was every-other-section, and a man could just use the in-between part. Cattlemen took government land, that which was lying there unused and unclaimed, rent-free, tax-free, putting it to use, with the cattle converting the wild native grasses to beef. The prairies for thousands of square miles were one vast pasture; the ranchers themselves maintained mutual understanding as to the amount of government land each one used as possessory rights. When a man sold his headquarters site, usually located near a stream or lake, the surrounding range for "as far as a cow could walk to water" went with it, even though he didn't own any of that land.

In the late spring, when the prairie grass was lush, the cowboys went out on the roundup, joggling thousands of miles back and forth across the unbroken prairie on their quick cow ponies to gather up the tens of thousands of cattle that had been grazing all winter long in the open pastures, even as the buffalo before them had done. The men collected the wild, roaming cattle, who often spooked at the sight and smell of man, and herded them to a central point or corral—since most of the early cowboys originally came from Texas, most ranching terms stem from Texas-Spanish—to check their brands, separating out those belonging to another ranch, to castrate the young bulls into steers, and to brand the new stock born since the last roundup. It usually took about three months, on into July, to finish the roundup, a strenuous, exhilarating time for the muscular young cowboys and a time of satisfaction for the owners totting up their profits.

By the late 1870s, the leading outfits in Nebraska—Bratt, Paxton, Boslers, Sheidleys, Pratt and Ferris, Newman Brothers, Hunter and Evans, Dave Rankin, and Cody and North—owned nearly 170,000 head of cattle located on a range stretching from the Republican on the south to the White on the north, from the forks of the Platte to the Wyoming border on the west, an area roughly thirty-five thousand square miles in size, more than twenty-two million acres. The Platte roundup alone, a small part of the total, called for the services of about two hundred fifty men, twenty-five or thirty wagons, and about twelve hundred horses. The cowboys represented all the ranches involved, and sorted out from the total the stock belonging to their own ranches.

By the early 1880s, news of the wealth that could be accumulated in western cattle ranches spread around the world; even before General James S. Brisbin's book, *The Beef Bonanza; or How to Get Rich on the Plains,* published in Philadelphia in 1881, reached England and Scotland, financiers there were sending their emissaries to Omaha or Cheyenne to buy ranches, combining in most cases with American capital from the East to create expansive spreads. They knew that anyone could quadruple his investment in no time while getting an annual return of twenty-five percent. Scottish and English money began to pour across the Atlantic to join with capital from Boston, New York, and Chicago on the range in Nebraska, Wyoming, and the Dakotas. Many of these ranches were enormous spreads that stretched across state boundaries, encompassing hundreds of thousands of acres of land. Since the ranchers paid neither rent nor taxes, it is difficult to tell how extensive their holdings really were, but a congressional investigation in 1886 showed that twenty-nine foreign companies controlled more than twenty million acres of ranchland in the Great Plains, some of it in Nebraska and most of it government land in the public domain.

Cattle companies came and went, changing names, directorates, buying and selling stock with rapidity during the 1880s. The Creighton and Coad spreads, large ones, were sold; the Bay State, started during the 1870s as Evans-Jackson, expanded with almost compulsive frenzy during those years, spending millions of dollars for stock, implements, and buildings—almost none for land, because it was free range, government-owned. The Swan Land and Cattle Company, with headquarters in Cheyenne, spent two and a half million dollars for its new holdings in the early 1880s, the whole enterprise failing in 1887.

The winter of 1885–1886, a blizzardy winter followed by a spring and summer of drought, and the winter of 1886–1887, a long and brutal, snow-covered winter, killed off thousands of cattle from Texas to Montana. The big die-ups, they were called. Although the Nebraska range was not so badly hit as were the Wyoming and Montana ranges, still the loss was tremendous. A number of the large, speculative ranches were bankrupt, and by the end of 1888 the cattle kingdoms in Nebraska were virtually gone.

Had these ranches been managed more carefully, the attrition need not have been so great. But so feverish was the desire for quick profits, so fast the expansion of the ranching operations, and so little the real understanding of ranch management that there were bound to be difficulties. Unsound financing and overstocking of the range, combined with two successive years of blizzards and drought, almost finished the ranching business. It was the small ranches in the Sandhills, sheltered from the wind, owned and operated by seasoned westerners who understood the range, which kept the cattle business going during the next few years.

The large cattle empires had been located in the broad expanses of the western part of the state, skirting the great oval that comprises the Sandhills. The thousands of square miles of grass-covered sand dunes there were for years considered a land of no return, eerie because in their labyrinthine expanses a man could become lost; they were thought to be fit only for Indians and for the occasional bad man—Kid Wade, Doc Middleton and others—who plunged into their vastness and were hidden from sight.

In the rush for farmland, some settlers had claimed land adjoining the Sandhills but found it marginal; the soil was so loose and light that when it was cut with a plow it blew away, creating naked blowouts, areas of sandy, desertlike land which the wind enlarged, eroding larger and larger areas. Because in those outlying areas there were few water sources, everybody assumed that in the heart of the hills, there was no water at all, that all beyond was desert.

Some ranchers had driven cattle north from Sidney to the Sioux agencies after 1874, and Captain James H. Cook had gone through the hills, too, in 1876. But the heart of the hills remained unexplored until the early 1880s, when working ranchers began to seek them out for spreads they could own and operate themselves; they saw that the grass was nutritious, the hills provided protection from the winds, and the hidden lakes and unexpected streamlets provided water. These ranchers lived on their spreads and worked them, handing them down to their sons and their sons' sons. These were the Abbotts, the Haneys, Thomas Lynch, James Forbes, J. H. Minor, later the Hannas and the Lees, among others; they grew up with the country.

The Sandhills, a formation unique to Nebraska, are a sort of Shangri-la, hidden from sight, unknown to most men, but providing serenity and peace. Their broad, lush meadows are sheltered from the prairie winds, their rolling dunes are covered with rippling grama grasses. The hills, extending beyond the horizon, are confusing; lifelong residents can easily become lost and disoriented in their wilds. Some people consider the hills desolate; others are so attuned to them that they believe them to be the last outposts of tranquillity on this earth.

Before 1900, the ranching business had recovered from hard times. Many of the familiar old outfits were gone, but others were coming in to take their places. A new danger threatened—settlers, farmers who plowed the land and opened it to erosion, fenced in the fields and interfered with cattle.

Warfare between the cowman and the farmer was not new; the first skirmishes took place in the late 1860s in the eastern part of the state when the first cattle drovers tried to run cattle from one place to another across Nebraska and were stopped by fences and by apron-waving farm wives trying to keep their garden patches from being trampled. It erupted into battle briefly in 1878 with the murder of two homesteaders, Ami Ketchum and Luther Mitchell, at the hands of men from the Olive ranch in Custer county. The Olives, Ira, Print, and Bob, were Texans who had come north to seek new pastures for their cattle, establishing their fifteen thousand head of shorthorns on the open range and their home at Plum Creek. The homesteaders in the region, some of them having struggled for several years to make a living, were upset when cattle rampaged through their yards, threatening to knock down their sod houses; the cattlemen detested the fences the settlers put up and accused the homesteaders of cattle rustling. The bodies of the two men were found one day in Devil's Gap, a desolate canyon; they had been hanged, shot, and burned. The case was a sensational one, which has become part of the Nebraska legend, the details amplified with each telling.

Little by little, as areas farther east were settled, homesteaders came into ranch country to take government lands; the completion of the North Western railroad in 1890 and branch lines of the Burlington made access to the land easier. "Nesters," the indignant cowmen called the settlers, thoroughly detesting them as they took up quarter-section homesteads, built soddies, fenced the land, broke the prairie sod. Cowboys took to slipping wire cutters in with their gear when they went out on the range, to snip the hated fences of the settlers; homesteaders began carrying loaded guns wherever they went. In 1894 settlers in Cherry County received threatening letters and before long three homesteaders were shot, killed in their own fields; one of them was Jason Cole, whose son D. J. later became a senator in the state unicameral legislature. Jason's brother, also a homesteader, left the country when he got a warning letter. The unsolved murders were assumed to have been the work of cowboys who had left Wyoming after the difficulties there between the cowboys and the farmers in Johnson County in 1892.

In some areas, especially those where the land was more suitable for farming than the Cherry County expanses, the homesteaders came in such numbers that they turned the range into farmland. Even Frontier County, organized in 1872 by cattlemen who named its county seat Stockville, later peaceably adopted the herd law, which required stockmen to fence in their stock to keep it from trampling farm crops.

From time to time, the cattlemen who were using free government rangeland tried to get lease laws passed, especially after the federal law of 1885 was passed, forbidding the fencing of public lands. Under laws existing until 1891, the most land an individual could acquire by homesteading was 480 acres, not enough for the extensive range that cattle needed, and in that year the Pre-Emption Act was stricken, canceling out 160 acres. As things stood, cattlemen could use public lands for their stock, but they could not lease them. Nor could they fence them in.

But they did. The Brighton ranch in Keith County, for instance, had 125,000 acres fenced in, and when the Coad ranch was sold in 1883, the sale bill listed four enclosed pastures, the largest one 143,000 acres. When the Nebraska Land and Feeding Company was incorporated in May 1899, the inventory listed 292 miles of fencing enclosing five hundred thousand acres of land.

Bitter homesteaders coming out to ranch country to file claims were sure the fences were put there to keep them out. Cattlemen were equally sure that homesteaders deliberately settled here and there to cut up their pastures by taking quarter-sections without any system but simply to ruin their range. They said, too, that they needed fences to protect their now-blooded stock from mingling with wild range cattle or the scrub stock the homesteaders brought in.

In December 1901, Congress voted a lease law to allow cattlemen to pay rental to the federal government for their lands, and the stockmen were jubilant. But in April 1902, President Theodore Roosevelt vetoed it. When a delegation of Nebraska cattlemen talked to him in Washington, his answer was clear. "Gentlemen," he said, "the fences must come down." [7] Although Roosevelt had been a rancher himself in Wyoming and Dakota in the 1880s, he had been elected to the presidency on a platform of trust-busting, opposing what he called the malefactors of great wealth. He was determined to make an example of the biggest cattlemen in the area to force the others into line.

In October 1903, Bartlett Richards and William Comstock, president and vice-president of the Nebraska Land and Feeding Company, were indicted in federal court on charges of illegally fencing government land. Their Spade, Bar C, and Overton ranches in Cherry, Sheridan, and Box Butte counties comprised one of the biggest spreads in the country. Both were experienced cattlemen; Richards had bought the original Spade ranch in 1888 and during the 1890s had lived in Chadron, where his family had established one of its banks; Comstock, his brother-in-law, had been in the ranching business for years in South Dakota and elsewhere.

Before the case came to trial, Congress considered various pieces of legislation which would enlarge homestead land in range country, finally passing in 1904 the Kinkaid Act, proposed by Congressman Moses Kinkaid of Nebraska, which provided that in thirty-seven counties of northwest Nebraska, settlers could claim not more than six hundred forty acres of nonirrigable land, receiving patents after five years of residence and proof of having made certain improvements on the land. Not all Nebraska newspapers were in favor of the law; some realized that the amount of land was far too small for family subsistence. But the Kinkaiders began to swarm into range

7. Mari Sandoz, *Love Song to the Plains* (New York: Harper and Row, 1961), p. 260.

country; in the first six years, some sixteen hundred patents were granted.

On November 13, 1905, Richards and Comstock pleaded guilty before Federal Judge Munger in Omaha to the charge of having illegally fenced 212,000 acres of government land but asked for leniency inasmuch as they were removing the fences. The judge fined each of them three hundred dollars and costs and sentenced them to six hours in the custody of the United States marshal, who turned them over to their counsel. The lawyer went shopping with them and then took them to the Omaha Club for lunch to fill out the required time. Newspapers picked up the story and heralded it all over the country. President Roosevelt was furious, removed the district attorney and the United States marshal, and roared that he wished he had the power to remove the judge. The men were taken to court again, charged with conspiring to secure title to public land through fraudulent entries, convicted, and sent this time to jail.

As federal prisoners, they could choose their place of incarceration, and in 1910, Comstock, Richards, and two employees of the Spade ranch entered the Adams County jail for their year-long sentences. Newspapers from all over the country printed stories about the special treatment the distinguished prisoners supposedly were receiving, and although federal inspectors checked the situation and found that the men were treated in the same manner as all other prisoners, a correction was never published nationally; for years the baseless story of the millionaire's club in jail was circulated. Richards became ill, was released to go to the Mayo clinic for surgery, and died on September 4, 1911, in the Nebraska Sanitarium in Hastings. Comstock's sentence was commuted so that he could attend the funeral services.

Fences down, Kinkaiders in, the range cattle business suffered. To make up for their loss of lands, cattlemen developed new ranching techniques. During the summer months ranch hands cut, raked, dried, and cured tons of wild hay for use in the winter; the town of Newport became the world center for the sale of wild hay. T. B. Hord, who had been associated with the Lance Land and Cattle Company from 1886 to 1891, began to preach the importance of supplemental feeding of cattle, and

before long had a long string of Hord elevators along railroad
sidings throughout western Nebraska to supply the stockmen.

Cattlemen could ship their steers to the Omaha stockyards
and there sell them to the various packinghouses. Efforts had
been made as early as 1876 to establish a stockyard in Omaha
and some hog-slaughtering had been done; in 1883, a syndicate
of cattlemen, headed by Alex Swan of the Swan Land and
Cattle Company, and including such others as William Paxton
and John McShane, organized the Omaha Stockyards Company,
bought two thousand acres in south Omaha, built pens, piped in
water, and were ready for business; an affiliated land company
sold lots later used for houses for packinghouse workers. In
1885, the stockyards company built a packinghouse and leased
it, inducing packers to come to Omaha with large cash and land
grants.

But for a while, only the Union Pacific brought livestock in;
the Chicago and North Western, whose lines through the northern part of the state covered much of the vast cattle country,
refused to take cattle to Omaha, shipping them on to Chicago
instead. In 1886, representatives of the Omaha stockyards,
threatening to lobby for legislation which would prohibit any
Nebraska livestock from going to Chicago, persuaded the North
Western to unload in Omaha. Shortly thereafter, the Burlington,
which had also been shipping on to Chicago, built lines into the
stockyards, and the success of the Omaha enterprise was assured. By 1900, enormous new slaughterhouses and packing
plants of the Armour, Cudahy, Swift, Wilson, and other companies were in operation; business buildings for livestock commission and brokers' offices erected; a Stockyards National Bank
established; and a Stockyards Hotel, and other facilities provided for the cattlemen who rode the cabooses to accompany
their trainloads of fat steers to market. South Omaha was meat
country.

The beef industry now stretched across the state, from the
weathered cow-tender on the ranches in the west to the muscled
cow-slaughterer in the packinghouse along the Missouri River.
By 1925, more than seven million head of beef, swine, and
sheep were processed in Omaha; and by 1955, the Omaha live-

stock market was the world's largest, Nebraska the leading beef
state of the country, and Cherry County the leading beef county
of the nation.

By 1975, however, the traditional patterns of meat processing
had changed; no longer was the business centralized in Omaha,
long strings of railroad freight cars disgorging their bawling
cargo into the holding pens in South Omaha. Most of the stockyards were gone, the land sold to be converted to other uses.
The Big Four of the packing industry—Swift, Wilson, Armour,
and Cudahy—were gone; only a few smaller packers had
slaughterhouses and packing facilities in Omaha. Instead, cattlemen hauled their stock in huge cattle trucks, on the highway
rather than on the rails, to regional packinghouses scattered
throughout the state—in Dakota City, York, and elsewhere—
where they were paid on a grade and yield basis after the animals were slaughtered and dressed. And most of those trucks
came from feedlots, far removed from the grassy ranges, for an
intermediate step had been added in beef production; cattlemen
sold their beeves to feeders, who penned tens of thousands of
head of cattle into confined quarters and fed them corn to finish
them for the packer. But although the procedures of getting
beefsteak from the ranchlands of the west to the tables of the
rest of the country have changed, the vast open stretches of the
Sandhills are still the point of origin for Nebraska beef.

In the meantime, the Kinkaiders were learning the truth of
what others had predicted; their new land was not suited for
general farming, and a six hundred forty acre spread was not
enough to work in cattle country. By World War I, many of the
homesteaders who had moved in under governmental protection
had been driven out by natural forces, their land bought by
ranchers.

The spectacularly large ranches of the old days are long gone,
but by the 1930s and since, as a result of the sale of Kinkaid
lands by discouraged farmers, Sandhills ranches comprise as
many as sixty thousand acres, a medium-large ranch including
ten or twenty thousand acres, with herds running from twelve to
fifteen hundred head. Some of the rangeland in the now-
irrigated North Platte Valley has been turned to sugar-beet production; other level lands turned into wheat production, rippling

acres of golden grain. The land that once produced only meat now provides bread and sugar as well.

Although the fabled days of gigantic cattle ranches are gone, the land is even more prosperous and productive than before.

13

The Immigrants

*T*HE settlement of Nebraska coincided with the flood of immigration from Europe that inundated the United States in the nineteenth century, and for several decades the federal census reported that one out of every four or five Nebraskans was foreign-born. Anyone in the towns of Wilber, West Point, Grand Island, or Osceola knew that was true; sometimes it was hard to hear English on Saturday night.

Almost all of the overseas immigrants in Nebraska came from northern Europe, more from Germany than from any other single area, but substantial numbers also came from the Scandinavian countries, Bohemia, Russia, England and Ireland. By 1870, two-thirds of the population was of foreign stock. By 1900, although many Nebraskans were second-generation Americans, many of them were still speaking the Old Country language, some of them bilingual, to be sure; they were eating rouladen or grebble or kolaches or östkaka, and otherwise following the European culture patterns their families had brought across the Atlantic.

Why they came is not surprising, for the new Nebraskans left their homes in the Old Country for the same reasons that other emigrants from Europe did: over-population, famine, and depressed economic conditions generally; political upheaval; military conscription; religious beliefs; a chance to make something of themselves in a new world.

Some of the earliest immigrants learned of Nebraska only

after they had arrived in this country and had settled in New York state or Ohio or Indiana or Iowa, and as the western fever caught up their new neighbors, the English or German immigrants were infected and decided to move westward, too. Most of the first newcomers from Europe to Nebraska came by way of somewhere else, the Schleswig-Holsteiners who settled Grand Island coming from Davenport, Iowa; the Brandenburgers who settled the Elkhorn valley communities of West Point, St. Charles, and Norfolk, coming from Watertown and Ixonia, Wisconsin; the Swedes in Stromsburg from Alton, Illinois; the Czechs in Wilber from Cedar Rapids, Iowa. In their letters to relatives back in the Old Country, they wrote glowing accounts of life in this new country, and envious villagers began to hoard their pfennigs so that they, too, could come to the fine new land called Nebraska. So impressive was this barrage of letters in publicizing Nebraska that from the early 1870s onward, many of the European immigrants came directly to the state, probably having talked of nothing else in their little villages in the meantime. Agencies that were beginning to stimulate immigration—church congregations, immigration societies, railroads—encouraged the writing of letters back to the Old Country as the most effective means of publicity.

Most of the immigration societies for Nebraska were affiliated in one way or another with the Union Pacific or the Burlington railroad, the two land-grant railroads, which formed land companies to work closely with the Nebraska State Board of Immigration, established in 1870, in encouraging settlement in the state. They distributed thousands of brochures, printed in the language of the country, throughout England, Germany, the Ukraine and Volga regions of Russia, and other parts of northern Europe, describing the beauties of the land, its fertility and its healthfulness, and how to acquire it, either through homesteading government land or by buying it from the land companies. The companies usually had land agents in the countries with the biggest source of potential business—Hamburg in Germany and Liverpool in England were important departure points—who arranged passage, usually steerage class, in boats crossing the Atlantic, and supplied practical advice about immigration procedures generally.

Once in this country and past the usually bewildering experiences at Ellis Island—where sometimes the newcomers were stripped of their names and assigned new ones, as in the case of one Swedish family named Johnson which was told, "We've got too many Johnsons now—your name is Ross,"—the immigrants to Nebraska boarded zulu cars, special railroad cars to take them to their destinations. Although many of the newcomers knew exactly where they were going, to join relatives or friends in Gothenburg or Sutton or Schuyler, others did not; the railroads employed bilingual "runners" to help the immigrants get on the proper trains. Sometimes the runners in their zeal deliberately misled the immigrants, steering them onto a train which took them to Minnesota, rather than Kansas or, in the case of Nebraska, to a Union Pacific destination rather than a Burlington one. For a brief time, the state of Nebraska hired a part-time agent in New York City to help encourage new arrivals to go to Nebraska.

The zulu cars were constructed with sections on each side of the aisle, each section containing two double berths made of wooden slats; no upholstery nor bedding was supplied; the travelers padded the slats with their own blankets and clothing. At one end of the zulu there was a cooking stove where passengers prepared their own food en route. When the journey was over, and the new Nebraskans were disgorged on the prairie, the railroad hosed the car. The trip from New York City to mid-Nebraska usually took four or five days.

Once in Nebraska, the travelers could stay at Immigrant Houses until they had located the land they wanted to acquire, homesites as well as farmsteads, either through purchase or homesteading. The principal Union Pacific house was at Omaha, with smaller ones along its trackage west; the main Immigrant House of the Burlington was at Lincoln, its long, two-story cluster of wooden, barnlike buildings connected by wooden sidewalks. The Burlington also maintained smaller houses at Henderson and Sutton. Newcomers could stay in these quarters for three or four days, rent-free, until they found suitable land. The shelter provided a refuge to the immigrants, a place to be free of landsharks eager to push undesirable land, a last chance to mingle with their compatriots before they plunged into a new culture.

Although most of the immigrants arrived as family groups, parents and a number of children together, some came to Nebraska as lone men eager to establish themselves before they sent for their families, and some came in colonies, groups of families settling together in a single community.

The first migration from England was a group of one hundred fifteen men, women, and children who left Liverpool together and traveled as an entity, settling in their newly established community of Palmyra in southeastern Nebraska in 1866. England was Burlington country, and most of the English immigrants settled originally in the southern part of the state. Other early English settlements were in Cass, Clay, Adams, and Fillmore counties; the first settlers in Hastings in Adams County were fifteen from Liverpool, city-bred men who had never done any sort of farming, let alone sodbreaking. They arrived in 1871, a year before the rails reached the area, and had to walk the last twenty miles to their destination, where they built soddies and struggled to master the intricacies of prairie farming.

Although the brochures in England describing Nebraska suggested that English immigrant families travel together as groups and settle in close proximity, as an antidote to the loneliness on the prairies, English immigrants tended to disperse after they arrived here; by 1880, English-born immigrants were settled in sixty-nine counties. Because the language was the same as their own, they did not need to huddle together for companionship; they shed their identity as English and became Nebraskans, retaining many British customs, however.

Most of the early English immigrants were farmers or laborers, although as early as 1870 there were Englishmen in Omaha representing medicine, law, teaching, the clergy, bookkeeping, merchandising, and the building trades.

The Germans, who became the most populous ethnic group in Nebraska, began to arrive shortly after the area was opened up to settlement. A German Catholic community at St. Helena, along the Missouri, was an early one, and when William Stolley and his party of thirty-one Germans went along the Platte to establish Grand Island in 1857, they passed eighteen dwellings of Germans at Columbus. There were enough German-speaking

Nebraskans that minutes of the first state legislative hearing in 1867 were translated into German and published. From then on, the numbers increased steadily until the flood of immigration in the 1880s, when emigrants from all parts of Germany streamed in to establish German Catholic communities, German Lutheran communities, and just plain German towns. To the Germans, to be a landowner was to be a somebody, and Nebraska and her free land provided the chance.

The first arrivals considered themselves Prussians or Hessians or Östfriesen or Westphalians, rather than Germans; they spoke such varied dialects that the Schwabians speaking *Schwäbisch* and the Östfriesen speaking *Plattdeutsch* sometimes had difficulty making conversation, although they could read the same German newspapers. On the Nebraska prairies, their provincial differences began to diminish and they developed a German ethnic identity; they were Germans, albeit Germans-about-to-be-Americans, rather than Bavarians or Holsteiners. The Union Pacific claimed Germany as its recruiting territory in Europe in the 1880s and 1890s, and throughout the central part of the state Little Germanies were established in which everyone spoke German, read German newspapers—by 1910, there were forty German-language newspapers published in Nebraska—sang German hymns and listened to German sermons in church, sent their children to German schools, did their banking at the German National Bank, held Sängerfeste (song festivals) at the Liederkranz Hall, ate wurst and drank beer at the Gemütlichkeit Lodge. In many communities, some second- and third-generation American-born persons spoke little English, so pervasive was the German culture.

Some, of course, were assimilated quickly into the American mainstream, particularly those in the rural areas where there were few other Germans, and the professional people who settled in cities and whose businesses were built on commerce with Americans, rather than German-Americans. They learned English quickly, forbade the use of the German language in their households, and joined the English-language Lutheran church; many of them Anglicized their names even before they had their naturalization papers. From Schmidt they became Smith; Mueller became Miller; Wilhelm, Williams; Schneider became

Snyder or even Taylor, the name translated into its English equivalent.

The church was the focal point in the lives of most of the German immigrants, particularly those who retained their German culture, serving not only as a religious center but as a social one as well. In the sixteenth century, Germany had been the starting point of the Reformation and, in the centuries since, had been the scene of various wars of religion; church identification was important to the Germans who immigrated to Nebraska. Although the German Catholics of necessity had to open their doors to Catholics who were not German— Bohemians, Irish, Poles, Italians—the Lutheran churches which were German remained German, subdividing into a bewildering maze of synodical organizations. To gain more members to help pay the costs of buildings and pastors, the churches in their own way became recruiting agencies for immigration, encouraging members to write letters to the Old Country to stimulate more settlers.

Many of the Lutheran churches established parochial schools, those of the Missouri Synod in particular; the synod had been established in 1847 and grew rapidly, its conservative theology of the infallibility of the Scriptures appealing to German-born Nebraskans and rural plainsmen generally. It was an immigrant church, dedicated to the ingathering of the newcomers and their children, preserving the German language and cultural heritage, substituting its own versions of fraternal lodges and other American institutions so that its members would not be tempted to assimilate into the American pattern. In heavily German farming areas, there often was a Missouri Synod compound with church, graveyard, school, and pastor's house perched on the plains, the cultural and social center for the German farmers for miles around. During church services, men sat on one side of the aisle; women and small children on the other side. Those who joined the Masons or bought life insurance (in defiance of the Biblical admonition "The Lord will provide") were dismissed from membership in the church, and therefore from the social functions of the neighborhood.

In addition to the various Lutheran churches, including the German Nebraska Synod, there were the German Evangelical

Synod, the German Reformed Church, and others, located more often in towns than in rural areas, less dogmatic in their theology than the rural churches and more amenable to assimilation into American culture patterns. Members of these congregations joined a myriad of German organizations, these *Vereindeutsche* (club Germans, differentiated from *Kirchendeutsche*, or church Germans)—the Sons of Hermann, a fraternal society; *Turnvereine*, social organizations; and *Männerchöre*, men's singing societies which had yearly festivals, sending the music to groups in other towns well ahead of the concert so that when the festival took place in Lincoln or Omaha or Hastings or at the Liederkranz Hall in Grand Island, everybody was already well rehearsed; the men and their families looked forward from one year to the next to these outings, chartering special cars on trains to go to them. In their lodge halls, there were family nights; babies swaddled in blankets were parked in the corner in prams or on benches, older children were assigned to look after toddlers, and mothers sat together discussing housewifely matters while the men puffed on their pipes and sipped their beer, discussing politics. When the fiddler tuned up, or on special occasions the three- or four-piece band, the waltzing began.

Every German community of any size whatsoever had a German butcher who made wursts of various kinds, dressed hundreds of geese for Christmas, and knew how to slice meats for rouladen or schnitzel; there were German bakers who made torten and heavy cakes and light breads. And any German town of any size had a brewery. The Germans were well fed, using sour cream, butter, lard, with loving, heavy hands; they enjoyed their German-ness.

Of all the immigrant groups who came to Nebraska, the Germans from Russia were the ones most likely to travel in colonies, sometimes most of a village moving as a group to Nebraska, building the same style of square, sawed-off, peak-roofed houses they had left behind, with the same neighbors on either side of them. They were diligent farmers, good husbandmen, whom Catherine the Great had lured into Russia in the mid-1700s to colonize the Ukraine and the Volga, assuring them they could retain their German identity. They would serve as a buffer region against the hostile Tatars of the East. A century later, in 1874, Czar Alexander II rescinded the privileges and tried to Russify them, whereupon more than a hundred thousand of them—for they were prolific and had multiplied ten-fold—packed up and left. They were a much-sought-after immigrant group; the Kansas Pacific, the Great Northern, the Northern Pacific, were as eager to herd them into Kansas or the Dakotas as the Burlington was to steer them into Nebraska.

The Germans from Russia, generally called "Rooshans" by the scornful native whites of the Plains, spoke no Russian, considered themselves German, and from a long tradition of nonassimilation in a strange country, kept to themselves after they arrived in Nebraska. Those who had lived in Catholic communities in Russia, as they had in Germany a century earlier, gravitated to German-Russian Catholic communities in Nebraska, the Protestants to German-Russian Protestant ones, and the Mennonites, followers of Menno Simon, a sixteenth-century Anabaptist, established Mennonite communities. Not only were they separate from other Americans, new or old, but they segregated into distinct groups among themselves.

Many of them, particularly the Mennonites who came with Peter Jansen into Jefferson County, bought farmland and farmed in the American style—that is, living on the farms they tilled, rather than going out from the village each day. In their luggage and pockets they brought surreptitiously from Russia the Turkey-red wheat seed, a winter-growing grain, which was to revolutionize wheat farming in the whole Great Plains area. They established Mennonite villages to provide services: implement shops, blacksmithies, general stores, but no lawyers—for Mennonites settle their own differences and to have lawyers implies lack of trust—and churches. For many years some Mennonite congregations in Nebraska wore drab clothing, the women wearing black bonnets, plain, long black dresses. The Jansen community, established in 1874, is dissipated now, as are many other Mennonite villages which thrived for perhaps a half century; the town of Henderson in York County is the single sparkling purely Mennonite community left, and when the fertile fields surrounding it change hands, they are sold only to other Mennonites. With a population of less than a thousand,

Henderson has four churches, all of them Mennonite, the largest one, Bethesda, having the largest sanctuary of any church structure in the state.

Others, especially Protestants from the Volga, settled in closely knit communities in already established towns—Lincoln, Sutton, and Hastings—to work as craftsmen or manual laborers. The men worked in brickyards, shoveled coal at the power plant, worked as carpenters or cabinetmakers; the women did domestic labor, particularly laundry, which their children picked up and delivered after school in their noncoaster wagons. Young unmarried German-Russian girls had fingers nimble enough to hand-wrap the ten million cigars that the Kipp Cigar Company in Hastings turned out each year, or to make candies that the Yager Candy Company manufactured. German-Russian homes were heated with lug-night, a sly ethnic term for coal the children collected along the railroad tracks. Small youngsters taunted coalcar tenders so they would throw coal, maybe big lumps, at them; when the coal sacks were full, the youngsters lugged them home at night.

In early May the German families from Russia in Lincoln and Hastings packed their blankets, clothing, a few pots and pans, some staples and home-canned meats; closed their houses; took their youngsters out of school; and boarded the special train to the sugar-beet fields, first in Michigan, after 1910 to the irrigated fields in the North Platte Valley near Scottsbluff. There for six months of the year the families labored in the fields, blocking, thinning, weeding, and finally digging tons of sugar beets, hand labor no one else would do, returning home at Thanksgiving. They lived in shanties, saved their contract money, and now own most of the Nebraska sugar-beet acreage, contracting at first with Japanese laborers, now with Mexican-Americans, to do the field work.

The American Historical Society of Germans from Russia has it headquarters in Lincoln; there are an estimated five million Americans now descended from the Germans from Russia.

The Czechs were the second most populous immigrant group in Nebraska, perhaps as many as 70,000 of them—immigrants and their American-born children—coming into the state in the years between 1865 and 1900; there were more Czechs in Nebraska than in any other state in the country. Early in American history, some immigrants from the provinces of Bohemia and Moravia came to the United States to live; as the frontier moved west, Cedar Rapids, Iowa, became one of the gathering places for those seeking western lands, and it was from there that the first Czech settler in Nebraska, Libor Alois Slesinger, came to Omaha to live on April 15, 1857, followed by many others who were already in the United States. In one great mass movement several years later, eight hundred families gathered in Chicago and Cleveland to migrate to Nebraska, settling in Knox County, taking homestead land and organizing villages with familiar names, such as Praha and Brno. Many of them had left their homeland after the abortive revolt of the Bohemians in 1848 against Austria, and when Nebraska lands opened up for settlement, they decided to colonize there. It was to be another generation or more before their homeland gained independence, for from 1727 to 1918, she was under the domination of either Austria or Hungary or both.

Other Czechs came directly from the Old Country to Nebraska, utilizing the services of the Immigration Societies; as with the Germans from Russia, many Czech villages emigrated as groups to America, sailing out of Hamburg or Bremen, steamship companies in both port cities maintaining Czech-speaking personnel on their staffs to take care of the rush of business.

The homestead land along the wooded river valleys, so like the land at home, was claimed early, so the later Czechs turned to railroad lands; one of the Burlington land agents in Omaha from 1877 to 1885 was a Czech, Vaclav Vodicka, who helped thousands of his countrymen buy land. The Burlington offered special arrangements to these settlers: if they would buy railroad land, they and their freight would be transported free, and if they had cultivated part of the land before the end of the first two years, they could have a twenty-percent discount, which was the amount of the first installment for the land. No other railroads made such liberal gestures toward settlers, and the Czechs became Burlington enthusiasts. By 1870, there were identifiable Czech colonies in Saline, Saunders, Colfax, Butler, and Knox counties, and they grew rapidly; the town of Wilber claims the title as the Czech capital of Nebraska, Verdigre as the kolache capital (Kolache are fruit-filled pastries, as much a part of Czech culture as the polka.)

Although many of the immigrants were skilled artisans and professionals—Antonia's father in Willa Cather's book *My Antonia* was a violinist—in Nebraska many of them became farmers at first. Among them were bachelors seeking to establish themselves as landowners before they began their own families, but with a dearth of young women of marriageable age within their colonies, sometimes they had to send back to the Old Country for mail-order brides. Some of these alliances worked out; others did not. One fifteen-year-old girl, sent alone to America to substitute for an older sister who had eloped with a local swain, discovered her bridegroom to be twenty years her elder, harsh and taciturn, her life in a windswept dugout one of bleakness; within two years she had produced two children, had learned no English to communicate with any non-Czech neighbors, and she went mad, spending the next sixty years of her life in an asylum.

Language was one of the most difficult problems for the Czechs, particularly those who lived in tight little ethnic colonies, where only their native tongue was spoken for several generations and where there was no chance to learn English; all of their business had to be conducted through interpreters. Those who were separated from their countrymen had more incentive to learn the new language. In later generations, Czech youngsters in mixed communities learned the advantage of having a second language, for they could speak Czech to each other on the playground at recess, to the annoyance of their American friends; in the classroom they spoke English. Those same bilingual children also learned how to settle the Americans who called them, in derision, "Bohunks." Although most of the Czechs in Nebraska came from the province of Bohemia, they did not want to be called Bohemians, equating the term with the artistic life that the word *Boheme* means in French. Long before there was a Czechoslovakia, they considered themselves Czechs.

Czechs are gregarious, particularly among their own, and quickly established ethnic organizations. Sokol clubs in South Omaha, Wilber, and Crete, provided training for gymnastics, logical activity for a group that enjoys folk dancing as much as the Czechs do; Sokol halls were combined gymnasiums and town halls, used also for theatrical productions and concerts. Czech folk dancers from Wilber performed at the inaugural celebration for Governor J. J. Exon in 1975. Czechs dominated the professional wrestling world for years—Joe Zikmund, Joe Stecher, John (Big Jawn) Pesek, and his son Jack winning world titles. Brass bands sprang into being, Frank Nedela's band in Crete playing at Governor Butler's inaugural in 1869, the Crete Military Band winning GAR state contests in the early twentieth century, and other oompah-pah bands sending toes tapping elsewhere in the state. Accordions are favorite Czech instruments, the first one many youngsters learn to play.

Czechs organized fraternal orders; the Cesko Slovansky Podporujici Spolek and the Zapadni Cesko Bratrska Jednota were the largest ones, providing low-cost insurance and sociability; they had weekly dances at the lodge with all generations present. Youngsters dancing the polka or schottische had to stay in the center of the floor or on the very outside, out of the way of their elders; always, however, parents would dance one polka or waltz with their children during the evening. The Czech Farmers' Mutual Aid Society in Nebraska, a crop insurance establishment, had fifty branches and one thousand members before it went out of existence in 1893; there were forty-six Czech banks in the state and twenty Czech-language newspapers before 1900.

Although most Czechs are Roman Catholic, a few who came to Nebraska were Protestant, followers of John Hus, and a few were freethinkers. A Czech Fraternal Presbyterian Synod was established in Omaha, and other Czech Protestants were also in Dodge County. A number of Czechs in Nebraska have gone into politics, a total of sixty in the state legislature; Hugo Srb, a Czech, was the first clerk of the unicameral legislature, Karl Stefan, born in Bohemia, served eight terms as a United States congressman from Nebraska, and Roman Hruska, a second-generation American, has served in both the United States House of Representatives and the Senate for a total of twenty-four years.

Czech family life was warm, expansive, full of music and heavy food—roast duck, pork, dumplings, sauerkraut. Possibly because they had to struggle for so many centuries for national identity, the Czechs are exceedingly conscious of their ethnic heritage; from childhood, youngsters are taught to walk tall and be proud of their Czech background. A generation ago, half-grown girls attended feather-stripping parties, learning to take the soft parts of duck or goose feathers from the quill to make down pillows or coverlets; only Americans would sleep on chicken-feather bedding. They learned the songs and dances of the Old Country, and learned to perpetuate ethnic customs. On Christmas Eve, for instance, once the mother of the household sat down, she could not get out of her chair again until bedtime; if she did, her hens wouldn't set early in the spring. Czechs had shivarees, loud noisy gatherings, not only for newlyweds but also for others on their patron saint feast days.

To preserve their heritage, Czechs arranged for the establishment of a department of Czech at the University of Nebraska in 1909 for the study of Czech language and culture; it is still functioning as are similar courses in public schools in Czech communities. In the 1960s various Czech towns united into a state organization, each chapter sponsoring an ethnic festival or program during the year. The two-day celebration in Wilber in August attracts upwards of fifty thousand persons annually to craft exhibitions, colorful folk-dancing and accordion contests, and polka bands in the beer gardens—for how the Czechs love their beer! Other Czech communities, Dwight and Verdigre among them, also sponsor ethnic festivals. Although by now the Czechs have become part of the Nebraska culture generally, they are still keenly aware of their own particular heritage.

When the Scandinavians began to flock into Nebraska, along with the other immigrants from northern Europe, they nostalgically named their communities after the land they left behind—Dannebrog, Gothenburg, Malmo, Stromsburg, even Wausa, named after Swedish King Gustavus Vasa—and added their languages to the polyglot on the prairie. By 1890, there were 24,693 Swedes, 12,531 Danes, and 3,632 Norwegians on the Nebraska census rolls, most of them in ethnic communities scattered throughout the central part of the state, Swedes near other Swedes, Danes near other Danes. A yarn, apochryphal no doubt, tells of a lone Italian settling in a Nebraska community and carefully learning the language of his new country, not realizing that it was Danish; for thirty miles around, that was the only language he heard.

Among the first Swedes were laborers lured to Omaha by the opening of the Union Pacific shops in 1865 and the building of the railroad bridge over the Missouri in 1871. They came from settlements farther east, in Illinois and Iowa, and they worked as machinists, blacksmiths, carpenters; later they worked in packing plants or as teamsters and coachmen. Young Swedish women were domestic servants. By 1900, two-thirds of Omaha was foreign-born, four thousand persons from Sweden alone settled into a colony predictably called Little Stockholm.

Almost concurrently, Scandinavian farmers arrived, homesteading or buying land along the Platte Valley, building dugouts or soddies. Although this was Union Pacific country, the railroad seems not to have played a significant role in Swedish or Danish settlement; the newcomers arrived in groups of three or four families at a time, not as whole colonies, influenced by the enthusiastic letters of their relatives already on the plains, not by immigration-society brochures. The Swedes were attracted by the availability of land—at home land was expensive and difficult to obtain—and to some extent by religious freedom.

Lutheranism was the Swedish state church, and until 1869, Swedish law prohibited any meetings not conducted by ordained ministers of the Established Church, a law that was responsible for some emigration from Sweden; a number of early Swedish settlements in Nebraska were Baptist, and a few were Covenant, Methodist, or Mission Friends. Most, however, were Lutheran, affiliated with the Augustana Synod, and social life in Scandinavian communities revolved around the little church on the prairie. Even among the Lutherans, however, there were doctrinal battles, so fierce that on occasion church services were held with armed guards from among the congregation standing at the door to keep out dissenters. Although the Lutheran hierarchy discouraged colonization efforts among its clergymen, saying they should devote more time to the flock (*jhorden*) than to the soil (*jorden*), a few of the early-day immigration leaders were Swedish pastors leading their flocks to new communities. The Rev. S. G. Larson, for instance, helped more than three hundred Swedish Lutherans acquire land in the Malmo-Mead-Swedburg area in the east-central part of the state in 1870, and the Rev. Theodore Hessel, a Baptist, led another group to Estina, near the Platte.

By 1875 there were Swedish settlements as far west as Red Willow County; within the next ten years the Swedes had organized a college, Luther College at Wahoo. (The town was named for an Indian shrub growing nearby.) Some of the synod ministers had to overcome their Scandinavian parishioners' distrust of an institution that, they feared, would foster laziness, and engender immorality. It was coeducational, and it cost too much to maintain; to the sod-house farmers battling blizzards, dust storms, and grasshoppers, almost any amount was too much. One man crawled under the bed when he saw the pastor approaching, but he sneezed. He had to come out then, and reluctantly he made a contribution to the church. The Swedish Lutherans started a hospital, Immanuel Deaconess in Omaha, and the Rev. K. G. William Dahl established Bethphage in Axtell, a home supported by the Swedish Lutherans for "those who are in bonds," epileptics and the feebleminded.

Those Swedes whose lives revolved around the church had no need for other activities; they had a Lutheran Brotherhood for men, the Women's Sisterhood, the Luther League for adolescents and children, and enough smörgasbords at the church to take care of all their social needs. They were God-fearing, rum-hating, self-sufficient souls. But other Swedish immigrants joined lodges, the Swedish Brotherhood offering insurance as well as sociability, a place for beer and *akavit* and dancing; the Swedish American Progressive Club to foster Americanism; and any number of other ethnic organizations. Most of the Swedish immigrants were diligent, hard-working people without outward levity or humor, strongly allied with the Republican ticket. Although children of immigrants learned their parents' language at home, they spoke English in school, and they gradually gave up the Old Country language. Most of the Scandinavians were eager to become Americanized, but Nebraska Swedes had their own newspapers, two published in Lincoln and others elsewhere; *Den Posten* is still published in Omaha.

The *Yul* season brought a flurry of activity to Swedish housewives, starting with St. Lucia day on December 13, when the daughter of the house, wearing a crown of lighted candles, served coffee and saffron cake to her parents and guests, and ending with the Christmas dinner of *lutfisk, kötteballer,* brown beans and *patata korf,* the in-between weeks occupied in baking *spritsar, vortlimpa* and other pastries. Even in the dugouts on the frozen prairie in bleak years, Swedish housewives did what they could to make a festive *Yul* season for their families, preserving eggs in waterglass (silica gel) during the laying period of summer to make sure of supplies for *Yul* baking. The Midsummer Day's festivities of June 24 were usually all-day community picnics with footracing and games later in the day.

It was not so much religion that brought Danes to Nebraska, but sheer population pressure; in the late 1800s, there were too many people for the land, especially after Denmark lost to Prussia the province of Schleswig-Holstein, whose ownership had switched back and forth between the two countries for decades. The animosity carried over to the New World, for although in Adams County both Germans and Danes attended a Danish Lutheran church at a township crossroads, the church fathers had to establish two cemeteries, one on either side of the road; Danes and Germans would worship together in peace if they had to, but they would not Rest in Peace together.

One of the first areas of Danish settlment in Nebraska was in Howard County. Dannebrog, the name meaning "Danish flag," was settled in 1871, and Nysted shortly afterward. The Danish folk high school at Nysted drew students not only from Nebraska but also from neighboring states to learn Danish and American culture. The peak years for Danish migration into Nebraska were between 1881 and 1890, later than that of the Swedes, and since seventy percent of the Danes who migrated were from rural areas of Denmark, most of them were farmers and dairymen who brought their skills and training with them. Although many of them settled in Howard County, others scattered throughout the state, dispersing themselves sufficiently to become Americanized more quickly than other Scandinavian immigrants. Communities which have sizable Danish representation include the Looking Glass Valley near Newman Grove in Platte County, Minden, Marquette, St. Paul, Kronsberg, Ord, Mason City, Pilger, Cozad, and Genoa.

In 1884 the Danes established a Danish Lutheran college, Dana, at Blair, the only Danish Lutheran college in the country. Dana now has an annual enrollment of about a thousand students, an active Danish language and literature department, and has been visited by Danish royal family members, Crown Prince Frederick and Crown Princess Ingrid in 1939 before they assumed the throne, and Queen Margrethe II in 1976.

Most Danes are Lutherans, and they established thirty-three churches in Nebraska, the United Danish Evangelical Lutheran Church—which had a Trinity seminary connected with Dana College—and the American Evangelical Lutheran Church. Some of the immigrants established other Protestant churches, primarily Baptist, when they arrived in Nebraska.

To the church Danes, dancing was considered a sin and only when folk dancing was reclassified as folk games could their children participate; these Danes were also Prohibitionists. The other Danes belonged to lodges. The Danish Brotherhood, whose national headquarters are in Omaha, had a membership of 22,000 in 1921, and still has seventeen lodges; and the Danish American Club has been in existence in Omaha for more than a half-century; most of these fraternal lodges provided insurance and sociability for the immigrants and their families. There were several Danish newspapers; *Den Danske Pioneer* in Omaha is still being published.

Danish communities on the prairie were always neat, tidy, almost picture-book villages, well scrubbed, with a fragrance of freshly baked bread hanging in the air, for Danish housewives take great pride in their breads and pastries. For festive occasions, such as Christmas or Danish Independence on June fifth, they roasted goose or pork or made *rullepølse,* meat rolls.

Because many of the Danish immigrants were young men, it was difficult for a bachelor to find a Danish girl to marry; frequently he would send back home for a wife from his own part of Denmark. Those families who had brought Danish girls to work as domestic servants discovered that the girls seldom stayed more than a few months, but quickly married Danish bachelors on neighboring farms. One Danish emigrant's wife explained that the last time she sent back to the Old Country for a household helper, she carefully specified that the servant was to be both old and ugly, to guarantee that she would have no suitors and would continue working for the family for a period of time. But not even that worked, for in this case within six months even the old and ugly servant was engaged to marry.

Most of the Norwegians who emigrated to Nebraska came not directly from the old country; they had settled first in other parts of the United States and later had moved on to the Nebraska prairies. There were small colonies in Boone, Madison, Platte, Webster, and Franklin counties, settling in ethnic colonies to be with people who spoke Norwegian and were Lutherans.

The yarn is told of a group of a hundred Norwegians who settled in the Shell Creek area of Boone County, only one of them understanding any English. To secure homesteads they had to declare their intention of becoming citizens and to take out their first papers. When they went before John Peters, the county clerk and an ardent Republican, they could not understand the words of the oath he administered, and when the English-speaking one asked for clarification of the words, Peters said, "It is like this: You are applying to become the citizen of a republic. Therefore, you must be a Republican in politics." [1] From then on, for many years, it was said, the Republicans could always count on a hundred Norwegian votes in that precinct.

When the Indians moved over, the Irish moved into Nebraska, they say, for Irish immigrants were among the first settlers in the territory. The contractor who built the first territo-

---

1. Cass G. Barnes, *The Sod House* (Lincoln: University of Nebraska Press, 1973), p. 161.

rial capitol in Omaha was Irish, using Irish workmen whenever possible; the first register of deeds and his assistant were also from Ireland. Several of the most influential men in Omaha were first-generation Irish-Americans. The most outstanding one, Edward Creighton, built the telegraph line from Omaha to Sacramento, thus opening up the West with communications. Creighton owned much of the real estate in Omaha; operated a lucrative freighting business to the Dakotas, Colorado, and Montana; and was one of the first men to realize the potential of the Sandhills ranchland, running cattle on spreads covering thousands of acres of western Nebraska. He was also the founder of Creighton University. Other early-day Irishmen in Omaha included Edward Cudahy, the Coads, the McShane brothers, Ben Gallagher, and others, all amassing fortunes in early-day Nebraska although none had gone beyond grammar school.

During the 1860s, when the Union Pacific Railroad was being built, Irish immigrants swarmed into the area as construction workers, going on to other parts of the state to start their own construction companies when the railroad was finished. Other Irish came in during the 1880s to work in the packinghouses. By the turn of the century, more than three thousand Irishmen had settled in Omaha, had built the cathedral of St. Philomena and a number of parish churches, had established two convents and St. Joseph's Hospital.

But not all the Irish were in Omaha. In 1871 an Irishman with a mission to serve his fellow men from Ireland came into Nebraska to look over the land. Three years later General John O'Neill returned with the first of what was to be four colonies of Irishmen to settle on farms in the West, free from the English oppressor's yoke. General O'Neill, born in Ireland, had distinguished himself as a Union officer during the Civil War and amassed a small fortune in business in Nashville, Tennessee. He had been an inspector general of the Fenian armies and later president of the Fenian Senate, and in 1865 he had conducted an unsuccessful raid on Canada to free it from the British. He was restrained by President Grant from launching a second attempt to liberate Canada and was imprisoned briefly. Realizing that he could not help his compatriots by arms, he decided to help them settle as independent farmers on American soil. In May 1874 he brought fifteen Irish immigrants to the village later named O'Neill, and immediately built an eighteen-by-thirty-six-foot sod house. The building, jocularly called The Grand Central Hotel, served as home for thirteen men, two women, and five children during the first year. In succeeding years General O'Neill brought other settlers, nearly two hundred men in all, some with wives and children, to establish towns in Holt and Greeley counties. Although he died in 1878, his Irish communities continued at Spaulding, Atkinson, Wisner, and other towns in the area.

The St. Patrick's Day festival in O'Neill, often held in snow flurries or blustering, chill winds, is a rollicking celebration; an enormous green shamrock is painted on the intersection of two highways in the middle of town, green beer flows copiously, and Irish jigs shake the floors at St. Mary's Academy.

There were other Europeans, too: the Swiss, mostly farmers, who tended to settle along the North Western railroad in northern Nebraska; the Scots; the French, some coming by way of Canada, where their families had lived for several generations; the Polish, who came to Omaha as stockyard workers and laborers; the Italians and Sicilians, who arrived in Omaha at the turn of the century; a few Greeks, a few Japanese, some of them going out into the Panhandle to work in the sugar-beet fields; and later, the Mexicans who came as farm laborers.

The 1900 federal census reports showed that of Nebraska's 1,066,300 people, 65,506 were born in Germany; 24,693 in Sweden; 12,531 in Denmark; 11,127 in Ireland; 9,757 in England; 8,083 in Russia; 2,773 in Scotland; 3,094 in Poland; 2,883 in Norway; and 2,340 in Switzerland; 156 of them couldn't wait but were born at sea. Another 503,336—half the population of the state—were born of parents who had come over from the Old Country.

The land, which only fifty years earlier had been occupied by eight or ten different tribes of Indians who spoke different languages, followed different tribal mores, moved after the now-gone buffalo, was filling up with as many kinds of white men; they, too, had different languages, different customs among themselves, and they were settling down on the prairie.

By 1914, when an assassination in Sarajevo ignited war in Europe, the varied citizenry of Nebraska was living together in relative peace and harmony, the unassimilated adults among the foreign-born happily speaking their native tongues, reading their foreign-language newspapers to learn about what was going on in their new country, following customs that already were being watered down from their original European beginnings. Assimilation was slow, particularly for those who lived in neighborhoods or whole communities of their own countrymen; there was no need to learn the new language, no opportunity to mingle with native-born Americans. Those who lived in settlements of mixed ethnic backgrounds, however, did learn the new language, new ways of doing things—Swiss, German, Czech and Swede priding themselves on being Americans now.

Most of the new Nebraskans were united in opposing woman suffrage, but they were sharply divided on the subject of Prohibition, recurring topics in state political circles. The Scandinavian Lutherans were on the same side as the churchly native-born white Protestants in deploring Drink, while the other immigrant groups and Catholics saw nothing morally reprehensible about schnapps, beer, and wine. Those who had relatives back in the Old Country were concerned about the war, but only as it affected their relatives; there seemed to be no reason for the United States, and therefore its citizens, to become involved; many of the new Americans had left their homelands to avoid military conscription and warfare.

By the end of the second year of the war, however, some of the German-born Americans began to question American neutrality, and some of the German-language newspapers in the state seemed to accept the reasons Kaiser Wilhelm gave for the war: Russia's hunger for land, France's hunger for revenge, and Britain's hunger for profit. Some of the German immigrants believed that the *Vaterland* had been attacked and was fighting in self-defense. When the United States declared war on Germany on April 6, 1917, the reaction in Nebraska—and elsewhere—was not universal approval. The German-born were appalled, and many native-born Nebraskans questioned the need for sacrificing American blood and resources over what they felt was a European matter. But the United States was officially at war, and almost overnight a hysteria of superpatriotism began to develop.

Congress established a National Council of Defense, and on April 25, the Nebraska legislature organized a state council and subordinate councils in each county, the bodies charged to create public sentiment for the support of the war, to detect and punish disloyal persons, suppress criticism of the war, supervise production of food and war supplies, and to serve as draft boards, ration boards, and financial agents for Liberty Bond drives and Red Cross campaigns.

Immediately, anything remotely German was suspect—language, customs, names, weiners and sauerkraut. Files were set up to record every family with a German name and that family's financial ability to subscribe to Liberty Bond and Red Cross campaigns; all Germans not yet naturalized were registered, fingerprinted, and strongly urged to begin naturalization procedures immediately;[2] lower echelons of Council of Defense workers were assigned to listen for any evidences of seditious or treasonous remarks in the countryside. The State Council of Defense urged people to use only English in public transactions, whether conversing on the phone or visiting on the street; clerks were told to refuse service to customers who could not speak English. Many Americans could not differentiate between non-English languages, and anything—Swedish, Danish, Czech—that was foreign was assumed to be German; often nationals from neutral countries were harassed.

A half-page advertisement in the *Hastings Daily Tribune* reflects some of the early wartime hysteria:

> The German National Bank has substituted the word "Nebraska" for the word "German" in its present name . . . This bank was founded thirty years ago by American citizens—its officers, directors, stockholders and depositors are American citizens with unswerving loyalty to American policies, American institutions and

2. Sheldon, *Land and the People*, 1:920.

American patriotism, practically everything they own or have was derived from American industries. They and their children have been educated in American schools, and each heart throbs and every fiber of their body vibrates with the spirit of true Americanism. Almost immediately after the declaration of war by the United States against the German Government, the German National Bank for patriotic reasons requested permission from the Comptroller of the Currency to change its title to "The Nebraska National Bank." It has taken considerable time to make the necessary arrangements.[3]

The announcement was made on April 20, not quite two weeks after the declaration of war.

During a parade in Omaha in April 1918, a crowd of several hundred persons watched as a man was taken from the Vienna Hotel for refusing to remove his hat during the playing of the national anthem. He was beaten and forced to kneel before the flag. The same punishment was doled out to John Schroeder in Lyons, who was also compelled to say "God Bless Woodrow Wilson" while kneeling, in late 1917.[4] Yellow paint was slapped on houses of persons thought to be slackers—that is—not buying enough Liberty Bonds nor subscribing enough volunteer service nor otherwise showing excessive patriotic zeal. In every community, German merchants and German individuals had to be the heaviest buyers of bonds, for their own health. In December 1917, William Volk of Madison County was forced to meet in closed session with the State Council of Defense to answer charges of disloyalty; he agreed under pressure to buy one hundred dollars worth of government securities. When the Kauf family in Hastings went to a synod meeting in Buffalo, New York, a representative of the Council of Defense came to the house and interrogated the children closely about the reason for the parents' absence. The Omaha Red Cross sponsored a "stein-breaking fest," and when the Minneapolis Symphony Orchestra presented a concert in Lincoln, the mayor ordered the music of all German composers eliminated from the program.

Individuals questioning anything concerning the war, espe-

3. *Hastings Daily Tribune,* April 20, 1917.
4. Sheldon, *Land and the People,* 1:925.

cially those with German names or heavy Germanic accents, were called into Council of Defense hearings without legal counsel; one man in Hastings, Harm Meester, was called in twice, once for being abusive when he questioned the need for sugar rationing, another time when he said that if he couldn't have more flour he wouldn't harvest his own wheat field— treasonous utterances; he was compelled to sign a statement of retraction which was later published in the local paper. A Gage County Lutheran minister was ordered to appear before both the county and the state Councils of Defense after he questioned America's alliance with Britain. The German language was dropped as a foreign language in Nebraska high schools, and in some communities public bonfires were lit on the main streets, superpatriots and gleeful students hurling the offensive German-language textbooks into the flames. In 1919 the legislature forbade the teaching of any subject in any foreign language, and prohibited the teaching of any foreign language itself until a pupil had successfully passed the eighth-grade examinations. The Nebraska Law, as it became known in educational circles, stood until the United States Supreme Court declared it unconstitutional in 1923.

University professors were suspect, sixteen of them tried by the University of Nebraska Board of Regents in June 1918. Eleven were exonerated, two were chastised, and three were asked to resign; the president of the Board of Regents, Frank Haller, a German-American, was himself a major target of abuse. The *Lincoln Star,* commenting on the case, said:

> So far as the public is concerned it has viewed the University situation for a long time with the utmost impatience. It has known that certain members of the faculty have been so saturated with bolshevikism, ultrasocialism, internationalism, and various other isms as to render them of no practical use as teachers of our Nebraska youth . . .[5]

The *Lincoln Journal* approved the return to "rugged patriotism and virile Americanism." [6] A committee was formed to investigate German books in the State Library Commission; it re-

5. *Lincoln Star,* June 20, 1918.
6. *Lincoln Journal,* June 20, 1918.

ported that the books were harmless but recommended that they be removed from circulation during the war.

German schools and German churches were the primary targets of suspicion. They were ordered to drop the use of the German language, even though neither students nor parishioners understood any other; ministers laboriously translated their sermons into English and memorized them to deliver to their uncomprehending congregations. On May 11, 1918, the Adams County Council of Defense asked the district court to deny preaching privileges to two German Lutheran ministers; on May 18, a Lutheran minister from Gresham was imprisoned. Many of those who were persecuted had sons who fought—and some sons who died—in the American trenches.

Nebraska was one of the first states to begin Americanization work; night schools and classes in citizenship for foreigners were urged in every community, "a campaign to elimination of the alien spirit, not only among the foreigners, but among the native born," an obvious reference to those first- and sometimes second-generation Americans who still spoke German.[7]

By the time of the Armistice on November 11, 1918, Nebraska was well on the way to becoming Americanized. The process had been bitter; animosities had been stirred up that took years to overcome. The superpatriotic wartime agitators put away their yellow paint and went back to their own smallnesses; Nebraska had somehow survived.

7. Sheldon, *Land and the People*, 1:924.

14

The Farmers

WHEN eager farmers swarmed into Nebraska to till her virgin acres, it never occurred to them that they would become pioneers in new agricultural procedures, developing a revolutionary system of dry-land farming to cope with unique problems of rainfall and wind.

All they knew was that the land was available and fertile. Possibly few of them realized that the four-hundred-fifty-mile breadth of Nebraska, from the ninety-fifth meridian to the one-hundred-fourth meridian, encompassed a wide range of climatic differences, and that crops and farming methods that produced well in one region might not work in all of them. The land east of the ninety-eighth meridian was not unlike land they had tilled in Illinois or Iowa—with a little less rainfall, to be sure— a mean of 27.74 inches as compared with a mean of 30.89 in Iowa and 36.61 in Illinois. The central area had less rainfall, a mean of 22.28 inches, and the west, 17.93. But the state geologist, Samuel Aughey, said in 1880 that "rainfall follows the plow," and that the great increase in the absorptive power of the soil was attributable to cultivation; he used a twenty-year study of Nebraska to prove his point.

Anyone who examines a piece of raw prairie closely must observe how compact it is. After the soil is broken, the rain as it falls is absorbed by the soil like a huge sponge. The soil gives this absorbed moisture slowly back to the atmosphere by evaporation.

Thus year by year as cultivation of the soil is extended, more of the rain that falls is absorbed and retained to be given off by evaporation, or to produce springs: this, of course, must give increasing moisture and rainfall.[1]

The opening of the new farms coincided with the transition from centuries-old methods of hand tilling to the invention of the first mechanical devices that were to make it possible for one man to plow more, cultivate more, harvest more, tend more acreage generally than ever before in history. Before then, farmers had only wooden plows which merely scratched the surface of the ground, sickles for cutting grain, and flailing as the only means of threshing. John Deere had invented a light iron plow in the early 1800s that made deep turning of the soil possible, and, from then on, ingenious tinkers on farms were to come up with new inventions to make farming possible on an increasingly larger scale.

As soon as the farmers located their homesteads, they began to plow enough land to put in their first year's crops. They did not have to strain to dig out rocks or boulders, nor chop trees and pull roots out, as their fathers before them had done farther east; all they had to do was plow the fertile soil. But it was heavy soil, for as Aughey told the farmers, "for vast ages the prairies have been pelted by the elements and trodden by millions of buffalo and other wild animals, until the naturally rich soil became as compact as a floor." [2] Breaking the thick prairie sod with its matted roots was a back-breaking job, hard physical labor; the sod-busting plow was a specially heavy one designed to cut a furrow and turn the resulting strip of sod upside down and leave it in a smooth pattern. The long moldboard, which was either a solid piece of steel or a number of rods bolted to the cutting edge of the plow, lifted the sod and turned it over so that the roots would be exposed to the elements and would decay. The grass turned underneath would die and the soil would be reduced to a good seedbed. A gauge wheel attached to the plow controlled the depth of the furrow to make sure the soil

1. Samuel Aughey, *Sketches of the Physical Geography and Geology of Nebraska* (Omaha: Omaha Nebraska Daily Republican Book and Job Office, 1880), pp. 2–3.

2. Aughey, *Sketches of the Physical Geography,* pp. 44–45.

was cut uniformly deep, and the plowshare was long enough to cut a furrow fourteen inches wide. To turn over an acre of sod required plowing seven miles of furrow, and a strong team could plow about two miles an hour. After the sod had dried out and the grass and its roots had died, a stirring plow was used to break the clods into smaller pieces so that a harrow, a horse-drawn rake, could be used to pulverize the soil.

Then the farmer planted sod-corn, known as flint or squaw corn, digging a hole, dropping a few kernels into it, covering the hole with dirt, and stamping it down with his heel, then going on to dig another hole a few inches away. It was a laborious, time-consuming process to plant even an acre of corn, which in good season would yield from ten to fifteen bushels of small, hard ears to the acre, the corn itself of low starch, needing to be ground in a mill before it could be used as food. The farmer sowed small grains—oats, barley, wheat—by scattering by hand, or broadcasting, then covered the sod by harrowing the dirt over it. Even as corn was needed for human food, acres of oats were needed for livestock feed, particularly for horses. The sowing procedures were those the farmer had used wherever he had lived before he came West; they were not peculiar to Nebraska. The next step was—it was to wait for rain.

Although Nebraska, and all of the Great Plains, have smaller amounts of rainfall than do farming areas the homesteaders were accustomed to, the moisture varies from year to year; as important to farmers as the amount of rainfall is the time of year that it falls—years of short rainfall can nevertheless be good growing years if the moisture comes during the growing season—and the amount of evaporation. The hot dry winds of July and August blowing across the prairie without let-up can sear the finest stands of corn, drying the surface of the soil to a hard crust.

During the late 1860s, the 1870s, and into the late 1880s there was generally sufficient rainfall, the moisture falling at the right times, the withering winds of late summer in abeyance. To be sure, there were some bad years—a drought in 1873 which dried up most of the field crops but not the gardens; the grasshopper invasion of late summer in 1874, which stripped every living thing—and some of the fainthearted and impoverished homesteaders left, scrawling signs, "Eaten out by Grasshoppers, Going back East to live with Wife's folks," on the tattered covers of the wagons they had lightheartedly driven to the prairies only a few months earlier. A Relief and Aid Society collected and distributed money, provisions, clothing, seeds, and other supplies, the army doled out surplus goods and rations, and the farmers survived, sure that next year would be better. It was. Thousands more immigrants flooded into the state to set up homesteads, and the great farming yields of the next dozen years justified their hopes. Farther and farther west the farms extended; it certainly seemed true that rainfall follows the plow.

Little by little, the farmers began to realize that methods that had worked for them back home, wherever that was, weren't right in Nebraska. Not until after the grim years of the 1890s, however, were they willing to try newly developed processes; they had learned that no amount of plowing could bring the rain. When the scorching winds of July 1890 swept across the state, corn wilted and died in the furrows even as the farmers watched. For more than twenty days the temperature was more than one hundred degrees, on two of them one hundred ten and one hundred fifteen. Then in 1894, starting on July 26, three days of furnacelike blasts of heat blistered all the crops in the state.

The reaction of the farmers in 1890 was political—the Populist Revolt. To the drought of 1894, the farmers reacted with despair. Some communities hired professional rainmakers who set off charges of explosives on the fairgrounds to force the water out of clouds overhead, but nothing happened; in others, the people who could leave, boarded up their houses and left. The panic of 1893 on Wall Street left banks so wobbly they could not loan money to farmers; what corn was left from last year was worth only ten cents a bushel, hogs were $2.85, and beef, $2.50 a hundredweight, and chickens were four cents a pound. Again the people of Nebraska had to call on relief societies for food and clothing to sustain them through the winter.

As soon as the drought was over and the fields began to glisten with moisture, the farmers started to listen to new ideas about farming methods, procedures that dry-land farmers still find valid. Hardy W. Campbell of Lincoln became the country's most outspoken advocate of dry-land farming, the techniques necessary to produce crops in areas where rainfall ranges from ten to thirty inches a year. The lack of rainfall keeps nutrients from washing away, Campbell said, so the soil in arid lands is more fertile than in humid ones; the clue to capturing the fertility is to conserve what moisture there is, storing it up in times of rainfall to use in times of drought. The soil itself provides capillary action; when the sandy loam is plowed deep and stirred, the water begins to come toward the top, in a wicklike action. Then the farmer harrows a sort of dust mulch over the top to keep the water from evaporating. During the growing season, he cultivates the rows of plants to stir up the moisture, and then harrows or rakes to keep it in. According to Campbell's philosophy of the soil, widely accepted by Nebraska plowmen, the successful dry-land farmer in Nebraska was one who had his corn "laid-by by the Fourth of July," cultivated for the last time before the kernels would form on the cob.

Even now the dry-land farmer who follows Campbell's theories does not use all of his land all the time; he allows part of it to lie fallow each year; summer fallow allows the soil to collect moisture while it is at rest. During the winter, land which is not seeded is left with stalks or straw still standing to catch the falling snow, and in the spring, the vegetable material is plowed under. The farmers themselves discovered that rotating crops helped preserve land fertility, and later, agricultural advisors suggested they alternate with leguminous crops, such as peas, beans, and clovers, which would add nitrogen to the soil. Since the land in the Great Plains was the first large semi-arid area to be put to farming use, all of the procedures were experimental; Nebraska became a test plot for dry-land farming.

Farm implements kept up with the changes in farm procedures, farmers themselves tinkering together some of the new inventions, professional engineers, others; in addition to the large, widely known implement companies, smaller ones sprang up in some Nebraska farming communities. Turning plows, disk plows, subsoil plows, spike-tooth, spring-tooth, and disk harrows to rake; various kinds of cultivators to stir up the soil; disk seed drills to plant seed; harvesters to cut small grain; grain headers to take the head or grain from the oats, barley, or wheat stalks; farmers needed more and more in the way of equipment. The first heavy implements were drawn by oxen, later by horses equipped with blinders so they could see only straight ahead and not be distracted by activities to the side. Long fringed netting of twine over their backs flipped in the breeze to sweep off the biting horseflies in the heat of summer. Some large-scale farmers bought heavy Percheron or Clydesdale horses for their powerful pulling ability. By the turn of the century, in every part of Nebraska some farmers were adventuresome enough to buy steam-powered equipment, ponderous coal-fired, cast-iron, locomotivelike contraptions that crawled heavily into the field and, with sputterings of scalding water and flapping of belts, provided the power for threshing machines and other harvest equipment.

At first the farmers planted corn, oats, and spring wheat; before the end of the century, Nebraskans learned of Turkey-red wheat, a variety brought to the Great Plains by Mennonite farmers emigrating from Russia, where the strain had proved successful. The seed was planted in the fall, and sprouted, but lay at rest during the winter months; it grew during the spring and early summer months and was ready for cutting in early July in Nebraska. Winter wheat, in its many variations, came to provide the backbone of much of the Nebraska agricultural economy. Certain varieties of sorghums grew well in Nebraska, providing sweetening, at first for people—almost every community or crossroads had a sorghum press that could crunch the juice from the fibrous stalks to be boiled into molasses—and later, to be used for animal feed.

The first farms were general ones, families growing garden crops for themselves, oats and hay for their livestock, corn or wheat or both for themselves and for sale, and enough livestock—a cow or two, pigs, chickens—for meat for their own use. During the growing season, the farmer's day started before dawn when he got up to care for the animals before going out into the field. He plowed, disked, harrowed, cultivated; he tended fences. When the wheat or other small grain was ripe, he cut it, bound it together—at first by hand, later with a binder machine—set it up in shocks in the field to dry. The cut wheat had to sit for about six weeks to harden, "go through the sweat" was the term, before it was threshed in a huge machine that separated the kernels from the straw. Threshing was a neighborhood undertaking with many men gathering at one farm to work together, then going to the next farm and the next, until all of the grain was harvested.

Women and children were as busy as the menfolk, cooking for threshers; noontime was dinnertime. They prepared mountains of fried chicken, mashed potatoes and good, rich gravy, plates of thick-sliced homemade bread still aromatic from the oven, a staggering selection of homemade pies—green-apple, gooseberry, raisin. From the windmill cooler they brought bowls of yellow homemade butter with the housewife's own distinctive design molded in the top; from the cellar they carried jars of homemade jellies and jams—wild plum, chokecherry, wild grape. A man was known by the eats his woman put out; if the wife served good, solid, substantial fare, and plenty of it, the farmer found it easy to round up adequate help for his threshing.

When the men in the field heard the dinner gong, they rushed to the house, washed their hands and faces at the pump in the yard, and stomped into the house to sit at the dining-table, which had all of its extensions in it so that it sometimes stretched across half the house. In the same workmanlike manner that they performed in the field, the men addressed the steaming mounds of food, piling their plates high and eating with gusto. While the women replenished the serving dishes from the kettles on the cob-fired cookstoves, the children watched hungrily, hoping there would be something left for them. Finally the men pushed back their chairs, picked their teeth, and then left to go back to the field. The women redded up the table, washed the dishes, and prepared for the second sitting, when the women and children could eat.

Midafternoon the eight- or ten-year-old girl children—for the boys their age were in the fields—were sent on the water detail. From the pump in the yard, the mother cranked cold, fresh water into crockery jugs, put in the corks, or stoppers of some kind, wrapped a wet burlap cloth around the crocks, and sent the youngsters to run as fast as they could, before the water got

warm, the quarter-mile or so over the furrows to the crews in
the field. There, in the shade of the threshing machine, the men
stopped their work to gulp the water, passing the jug from one
man to the next.

Between threshing the small grain and picking the corn in the
fall, farmers had to put up hay, cutting it, sweeping it into
windrows to cure in the sun—green hay rots in the stack—and
then piling it into huge stacks to provide feed for the horses and
other livestock in the winter. Much of the farmland and farm
labor was channeled into supplying food and lodging for the
horses which provided transportation and power for the farms;
when gasoline-powered equipment replaced horsepower on
farms shortly before the beginning of World War II, land and
labor were released for other duties.

In the fall, about the time of the first frost, the corn was ready
for harvesting, the kernels dented, or dimpled, and hard. The
farmer rigged up his wooden wagon—added a couple of boards
on one side of it to form a bangboard—hitched up the horses,
and headed for the field. While the horse plodded through the
field, the wagon straddling a row of corn, the farmer picked the
corn, using a curved husking knife or a peg strapped to the palm
of his heavy cotton husking gloves to slash off the dry husk
around the ear of corn. Then he twisted the ear free of the stalk
and tossed it into the wagon against the bangboard so that it
would fall into the box, each movement so deft and controlled
that a good workman could pick as many as seventy or eighty
bushels in a single day, if the stalks were tall and close together.
(Some bad years when the stalks were sparse and short, the
huskers got kinks in their backs from having to lean over; they
could husk no more than twenty bushels a day because of the
extra physical labor of having to walk from stalk to stalk and
bending over for the corncob.) Slash, twist, bang. Slash, twist,
bang—there was a regular, rhythmic, almost ballet motion to
the procedure. The horse, from years of practice, could tell
from the thumps how fast to move through the field. When the
wagon box was full, the husker unloaded the ears with their
hard orange kernels into the corncrib, a circular enclosure made
of wired slats which allowed air to circulate to finish the drying
process for the corn. As the corn was needed for feed, it was

shelled, at first by a hand-cranked apparatus, later by a powered one; the kernels went to the livestock, the cobs to the kitchen to fuel the cookstove.

Husking bees were social events, neighborhood get-togethers, families gathering at a farm in the area to work together. While the men were in the fields, moving from row to row to husk the corn, back at the house the women unwrapped tea towels from the bowls of food they brought and set up the picnic tables; the children played tag in and around the implements in the farm-yard and petted the new kittens in the barn. A husking bee could also be a philanthropic occasion; whenever a farm family had a crisis—particularly if the man was laid up with illness or in-jury—the neighbors were sure to come in to help get the corn in, or the wheat, too, for that matter.

During the late 1920s and 1930s, husking contests developed on county, state, and national levels. Men assembled at a farm where the corn rows of uniform length were marked off, and, at a signal, the contestants started out, one to a row, husking, twisting, flinging their ears of corn into the wagons; the first man through was declared the winner if his ears were cleanly husked. In 1933, Sherman Henrikson of Lancaster County was the national cornhusking champion, husking 27.62 bushels in thirty minutes.

Although the homestead laws and railroad land sales were in-tended to create a region of landowners rather than tenants, and the farmers who were attracted to Nebraska came so that they could be landholders, various financial disasters through the years brought the banker—or someone else—to Foreclose the Mortgage. In other ways, too, ownership of land shifted; some farmers, having proved up their land, moved to town to live, renting out their farm property; others leased land to a son, who hoped to inherit it eventually. In some cases, speculators bought up farmland and leased it to tenants. Even so, however, the ag-ricultural census of 1880, taken after the few disastrous years of the 1870s, showed that only eighteen percent of the farms in Nebraska were operated by tenants.

Nebraska's most celebrated landlord was William E. Scully, an Englishman who owned what was termed at the time probably the largest improved farmland accumulation in America. He came to the United States in 1851 and with a horse and spade investigated the depth and quality of soil from Pennsylvania to Nebraska, eventually accumulating 210,000 acres in Nebraska, Kansas, Missouri, and Illinois; between 1881 and 1886 he bought 65,000 acres in Gage and Nuckolls counties, Nebraska, leasing it to tenants. The Nebraska granger of the day did not approve. An editorial in the *Nebraska State Journal* of February 2, 1887, deplored the

> . . . tendency among foreign capitalists to hold large sections of Nebraska land as permanent investments, for the introduction of the landlord system of Great Britain which has proved such a curse to Ireland, Scotland and some parts of England. One Irish capitalist has today over 40,000 acres of land in Nuckolls county that is being peopled by tenants.[3]

The indignant legislature joined those of Illinois and Kansas in passing a law in 1887 calling for forfeiture of all lands belonging to nonresident aliens and barring them from acquiring or inheriting farmland; when the United States Supreme Court held the Illinois law unconstitutional, Nebraska amended her law enough to make it enforceable. Scully then took out naturalization papers and became an American citizen, residing in Washington, D.C. Upon his death, his lands were divided between his sons, and upon their deaths, among his grandsons. Robin and Bill Scully, whose office is in Beatrice, Nebraska, now own the Nebraska lands. Under the tenancy contracts, the managers of the Scully farms, who usually remain for twenty years or more, sometimes for generations, are required by their leases to rotate crops, plant legumes, and diversify their crops, practicing careful husbandry; they make surface improvements themselves and own them. Although the Scully lands remained intact, despite the Nebraska law intent upon breaking them up, the dire prediction of absentee landlordism and subsequent serfdom in the state never took place.

---

3. Quoted in Addison E. Sheldon, *Land Systems and Land Policies in Nebraska,* (Lincoln: Publications of the Nebraska State Historical Society, 23, 1936), p. 323. The newspaper reference to Scully as an Irishman was misleading; he was an Englishman who happened also to own some lands in Ireland.

By 1900, following the grim years of the 1890s, the tenancy rate on Nebraska farms rose to thirty-six percent, where it remained, off and on, for the next six decades or more, except for the wretched years of the Dust Bowl, when anybody was fortunate to keep anything; the tenancy rate then was almost fifty percent, the banks who owned most of the foreclosed farms sometimes almost begging the former owners to remain on them simply to have them occupied. From 1954 to 1969, however, as individual farms became larger in size and fewer in number, the tenancy rate dropped, so that at the beginning of the 1970s, it was down to twenty-five percent, only one out of four farms operated by a tenant rather than the owner.

The early years of the new century were good for Nebraska farmers; yields were good, expenses low enough and prices high enough that they could afford new implements to take some of the drudgery out of the work and occasionally leave the farm in the summertime to go to Chautauqua—week-long programs of inspirational speeches, singing groups and band concerts, nondenominational sermons, and an occasional travelogue. Performances took place under a spreading tent or a frame pavilion in any of a dozen towns throughout the state. The farmer would have the hired man—for almost every farm now had at least one—drive the family in the wagon to the nearest railroad stop, where they boarded the special train to take them to Crete or Hebron or Long Pine or Fullerton, for instance, or Lincoln, where they would rent a tent and spend an exciting several days at the campground. For a score of years, from the late 1890s onward, Chautauqua was an exciting cultural, sociable event in the lives of Nebraskans, townspeople as well as farmers. William Jennings Bryan, their own perennial candidate for the presidency, was often a headline speaker on the circuit, his mellifluous voice stirring them, soothing them, always pleasing them. Senator Bob LaFollette of Wisconsin was another favorite, as was Madame Ernestine Schumann-Heink, the contralto with the big voice. For many in the audience, Chautauqua was their only exposure to the arts.

Farmers experimented with new crops; sugar beets, potatoes, and alfalfa did astonishingly well in the Panhandle areas of the

North Platte Valley, for instance. New strains of familiar crops, winter wheat in particular, brought improved yields, and what was more important, more assurance of success on the dry-land farms of the most arid reaches of western Nebraska. During these years, farmers began to specialize, the ones in the more humid eastern areas concentrating on growing corn, those in the broad, sweeping dry flatlands of the west, planting wheat.

World War I erupted; the world needed food—food which Nebraska farms could produce. Prices spiraled; wheat, which was eighty cents a bushel in 1910, was a dollar sixty in 1916, and by 1918, almost two dollars. Corn leapt from thirty-six cents in 1910 to more than a dollar and a quarter in 1918. The Council of Defense, and all other governmental bodies concerned with the war, kept crying, "Wheat Will Win the War!" The farmers saw their duty. They plowed up their pastures and planted them to wheat; they stretched out into the southwestern parts of the state, into Cheyenne, Deuel, Kimball, and Perkins counties, and parts of Banner, Garden and Keith counties, and into the high plains west of the Sandhills, plowing them and discovering that their hot, dry acres produced two-dollar wheat. Almost three million acres of land were added to production during the war years, almost forty percent of it in the wheatlands of the west.

To help bring in the abundant wartime harvests, hundreds of itinerant farm workers came into the state in 1916, members of the Industrial Workers of the World, more commonly known as "Wobblies," intent on organizing farm labor. Although farmers always depended on transient workers during the harvest season, this was the only time that the Wobblies came onto Nebraska farms in any numbers. In some courthouse squares, where traditionally farmers and would-be harvest hands got together, there were skirmishes between the outsiders and the regular neighborhood laborers, but in most Nebraska communities where the Wobblies came in, the men got their assignments and worked well in the fields, providing badly needed labor. Their lasting contribution to the farm scene was that in many communities they succeeded in breaking up the broker system of hiring casual farm labor. Until then, an intermediary between farmer and farmhand made the arrangements, claiming a sizable fee, as much as a dollar a day, from the worker in return for securing his job.

When the war ended and prices continued to soar, farmers assumed that a new era of farming had arrived; they bought whatever land they could find, at whatever price, mortgaging what they already had. From 1910 to 1920, mortgage debt on Nebraska farms increased one hundred seventy percent. And then the bottom dropped out; from 1921 to 1923, one-fourth of the farmers failed. Although for townspeople, the 1920s were a period of prosperity, for most Nebraska farmers the decade was one of struggle to pay off debt, high-interest loans for high-priced land with low-priced wheat and corn. Although from 1923 to 1926 there was a brief period of recovery, prices collapsed again. Six hundred fifty Nebraska banks, most of them country banks, closed their doors during the 1920s, too far extended on credit to farmers.

The crash on Wall Street in 1929 affected Nebraska farmers only indirectly; few of them were gamblers in the stock market. What did hurt them was that even more banks closed. In looking back—which is always easier than deciphering now—it seems that the great crises in financial markets that have upset the United States as a whole have somehow been followed, in Nebraska and in the Great Plains generally, with disastrous climate, which has been even more devastating than the economic debacle: the panic of 1873 was followed by drought and grasshoppers; the panic of 1893, by drought and unbelievable heat; the crash of 1929, a cataclysmic combination of natural disasters. It was not the collapse of the stock market that hurt Nebraska; it was the years of drought, dust, heat, and despair that followed in the 1930s, years so harsh they left psychological scars that remain even yet, almost a half-century later.

The farmers' financial condition was precarious to begin with. When the unrelenting heat and dryness and wind seared the crops in the field, there was no produce to sell, no feed for the livestock, mighty little food for human consumption. As the winds blew day after day, eventually the topsoil went with them, the soil that was the lifeblood, the means of existence, for Nebraskans. At that moment, then, and for most of the decade

of the 1930s, Nebraska became truly the Great American
Desert.

The rains stopped, the heat rolled in, and the winds swept up
tons of fine, powdery soil and blew it from Oklahoma to the
Dakotas and beyond, red soil from Oklahoma, yellow from
Kansas, other colors from other states, all mixed together in
frightening clouds that swirled through the sky, obscuring the
sun, creating a darkness at noon. When the winds finally died
down, the dust settled in drifts around the tumbleweeds piled up
against fence rows or sheds or chicken houses, there to rest until
the next winds picked it up and swept it somewhere else.

The approach of a dust storm was an awesome sight; the air
would become murky, and then from the southwest a huge
roiling mass of dust, visible for miles, would roll across the
prairie, encompassing everything in its way, shutting out the
sun, then moving on in its course. The year 1935 was the worst
of all, for the dust storms were more frequent, more dense, the
heat more intense and longer lasting. Despite dust masks and
respirators, which many persons in the southwestern part of the
state wore, there were dust-related illnesses, particularly pneumonia and appendicitis, but country doctors developed new
techniques for handling such cases; they did not remove a rup-
tured appendix but put in drains so that the infection could drib-
ble out, and their rate of recovery was phenomenal.

Although summertime days in Nebraska are hot, the elevation
of much of the state means that at night, temperatures fall to tol-
erable limits, but during the mid-1930s, the heat rolled in at
midnight almost as much as at noon. Farmers and townspeople
alike went outdoors to sleep on porches or in back yards, wherever they could find an errant breeze to cool them off, to escape
the unbearable heat trapped in their houses. Many housewives
learned that a bathtowel dripping with water and placed where
the wind could reach it would cool the house a little, but it had
to be changed often because it would trap some of the gritty
dust and become mud. The silt seeped into everything—sills,
floors, blankets, dishes, food, everything in the house.

At infrequent intervals, there was rain—sometimes just a
shower falling with enough dust that it was mud by the time it
hit the ground, other times a gully-washer, little of the moisture

falling at a time to benefit farmers. In May 1935, a torrential rainstorm flooded the Republican River, leaving a hundred persons drowned and ninety missing. The next year there were grasshoppers, eating what little the farmers had been able to grow during the hottest summer yet. At least there was variety in the calamities that swept the state during the 1930s, the most prolonged period of disaster the state has ever known.

Each spring the farmers who were left plowed their fields and sowed their crops; some years all the corn from a quarter section of land could be piled into a couple of bushel baskets, and some years there wasn't even that much. They raked tumbleweeds into stacks to provide some sort of forage for the stock, but sometimes the hungry jackrabbits beat the cattle there. Heavily mortgaged farms were claimed by banks; even those farms which were clear often went on the auction block for nonpayment of taxes. Many farmers moved into town to work on federally sponsored works projects—never admitting it was going on relief—to earn cash for food for their families. Others by the hundreds piled their possessions into their cars and headed west to California; between 1930 and 1940, the population of the state dropped by sixty-five thousand people.

In 1932 alone, more than six hundred thousand acres of Nebraska farmland were abandoned, much of it land that had been opened during World War I to wheat cultivation. Marginal land at best, it should never have been cultivated but left in pastureland; twenty years after the fact, farmers were paying the price of their wartime folly.

Had it not been for massive infusions of federal aid, Nebraska could not have survived the 1930s. Aid for the farmers came through the Agricultural Adjustment Administration, later the Federal Land Bank and the Farm Security Administration. In 1933 the Triple A offered farmers a dollar an acre for limiting wheat and corn production and began promoting soil and water conservation; that same year it embarked on a program that indignant farmers called Henry Wallace's pig-killing, the slaughtering of a half-million pregnant sows to force pork prices up. With families hungry, farmers could not figure how wanton destruction of food could help the situation. The next year, they began to understand. Then the government bought five hundred thousand emaciated, ribby cows—those that had survived the pneumonia caused from poking around in the tumbleweeds to find a mouthful of food—and many were too weak to ship to market; they had to be shot on the site. Figures for 1933 alone—and that was not the worst year, 1935 was—show that Nebraska farmers received ten million dollars for warehoused corn loans, forty million for the corn-hog program, five million for the wheat-adjustment program, and one million for the pig- and brood-sow slaughter.

By the late 1930s, the rain began to come back, the winds dropped, the heat abated, and farming in Nebraska was possible again. Convinced now of the importance of soil conservation, which Dr. George E. Condra of the University of Nebraska Conservation Division had been preaching for years, farmers began to plant shelter belts of five or more long rows of trees through the countryside to trap the snow in winter and block the wind in summer, and to adapt contour planting to their own lands to prevent erosion. They began to apply what they had learned about dry-land farming and to think in terms of conserv- ing the fertility of the land rather than spending it, realizing now that they must husband their resources carefully.

In 1938 a new Agricultural Adjustment Act provided for crop-production control by direct allotment of acreage, provided for parity payments, and standardized the conditions under which commodity loans would be offered. From then on, the federal government was part of the farming scene, not only in Nebraska but in the rest of the country as well.

Although the rainfall in Nebraska is unpredictable, the state has more miles of surface streams than any other state and more usable, fresh, underground water. From the beginning of Ne- braska as a farming region, scientists and farmers alike looked at the running streams and dreamed grandiose dreams of irriga- tion, of somehow channeling that water into usable form for farmland and pasture. The mayor of Omaha, for instance, mak- ing a Fourth of July speech in York in 1878, went on and on about what he called the abundant natural irrigation through the spreading rivers of Nebraska, the winding creeks and numerous streams and never-failing springs; others before and after him orated in similar vein.

In the late 1880s, farmers along the South Platte in western Nebraska constructed a few ditches and diverted water into about ten thousand acres, drawing sneers or contemptuous laughter for their efforts. But after the dry years of the early 1890s, thoughtful men all over the state looked at their nearby rivers and mused; a state irrigation convention was held in 1891, with Robert W. Furnas, former governor and longtime agricultural enthusiast, its first president. By 1895 the legislature created a state Board of Irrigation, and by 1899, almost one hundred fifty thousand acres in western Nebraska were irrigated from the Platte, and in other parts of the state other lands were irrigated from the North Loup, Republican, and Elkhorn, all of the ditches built with private capital. Others were planned, but the cost of digging ditches was too great for individuals to contemplate, even those banded together.

Two federal laws, one in 1902 and another in 1911, established the means of government financing, and in 1910, the Pathfinder Reservoir on the North Platte, in Wyoming, was built, with a canal on either side of the river bringing irrigation water down into Nebraska. The water that trickled out of those ditches provided the start for the sugar-beet industry in the Scottsbluff area, which now produces more than a million and a half tons of beets a year. Another reservoir was built in Wyoming in 1928.

In 1935, central Nebraska learned to its jubilation that the long-dreamed-of series of dams, reservoirs, and diversionary canals necessary for irrigating a half-million acres of land in Gosper, Phelps, Kearney, and Adams counties had been approved by President Roosevelt; construction on the ten-million-dollar project began during the depths of the depression. The project, known later as the Tri-County Project, had been the dream of dedicated men for more than twenty years, but before it was much more than started, the state supreme court, in a monumental decision, declared that water could not be diverted to lands or projects outside the watershed, a decision that hampered complete utilization of ditch irrigation in the state.

Another irrigation project started on the Loup River and, in subsequent years, others on the Elkhorn, Republican, and Niobrara rivers, all of them providing the means for impounding water for release upon demand into irrigation ditches, for generating electrical power, and for creating recreational areas. Beside the ruts of the Oregon Trail along the North Platte River, for instance, the second-largest earthen dam in the world impounds water for Lake McConaughy, where sailing regattas are held each year, sailboats scudding across part of the area once considered the Great American Desert. From the hydroelectric part of the irrigation systems, some of the electricity for Nebraska is generated.

While some men planned ditch irrigation, others were considering pumps, and during the 1890s, an amazing variety of homemade windmills pumped water in the Platte Valley. But the mechanical means for pump irrigation were slow in developing, even though scientists had discovered that Nebraska lies on the largest underground water supply in the nation. Ditch irrigation, the oldest form known to mankind, depends on trenches carrying water from the source to the fields; the land should be level so that the water can flow easily. Water-bearing trenches use a considerable amount of land, and only the acreages that are close by can utilize the water from the irrigation ditches. Those farms which lie fifty or a hundred miles away from irrigation canals had no access to the water.

Farmers who were digging wells to secure water for their own household uses realized that if they could pump water out of the ground to drink, surely they could pump enough more to irrigate their fields, so that even though they were far from canals they could have the life-giving water for their crops. The development of pump irrigation was dependent upon the manufacture of internal-combustion engines; some of the earliest irrigation pumps in Nebraska were merely tractor engines or small truck engines, cemented into place beside the well, whirring away to lift the water from the well to the top of the ground where it flowed between the rows of corn.

By the early 1930s, manufacturers in Nebraska were producing irrigation pumps, but the farm economy was in such straitened conditions that few farmers could afford to buy them, and by 1939, only eighty thousand acres of land were under pump irrigation. But from then on, as farmers could afford the cost of wells, pumps, pipes, and other equipment necessary for irrigation systems, they installed them, and by 1954, more than one million three hundred thousand acres of land were under irrigation, either open-ditch or pump. Many of the pumps were manufactured in the state, as was most of the pipe—miles of it—necessary to carry the water from the pump to the furrows to be irrigated; the gated pipe, with holes to allow the water to run into the furrows, was made of aluminum, its light weight requiring less manpower to handle the pipe in the fields.

Although the climate did not change, and recurring dry years still came, farmers realized the value of installing irrigation systems on their farms; they could see that their neighbors' irrigated fields produced crops despite drought. The initial cost of putting down a well and installing equipment was high, but the astronomically increased farm yields justified the investment because a few years of bumper crops paid for the installation. Various types of fuels powered the pumps, electricity occasionally, but usually diesel or tractor gasoline, or propane which had to be supplied in drums or barrels taken to the site. In the early 1950s, low-cost natural gas became available as an irrigation fuel when Kansas-Nebraska Natural Gas Company, a farm-oriented pipeline company, built networks of lines for irrigation purposes through the central and western parts of the state, making it possible for farmers to connect their irrigation pumps to an inexpensive, convenient source of fuel. In 1953 the company supplied 700 irrigation wells in Nebraska; in 1976 the number had grown to 10,330.

In the mid-1950s, the Valmont Company in Valley began production of a water-driven center-pivot system of overhead sprinklers, an irrigation procedure which watered the land from above, as from a shower, rather than from the ground near the roots. This invention, a modern-day refinement of an ancient principle, made possible the irrigation of uneven land, for it did not depend upon gravity flow for the water to move across the field on the ground, and it simplified the irrigation of non-row crops. Furrow irrigation on the ground meant that water had to trickle between the rows of corn or milo, but wheat, alfalfa, and pastureland are not planted in widely separated rows. The new system saved manpower, for once it was installed, it stayed in place, and it proved to be far more efficient in its use of water, with much less running off the field, going below the root-line of crops, or evaporating than in the furrow system. Any furrow or gravity-flow type of irrigation, whether the water comes from canals or from a pump, is from fifty to sixty percent efficient, whereas the overhead sprinkler utilizes from eighty to ninety percent of the water.

Perhaps a score or more of manufacturers are now producing center-pivot overhead sprinkling systems, almost all of them based in Nebraska. To install the well and pump, the pipes, and the other necessary equipment for such a system costs fifty thousand dollars or more for a quarter-section of land, one hundred sixty acres, but such is the advantage of irrigation that the high initial cost is justified. By 1965, almost three million acres of Nebraska farmland were under irrigation, and by 1975, more than five million, a quarter of the croplands of the state. The whir of pumps across the farmlands is a reassuring sound to farmers whose fathers and grandfathers spent days of anxiety looking up into the skies wondering if the rains would ever come.

The revolution in Nebraska farming began with irrigation, and in the next few years agricultural procedures had changed so greatly that they bore only slight resemblance to those of a quarter-century past. Important though it is, water alone cannot produce crops in the field. Early students of irrigation wondered whether the fertility of the soil would be affected by irrigation runoff, and from the middle 1950s onward, Nebraska farmers concentrated more and more of their efforts on replenishing nutrients to the soil.

When the first sod-breaking farmers discovered that the new soil was fertile, they assumed that it would always be productive. What fertilizers they had were simply animal wastes that collected in the barn; from time to time farmers would haul out the manure and plow it into the soil in the field; the procedure of fertilizing the soil was not generally considered to be of great importance. As they developed more sophistication in farming techniques, farmers rotated crops to prevent wearing out of the soil, and planted leguminous crops to replenish the nitrogen; a few learned firsthand of the damage that too much nitrogen can create, for a few thrifty Nebraska farmers left the nitrogen-bearing nodules in the soil too long, assuming that if a little enrichment is good, more is better. In one season, they learned the damage that nitrogen burn can cause, and were more cautious in years to come.

In the late 1950s, chemical fertilizers began to be available in commercial quantities, the nitrogen fertilizer manufactured from natural gas supplied either in liquid form to be sprayed on the soil or in dried pellets which were disked into the ground. The enrichment of the soil boosted crop yields dramatically, particularly when irrigation plus natural rainfall supplied sufficient water to the land.

More chemistry came into agriculture with the development of insecticides and fungicides designed to control the various bugs, beetles, worms, nematodes, and rusts that had caused loss of crops in the field from year to year. Whereas a generation earlier, Nebraska farmers poured kerosene on grasshoppers to destroy them, they now used sophisticated new versions of petroleum distillates, some of them, it turned out, as toxic to man as to the bugs they were designed to destroy. The old Paris green and other primitive poisons which farmers had used spasmodically in earlier years, pumping by hand onto the plants, were probably even more dangerous than the new chemicals, but they had not been used in the same lavish amounts.

Almost concurrently various herbicides came out of the test tubes, chemicals designed to keep down weeds in the fields, eliminating the need for hoeing, either by hand or with harrows or disks. No longer, then, was the farmer committed to have his corn laid-by by the Fourth of July; he planted the seed and then, with his chemical sprayer, fertilized and wormed and weeded it. He did not stir the soil after that.

By the late 1920s, too, the seeds the Nebraska farmers planted, and even the crops they sowed, began to be vastly different from those of a generation before. Plant geneticists had been at work in their laboratories and test plots, and by the 1940s, most farmers planted hybridized corn, the new seed containing the best qualities of many strains, producing more kernels, of higher nutritional content, on sturdier, drought-resistant plants than earlier varieties. The new corn had only slight resemblance to the flint corn or later open-pollinated corn the early farmers in Nebraska had planted; as the science of plant genetics becomes more sophisticated, the quality of the seed improves. Farm youngsters who in an earlier generation would have been working with their fathers in the fields, driving teams of horses or binding shocks of wheat, now spend part of the summer working for seed companies detasseling corn, the first step in hybridization. Seed companies have been working for years on hybridizing wheat, but the seed of wheat is much more complicated than that of corn, and the dramatic changes which have been made in corn production have not yet come to wheat.

Among the new crops were various kinds of milo, a sorghum whose clusters of grain range in color from golden to chestnut to black, providing highly nutritious feed for cattle. The milo was an improvement on the early-day kaffir corn or millet of earlier years, but planted far more extensively than its predecessor; in 1973 one hundred twenty-five thousand acres of Nebraska farmland were planted to sorghums. Soybeans, too, were added to the roster of crops, producing feed for animals as well as oils for industrial uses. Almost three hundred thousand acres were planted to alfalfa. Much of the alfalfa is dehydrated into pellets, which are easier to handle than the cumbersome old bales for livestock feeding.

With new seeds and chemicals, basic farming procedures also changed; rather than planting crops in rows sufficiently far apart for a man and a team or tractor to drive between them to cultivate the soil, the Nebraska farmer of the 1970s planted his corn rows close together to raise more plants per acre. Once the field was seeded, he did not till it or cultivate it unless the herbicide floated off; only a few farmers believed that tilling helps corn growth. The acre that yielded twenty to twenty-five bushels of corn in a good year a generation earlier made as much as two hundred bushels; wheat yield increased from thirty to sixty bushels to the acre.

The end of the Dust Bowl days in Nebraska marked the advent of the mechanized farm. Although engineers earlier had hoped that steam-powered equipment would boost farming methods, it was the development of farm machinery with internal-combustion engines that mechanized farming. Gasoline-powered tractors had been in production for years—any youngster on the farm who could drive a Model T yearned for a tractor—but faithful old Dobbin remained a barnyard fixture during the 1920s and 1930s simply because mechanized equipment cost money. Federal support of agriculture during the days of the late 1930s meant that through soil-bank payments and others, farmers had cash, and by the early 1940s every farmyard had a gasoline tank near the barn to fuel the various pieces of new equipment. Dobbin was finally gone, and the acres that had been used for his pastureland and his oats were now plowed into food production for human consumption.

Reapers, binders, headers, and threshers were replaced with one single machine, a combine whose gigantic structure moved through the fields cutting wheat and threshing it, accomplishing in hours what many primitive machines, many men, and many horses had taken weeks to do a generation earlier. With a change of attachments, that same behemoth machine replaced all the manpower in the cornfield, picking, husking, and shelling the corn in one tour across the field, turning out in one afternoon the equivalent of hundreds of man hours of hand labor. Even a single small utility tractor, the most insignificant machine of all in the large implement shed, had more pulling power than a team of Percherons, the heavy draft horses of a generation ago, who moved slowly even when they were not tugging.

Whereas the farmer of a generation or two ago in Nebraska developed calluses on his hands—corn husking lotion is still available in drug stores, but few farmers buy it any more—the farmer of today develops his as he sits in the air-conditioned cab of his $50,000 machine, earplugs in his ears connected to the audio equipment of his tape player, the music displacing the noise of the machine as it roars through the field. The trucks that the kernels roll into as he picks, husks, and shells the corn cost him from twelve to eighteen thousand dollars each. Before he could harvest the field, he had to plant it, using his thirty-thousand-dollar tractor to pull his seven-thousand-dollar planter, and he disked it with the nine-thousand-dollar tandem disk attached to his tractor.

Excluding land, buildings, and livestock, the average Nebraska corn farmer has from $120,000 to $145,000 invested in simply the mechanical devices that enable him to farm his section; the general farmer, who may also grow some wheat and have some livestock, probably swine, will have from $160,000 to $185,000 invested in his machinery. Land, buildings, irrigation equipment, seed, and chemicals are all extra.

Farming in Nebraska has become big business. The capital expenditure necessary for any operation is so great that a farmer is not justified in tilling only a few acres; he buys more and more land, as it becomes available, so that there are fewer farms now than there were a generation ago, but each individual farm is much larger. The fields his father or grandfather worked are not big enough now, in many cases, for him to get his enormous rigs into; sometimes he has dug out the shelter belts—five rows of full-grown trees now—to connect one field with another for more efficient tilling of the soil. Whereas his father talked of the "south forty," meaning acres, he himself talks of his land in terms of sections, or six-hundred-forty-acre plots.

No longer is he dependent on the hired man or threshing crews or cornhusking gangs. He works alone. The Nebraska farmer of one hundred years ago provided enough food to feed four people; now he provides enough for fifty-nine. He relies less on muscle power and more on brain power than did his forebears; he must be a mechanic to keep his machinery in working order, a chemist to understand the materials he applies to his fields, an economist to figure out his long-range plans, and an accountant to figure his immediate profit and loss. He fills out papers, returns, charts, forms. But no matter the differences, he has striking similarities with his ancestors: he loves the soil.

15

The Cornhuskers

OMEHOW, sometime along the way, the diverse peoples who make up the state achieved cohesiveness. Rather than identifying themselves as ranchers first, or farmers, or townspeople of this community or that, they considered themselves Nebraskans. Although the cowhand on the ranch in the far western reaches could not understand all the problems of the worker in an insurance office in Omaha, four hundred miles away, he felt a bond of kinship with him: both were Nebraskans.

And as Nebraskans, they helped create some unique institutions. The first was the unicameral, or single-house, legislature, the only one in the nation. Although the idea was not new in the United States—some early colonial assemblies had had only one legislative body—by the time of statehood all the states had two-house legislatures, one body presumably to act as a check upon the other. Even though the Nebraska legislature was probably neither better nor worse than any other, for almost a score of years, starting in the mid-1910s, political reformers tried to interest the state in changing its legislative structure to a single-house body, but never quite succeeded in getting the proposition on the ballot. Early in 1934, Senator George W. Norris, who at that time had served in Congress for more than thirty years and had only recently promoted administrative reform in Congress, assumed active leadership in promoting the new legislative system. This time the state was receptive. It was in the depths of the Great Depression, the dust was blowing, and the heat was rolling in; in times of drought and distress, the state seemed interested in innovations, as it had shown during the 1890s. The new system promised efficiency and, even better, economy in government; and the voters had faith in Norris. Within four months he succeeded in getting enough signatures on petitions to place the issue on the ballot, and from then on, the movement for a unicameral legislature rapidly gained strength. With the help of civic leaders, political-science students, and others, Norris visited every part of the state during the campaign, and when the ballots were counted in November, the unicameral amendment had won by a majority of almost sixty percent.

The amendment provided for a one-house legislature of no fewer than thirty nor more than fifty members, to be elected for two-year terms on a nonpartisan basis. Although the nonpartisan provision brought opposition from leaders of both political parties—who still try, intermittently, to change it—the voters approved; they had been crossing political lines, switching political allegiance, for years. (In fact, they re-elected Norris the next year as an Independent; in all previous elections he had run as a Republican candidate.)

During the last session of the bicameral body, the sixty-nine members of the house and senate redistricted the state and established the number of members for the new unicameral body at forty-three—six more have since been added—and on January 5, 1937, the first session of the unicameral legislature of Nebraska opened, with Senator Norris addressing the group of twenty-two Democrats and twenty-one Republicans who had been elected on the nonpartisan ballot.

One of the first acts of the new legislature was to establish procedures for a public hearing on every bill while it is in committee. Another early action was the creation of a legislative reference service; twelve years later the Legislative Council was enlarged to include all members of the legislature, functioning as a committee of the whole in the interim between sessions; the council was provided with a professional staff. In 1961 a fiscal analyst was added to the Legislative Council and in 1965 the Department of Administrative Services was created. At the time the state was redistricted and six more legislative districts formed, the term of the senatorial office was lengthened to four years, senators in odd-numbered districts elected at one time, those in even-numbered districts two years later.

Despite the gloomy fears of its opponents, the unicameral legislative system has worked well in Nebraska. Although the legislative process can never be speedy, the single body provides more efficiency that the old two-house system did, and through the committee structure provides its own system of checks and balances.

The legislature meets in a building which is a departure from traditional capitol architecture. The cornerstone was laid on November 11, 1922, and state offices moved into it before the legislature met in 1925. Designed by Bertram G. Goodhue, it is a low-lying structure hugging the plains, dominated by a great central tower rising four hundred feet into the sky, a twenty-seven-foot sculpture, The Sower, crowning the rounding spire. The building symbolizes the strength and foundation of Nebraska.

To accommodate proliferating state offices, a new, angular, white office building was constructed fifty years later, of less striking lines than the nearby capitol; various departments of state government moved into it in the winter of 1976.

The second institution unique to Nebraska is its statewide public power system, for Nebraska is the only state in the nation to have all its electricity generated by publicly owned plants.

Whereas the idea of the unicameral legislature was fully developed when it was presented to the public, the institution of public ownership of power did not spring full-blown but developed by degrees. During the drought-ridden 1930s, the people of Nebraska realized that their salvation lay in harnessing the vast network of rivers for irrigation purposes; for decades, various dreamers had promoted the idea of impounding the water and diverting it to supplement inadequate rainfall. As they looked at the water then, they could see its potential for hydroelectric generation, an idea encouraged by Nebraska's Senator Norris, father of the Tennessee Valley Authority (TVA), which had combined flood control with hydroelectric generation.

The Reconstruction Finance Corporation Act of 1932 provided the first federal legislation for the construction of dams and power plants, incidentally creating work for depression-idle workers. A state law in 1933 provided for the organization of public power districts with authority to borrow money backed by revenue bonds. The Loup River Public Power District was the first to be started, generating power in March 1937; with the organization of the Omaha Public Power District in 1945, all electricity generated in the state came from government-owned plants.

Curiously enough, although the idea of public ownership originated with these hydroelectric plants, only a small part of the state's electricty now is generated from water power. The water supplies are sufficient, but on the flat prairie the water does not drop enough to create the force necessary to turn the turbines. Another irony is that more irrigation water now is supplied from wells than from the ditches leading from the dams.

Nebraska now has four public power districts: the Loup River Public Power District, the Central Nebraska Public Power and Irrigation District, the Nebraska Public Power District, and the Omaha Public Power District; these are augmented with thirty-two rural electrification districts and fifty municipally owned electrical plants, many of those being small generating plants. All of them are connected by a grid system to the lines of the federal Bureau of Reclamation, whose power is generated by dams in North Dakota and South Dakota, a sophisticated interconnection to be used in times of dire emergency. Two of the plants of the Nebraska Public Power District are powered with atomic energy; most of the other plants in the state operate on fossil fuels. Recent regulations of the Federal Power Commission proscribing the continued use of natural gas to produce power have resulted in the development of plans for new coal-fired plants.

Practically every step in the evolution of the statewide public power system has been accompanied by controversy. Now that the cries of "Socialism!" have abated and the system is an accomplished fact, new controversies deal with the effect of coal as a fuel and with the development of a proposed coal slurry pipeline to carry powdered coal in liquid form across the state.

A third institution peculiar to Nebraska is its network of twenty-four natural resources districts, organized along natural watershed boundaries, to conserve soil and water, the most valuable of the state's natural resources. Although many other states have conservation agencies, no others are so encompassing nor organized along the watershed boundaries of the rivers.

The natural resources districts are the result of the merger of a number of earlier conservation agencies. The disastrous loss of topsoil in Nebraska during the dust-bowl days of the 1930s stimulated the legislature to create soil conservation districts in 1937; in later measures the legislature enlarged the scope of the Nebraska Soil and Water Conservation Committee, as it was later known, to include water conservation, watershed protection, and flood control. The natural resources districts were created by legislative action in 1972, charged with conserving soil and water by supervising erosion prevention, floodwater and sediment control, flood prevention, pollution control, ground and surface water utilization, sanitary drainage, fish and wildlife protection, water supply, recreation and parks usage, and forestry and range utilization. The districts have the power to levy a tax of up to one mill on all tangible property within the district and to levy special assessments on property owners receiving benefits of local special-benefit projects.

Many of the political changes which occurred in Nebraska, and indeed in the nation, during the first half of the twentieth century were the work of Senator George W. Norris, either directly or indirectly. Some scholars considered him the preeminent example of an effective United States senator. Elected to the House of Representatives in 1903 and to the Senate in 1913, he served Nebraska in Congress for forty consecutive years, longer than any other Nebraskan. Although for thirty-six of those years, he was elected as a Republican, he did not adhere to the party line, voting independently and criticizing whatever principles he thought harmful; he voted according to his conscience, saying that he'd rather be right than regular. (He endorsed Theodore Roosevelt in 1912, Robert La Follette in 1924, Alfred Smith in 1928, and Franklin D. Roosevelt in all four of his presidential campaigns.)

His political contribution lay in four major fields: administration, rural electrification, farm relief, and labor. In the House, he was the leader of the reform group which reduced the control of the speaker; later in the Senate, he sponsored the Twentieth Amendment to the Constitution which abolished the so-called Lame Duck sessions of Congress. He fought for other political reforms, such as presidential primaries and the direct election of senators, principles which his compatriot, William Jennings Bryan, had espoused earlier. On the state level, Norris was instrumental in gaining approval for the unicameral form of legislature.

Like Bryan, he had strong antiwar convictions. He voted against the entry of the United States into World War I, and denounced the Versailles treaty.

Realizing the need for rural areas to have access to electricity, he sponsored government power-development, primarily in the Tennessee Valley Authority; the first TVA dam, completed in 1936, was named in his honor. Although he did not bring about such dramatic progress in power-development in his own state, his influence was responsible for Nebraska's eventual move toward complete government-supplied electric power.

Norris was also a leader for farm-relief legislation and for soil conservation through tree planting. The Norris-Doxey act provided for planting of shelter belts of trees throughout the prairie states.

But his interests were not parochial, determined only by his geographical boundaries. He was the coauthor of the Norris-LaGuardia act, which restricted the use of injunctions in labor disputes and opened the way for a changed legal concept of labor-management relations. Norris also supported social security and old age pension legislation.

Although many of the principles for which he worked were the same as those of William Jennings Bryan, Norris was able to put them into action from his position in Congress; he was skilled in the ways of political maneuvering in Washington.

Certainly no other man in the twentieth century had so much effect upon Nebraska as did Norris, and few surpassed him in Congress in effecting changes nationally.

16

The Prosperous Years

$\mathcal{A}$S Nebraska began to recover from the ten-year drought and Depression of the 1930s, World War II erupted. But this time the state was not thrown into the emotional turmoil that had been part of the home-front activity of World War I a quarter-century earlier.

Hordes of people left Nebraska to work in war plants on the West Coast, but as some war-related industries were established in the state—ordnance plants at Hastings, Mead, Grand Island, and Sidney, a bomber assembly plant in Omaha, and others— other workers came in. Rainfall was plentiful, crops abundant, farm prices high; the state was in a period of prosperity unknown since the golden years of the 1880s.

The thirty years since the end of World War II have been years of growth and continued development. Although there have been intermittent periods of dryness—during the mid-1950s, for instance—and periodic declines of farm prices, the state is still in an era of plenty. The farmers complain, to be sure, and the ranchers, too, at the slightest suggestion of a drop in either rainfall or prices; they are Nebraskans, after all, reared in the tradition of vocally expecting the worst but inwardly knowing that everything will be all right—Nebraska farmers talk pessimism but think optimism. New farming procedures, especially the use of irrigation, make the spectre of drought less frightening now than it was to generations past. Wheat and beef prices fluctuate but in the past three decades have managed to average out so that the year of loss is compensated for in the next years of profit.

Where once the population of Nebraska was scattered throughout the state, the little dots on the map marking crossroads settlements have become tinier, and the blobs marking the cities have become larger. Although the population of the state as a whole has remained fairly constant, it has shifted; the crossroads village which once had banks, grocery stores, doctors' offices, and even weekly newspapers is diminishing in size, in some cases evaporating entirely. The change, begun in the 1920s as automobiles and highways made access to larger communities easier, has accelerated in the last thirty years. Whereas in 1940 only six communities outside of Omaha and Lincoln had populations of ten thousand or more, the move from farm to town brought that number to ten in 1970. They include Grand Island, Hastings, Bellevue, Fremont, Kearney, North Platte, Norfolk, Columbus, Scottsbluff, and Beatrice. Each serves as the commercial center for the wide geographic area surrounding it, as an industrial center for manufacturing and servicing farm-related equipment, and as a cultural nucleus as well.

Because distances on the prairie are vast, even with sophisticated automotive equipment to bridge them, the town that serves as a shopping area provides goods and services far in excess of the size of the population; customers drive in from miles around to buy their groceries, their clothing, their household necessities; to go to the doctor, the dentist, the hairdresser. It is as cultural centers, however, that out-state Nebraska towns have made the most astonishing changes. Although Hastings has had a symphony orchestra continuously since 1926, other communities have started theirs more recently—the Sandhills Symphony in North Platte, for instance, whose players drive fifty miles or more one way to attend rehearsals. Art galleries, workshops for painters and sculptors, community theaters—most of them providing artistic release for amateurs, to be sure—are almost as much a part of the community now as the new shopping mall with its acres of concrete parking spaces. In developing cultural awareness, Nebraska communities are atypical.

Lincoln and Omaha have grown proportionately in the decades since the end of World War II. As the capital city and home of the state university, Lincoln has a population of one hundred sixty thousand—except on the five or six home-game football Saturdays in the fall, when an additional eighty thousand or more red-clad Cornhusker enthusiasts pour into town; on those days, the Nebraska stadium becomes the third-largest population center in the state. The streets of the Lincoln business district are wide; some of them have fountains with sprays that dispel the Nebraska heat; streets in the residential areas are tree-lined. The town retains the quiet, intellectual atmosphere of its early days, when meetings of discussion clubs, temperance societies, and concerts at the rococo opera house provided the entertainment of the town. Lincoln did not allow bars until late 1966, the first legal drink served in town being a bourbon-and-water poured at 8:55 a.m. on December 14 to a customer from Omaha.

Lincoln's social structure supposedly is divided into four groups: the university; the governmental, or legislative, group; the so-called Old Families; and others. All of them support the Lincoln Symphony Orchestra, the locally produced drama at the Lincoln Playhouse, the Art Guild, and the Sheldon Art Gallery, which is known internationally.

Omaha is the commercial center of the state, its metropolitan population of a half-million sprawling over the hills overlooking the Missouri River. Through the years, Omaha has been many things—outfitting center for the westward travelers, hub of the Union Pacific railroad empire, site of the Strategic Air Command whose red telephone, connected to the White House, controls the military fate of the United States—but generation after generation, her reason for being has been to supply food. Along the Missouri River bottoms, cranes dump truckloads and trainloads of grain into huge barges which meander down the muddy swells to take corn and wheat and soybeans to the port of New Orleans and the world; in offices with phones and ticker tapes, men in the Omaha Grain Exchange sell grain, and in the offices of the Omaha Livestock Market, cattle and swine; in slaughterhouses and packing plants, butchers carve T-bones and prime rib roasts and create salami; and in factories scattered throughout the town, men and women in assembly lines produce corn flakes, bakery products, ice cream. Frozen TV dinners originated in Omaha. Half the entire industrial structure of Omaha is devoted to food processing.

Brash and boisterous since her raw beginnings, Omaha has settled into respectability, having survived her lusty past when she was a wide-open, sin-supplying city. She started out as a rip-roaring frontier town, the jumping-off place for the West, and for years afterward continued to provide entertainment. "Mayor Jim" Dahlman, the colorful former cowboy who served as mayor from 1906 until his death in 1930, lauded personal liberty—which meant the open saloon and other sporting establishments; he took his orders from Tom Dennison, the gambler who was the political boss. Although reform groups periodically tried to clean up the town, it was not until Dennison's death in 1934 that they succeeded.

The Depression of the 1930s flattened Omaha, so much so that a sociologist-historian wrote in 1939 that "her glory has departed." [1] But he was wrong. In the years since, Omaha has thrived as an industrial, commercial city, with insurance companies setting up headquarters there, construction firms based there handling jobs world-wide, and medical complexes included among the business institutions. Father Flanagan established his Boys Town in Omaha, the Joslyns gave a distinguished art museum to the city, and in more recent years a symphony orchestra, the Omaha ballet, and the Omaha Playhouse have thrived.

Much of the top-drawer social life of Omaha centers around Ak-Sar-Ben, Nebraska spelled backward, whose board of governors represent the power structure of the city. Organized in the 1890s, the Knights of Ak-Sar-Ben dreamed up the Trans-Mississippi and International Exposition of 1898, a grandiose world's fair in a setting of dazzling white classical-style buildings. Almost a hundred thousand people trooped in to see the sights, some of them shaking President McKinley's hand. Since then, the Knights have operated as a non-profit civic organization to sponsor entertainments and livestock shows, run pari-

---

1. George R. Leighton, *Five Cities: The Story of Their Youth and Old Age* (New York: Harper and Brothers, 1939), p. 140.

mutuel horseracing, using their profits to underwrite livestock
and conservation programs throughout the state. Every October
even now they hold a glittering coronation ball, crowning the
king and queen of the mythical kingdom of Quivira, daughters
of prominent businessmen throughout the state serving as coun-
tesses and princesses.

The immigrants now moving into Omaha to seek a new life
on the prairies are blacks, joining the descendants of German,
Czech, Irish, Swedish, and Jewish immigrants of generations
past. In the 1940s there were an estimated 6,000 blacks living in
Omaha; by 1976 the number had increased to an estimated
45,000.

In the past quarter-century, new industries have appeared on
the Nebraska prairies. Some of them are homegrown, factories
which sprouted up to produce farm-related equipment in such
towns as Henderson, Hastings, Grand Island, and Columbus.
Others are plants which have been moved inland from urban
areas in the East, businessmen eager to use Nebraska laborers
because of their adaptability and capacity for hard work. Many
of these plants are small, employing only a few hundred people,
but they contribute to the economy of such towns as Norfolk,
Holdrege, Cozad, Scottsbluff, Ogallala. Some of the workers
who assemble delicate precision instruments on assembly lines
by day are able to combine the best of two worlds, living on
small farms nearby and tilling the soil after their 40-hour weeks
are finished; others are those who have sold their acreages to be
merged into larger, more economically viable farm spreads and
have come into town to work. The entire nonagricultural industrial output of the state is only a small proportion of her economic contribution to the world.

To train young Nebraskans in technical fields, such as elec-
tronics, diesel mechanics, and others, the state has developed a
system of technical community colleges. For years the only
state-supported one was at Milford, and its waiting list was
long. In 1966, seventeen counties in mid-Nebraska secured legislation to create a regional tax base for an area technical school
in Hastings, utilizing the buildings and some of the nearly fifty
thousand acres of the by-then vacated naval ammunition depot

as its campus. The new technical school held its first classes in September 1966, its individualized instruction through audiovisual equipment causing a great stir in academic circles throughout the country. Other regions sought to start similar institutions. In 1971 the legislature created a new statewide, independent system of locally governed technical community colleges, combining new technical schools with already existing two-year community junior colleges that until then had been supported by local mill levy. The six technical community college areas are Western Nebraska at Scottsbluff, Mid Plains at North Platte, Central Nebraska at Hastings, Northeast Nebraska at Norfolk, Southeast Nebraska at Milford, and Metropolitan in Omaha.

But other educational problems in Nebraska have not been so easy to solve. Nebraska has more school districts than any other state in the Union, 1,241 of them, more than eight hundred of those with country schools and a handful of students; 161 of them still have outdoor privies. With vast distances to bridge, farmers and ranchers in isolated areas are loath to give up their neighborhood schools and resist efforts to consolidate or merge districts. Small villages do not want to lose their high schools, feeling perhaps that so long as they have enough boys enrolled to field a team for the state basketball tournament, their communities still have identity. The issue of redistricting schools is a charged, highly emotional one that has been battled in Nebraska for thirty years or more. With the great disparity of population, no single solution will work. Small changes are made, year by year, but not even legislative mandate seems able to speed the process of amalgamating school districts into logical, efficient-sized units. Despite the inadequacy of many of the schools in their physical plants and size, students seem to receive sufficient education to rank high in national testing programs. Who knows what they could do if their schools were smaller in number, larger in size, and better equipped?

By the 1960s, it was obvious that Nebraska needed a change in her tax structure. For years she had prided herself on having no income or sales tax, no bonded indebtedness, advertising herself as the White Spot of the Nation. But in 1966, the constitution was amended to introduce sales and income taxes and to prohibit the state from levying property taxes for state purposes.

Recent legislative action has been concerned with conservation, for Nebraskans learned long ago, earlier than most other Americans, that the land, the water, the air, all natural resources are a trust, that man cannot be profligate with the gifts of nature but must conserve them. The most serious problems facing Nebraska in the late 1970s are those of water ownership and distribution, for Nebraska has never decided legally who owns the water. The legal problems of diverting water from one watershed to another are still being discussed; so, too, are riparian rights, not only within the state but also with Colorado and Wyoming for their usage of Platte River water. Nebraskans realize that survival in their semiarid climate depends upon judicious use of water supplies, and the construction of dams and escalation of underground-water use in irrigation systems are matters of concern.

Because so much of the economy of Nebraska is based on fossil fuels—to power farm machinery, to provide fertilizers that produce enormous farm yields, to suspend chemicals that control weeds and pests, to create electricity—the shortage of natural gas and petroleum products looms as a tremendous, immediate problem. But unlike other parts of the United States, Nebraska still possesses two great inexhaustible sources of power: the sun and the wind. So long as there are few particle pollutants to interfere with the sun's rays, the possibility of efficient utilization of solar energy exists in this land of almost constant sun. And so long as the wind can sweep across the broad unbroken expanse of prairie, the wind—which the early pioneers harnessed through their windmills—remains a powerful source of energy.

With the can-do, make-do spirit of their forefathers to encourage them to develop a sophisticated application of these two great sources of power, Nebraskans need not be as dependent on fossil energy as persons in other parts of the United States.

In less than a century and a quarter, the people of Nebraska have transformed what was once part of the Great American Desert into a land of plenty. In the early days, their job was to break the land, using physical brawn, endurance, and faith. But they have learned that they must save the land, using it wisely. Their creativity now lies not in their muscular power but in their thoughtful, imaginative mental powers.

Frugal, hard-working, independent sometimes to the point of stubbornness, Nebraskans are an astonishing breed. Their ethnic backgrounds are varied, their geographical surroundings diverse, the lives of the eastern urban dwellers unlike those of the western ranchers and farmers. Yet they have unity. It stems from a common history of sharing the land, the broad sweep of the prairie, the dunes of the Sandhills, the canyons of the Niobrara. For wherever they live, on farms or ranches, small towns or cities, Nebraskans feel a close kinship with the soil and the fruitfulness thereof. This is the story of Nebraska.

Suggestions for Further Reading

Books about the Great Plains generally, and Nebraska specifically, are almost without limit. Because the development of the area has been so recent, it has been relatively easy to chronicle; journals, diaries, and other primary source materials have not yet been destroyed and are available to researchers.

The books which are listed here for further reading are only a few of those that are generally available, many in paperback editions.

The best general, overall history of Nebraska is James C. Olson's sparkling *History of Nebraska* (Lincoln: University of Nebraska Press, 1955, 1966), a scholarly, balanced, readable account of what has taken place in the state and why. Another general history, based on Olson's but including tall tales and more details about Indians, is Mari Sandoz's *Love Song to the Plains* (New York: Harper and Row, 1961; reprinted Lincoln: University of Nebraska Press, 1966).

For an understanding of the land, Walter Prescott Webb's classic *The Great Plains* (New York: Ginn and Company, 1931; New York: Grosset and Dunlap, 1972) is essential.

Other good general reference books about Nebraska, written at earlier dates, are Addison E. Sheldon's 3-volume *Nebraska: The Land and the People* (Chicago: Lewis Publishing Company, 1931); the 3-volume series *Illustrated History of Nebraska,* edited by J. Sterling Morton and Albert Watkins (Lincoln: Jacob North and Company, 1907–1912); and A. T. Andreas's *History of Nebraska* (Chicago: Historical Company, 1882; Lincoln: Nebraska State Historical Society, 1976).

Books about Plains Indians are legion. Waldo R. Wedel, *Prehistoric Man on the Great Plains* (Norman: University of Oklahoma Press, 1961) is the classic about early cultures. For Indians of later periods, Robert H. Lowie's paperback, *Indians of the Plains* (New York: American Museum Books, 1963) is a concise reference book, giving details about social organization, art, recreation, and religious

211

beliefs of various tribes. George Bird Grinnell's books about the Cheyenne, particularly *The Cheyenne Indians, Their History and Ways of Life* (New Haven: Yale University Press, 1923) and *By Cheyenne Campfires* (New Haven: Yale University Press, 1926, 1962) combines scholarship with a firsthand knowledge and understanding of the Indians. George E. Hyde's writings on various Plains tribes are well done. They include *Red Cloud's Folk* (Norman: University of Oklahoma Press, 1937, 1957), *The Pawnee Indians* (Denver: University of Denver Press, 1951), *A Sioux Chronicle* (Norman: University of Oklahoma Press, 1956), *Spotted Tail's Folk: A History of the Brule Sioux* (Norman: University of Oklahoma Press, 1961). Mari Sandoz, who was closely associated with the Indians during her childhood, provides a rare quality of involvement and understanding of the Indians in her writings; *Crazy Horse: The Strange Man of the Oglalas* (New York: Alfred Knopf, Inc., 1942; Lincoln: University of Nebraska Press, 1959) is written in an almost Siouan cadence. Her *Cheyenne Autumn* (New York: Hastings House, 1953; New York: Avon Books, 1964) is a dramatic account of the flight of a tribe forcibly removed to another location; and her two books for young people, *The Horse Catcher* (1956) and *The Story Catcher* (1963), both Westminster Press, Philadelphia, capture the essence of Sioux everyday life. Dee Brown's *Bury My Heart at Wounded Knee* (New York: Rinehart Holt Winston, 1970) tells of the subjugation of the Indians. There are scores, even hundreds, of other books of varying qualities of scholarship and understanding about Plains Indians.

For an account of the early explorers in the West, Bernard DeVoto's *The Course of Empire* (Boston: Houghton Mifflin, 1952) is a good general reference. Various books have been written on the Lewis and Clark expedition; their *Journals* (New York: The Heritage Press, 1962) is a good edition. The best work on fur-traders is still Hiram M. Chittenden's *The American Fur Trade of the Far West* (1902; reprinted in two volumes, Stanford: Academic Reprints, 1954). Everett Dick's *Vanguards of the Frontier* (New York: D. Appleton-Century, 1941; Lincoln: University of Nebraska Press, 1965) tells of fur-traders and missionaries.

The most comprehensive book about the Overland Trail is Merrill J. Mattes's *The Great Platte River Road* (Lincoln: Nebraska State Historical Society, 1969) which contains material from hundreds of diaries and journals telling about life on the trail. An old classic is Francis

Parkman's *The Oregon Trail*, first published in 1849, most recently reprinted by New American Library, New York, in 1950. For accounts of the Mormon expeditions, *Handcarts to Zion*, by LeRoy R. and Ann W. Hafer (Glendale, Cal.: Arthur H. Clark Company, 1960) is a detailed, authoritative book; Bernard DeVoto's *The Year of Decision: 1846* (Boston: Houghton Mifflin, 1943) is a good overall study. William Lass's *From the Missouri to the Great Salt Lake* (Lincoln: Nebraska State Historical Society, 1972) is a definitive study of the freighting business.

Wesley S. Griswold's *A Work of Giants* (New York: McGraw Hill, 1962) tells about the Union Pacific construction; Richard C. Overton's *Burlington West* (Cambridge: Harvard University Press, 1941), of the Burlington, particularly its colonizing efforts. Reminiscences by an old railroad construction man are given in *End of Track* by James H. Kyner, published privately in 1937, by the University of Nebraska Press, Lincoln, in 1960.

For material about the homesteading years, scores of books are available, among them Everett Dick's *Tales of the Frontier* (Lincoln: University of Nebraska Press, 1963, 1970). Richard A. Bartlett's *The New Country: A Social History of the American Frontier, 1886–1890* (New York: Oxford Press, 1974) is an excellent account of family life, towns, and institutions on the frontier. Various volumes of *Sod House Memories*, edited by Francis Jacobs Alberts, published by the Sod House Society, Hastings, give firsthand accounts of sod-house living. Solomon D. Butcher's *History of Custer County* (1902; reprinted Denver: Sage Books, 1965) is a remarkable collection of firsthand reminiscences.

Although a number of Nebraska communities have published books of varying size and authenticity about the history of the town involved, one of the most detailed and scholarly is Dorothy Weyer Creigh's *Adams County: A Story of the Great Plains* (Hastings: Adams County-Hastings Centennial Commission, 1972). Since the stories of the towns are so similar, this serves as a prototype of all the others.

The standard work on Populism is John D. Hick's *The Populist Revolt* (Minneapolis: University of Minnesota Press, 1931, 1961). A scholarly biography of William Jennings Bryan's life is *The Trumpet Soundeth* by Paul W. Glad (Lincoln: University of Nebraska Press, 1960).

The best account of the buffalo slaughter is contained in Mari Sandoz's *The Buffalo Hunters* (New York: Hastings House, 1954). Andy Adams's *The Log of a Cowboy* (Boston: Houghton Mifflin, 1903; Lincoln: University of Nebraska Press, n.d.), gives a firsthand account of the cattle trail to Ogallala. For accounts of the cattlemen, Harry T. Chrisman's *The Ladder of Rivers* (Denver: Sage Books, 1962) details the story of the Olive brothers and their troubles; Gene Gressley's *Bankers and Cattlemen* (New York: Alfred Knopf, Inc., 1966; Lincoln: University of Nebraska Press, 1972) is a scholarly account of the total ranching business on the Great Plains. Nellie Snyder Yost's *Call of the Range* (Denver: Sage Books, 1966) a rollicking book not accurate in all details but capturing the color of ranching, concentrates on the Nebraska cattle business. Mari Sandoz's *Old Jules* (Boston: Little Brown and Company, 1935; Lincoln: University of Nebraska Press, 1966) tells of the homesteaders' view of cattlemen.

Index

215